STATE SOVEREIGNTY

The Power Lies with Us,
Not the Federal Government

FEDERICO LINES
States Rights Radio

STATE SOVEREIGNTY

Paperback ISBN: 978-1-7346385-2-3

Printed in the United States of America

16 17 18 19 20 21 9 8 7 6 5 4 3 2 1

CONTENTS

ACKNOWLEDGEMENTS

THIS BOOK IS DEDICATED to my late father, Fernando V. Lines, a strong admirer of the American Federalism system. My father was like me, a naturalized American citizen who truly believed in the rules of federalism, the Sovereignty of the individual and autonomous state over the federal government. I would like to thank him for giving me the tools and means to pursue my education, for instilling in me the courage to stand up for what I believe in and to educate others in the American federalism principle. I'd also like to dedicate this book to my mother Sylvia Lines and my sister Alejandra Lines -- two strong members of my family whom I am just as proud of as I am of my father.

I would like to thank my former colleague Geoffrey Stone, who taught me everything I know about how to write, edit, design, and publish books. Thank you.

And I would also like to express my appreciation to Brian Hetzman and Felicia Dionisio for helping me with the editing of the manuscript and design of the book cover. Thank you.

INTRODUCTION

THIS BOOK IS ABOUT the issue of State Sovereignty and how it functions in our American federalism republic.

I am going to discuss issues that were brought before the national court of the land - - issues that should have been heard and debated at the state level and not at the national level. There are certain issues that should be left to each individual state – like education, commerce, abortion, family issues, and immigration. However, slavery and segregation were exemptions, as they were not issues of state sovereignty, despite many people before, during and after the Civil War making this outrageous claim. They were issues involving human-rights violations, not state-sovereignty violations. The Thirteenth, Fourteenth, and Fifteenth Amendments settled the matter and states had to abide by and not contradict federal constitutional law. That is a very important point. States can create their own set of laws if they are not contradictory to the constitution.

The biggest topic of nationwide discussion these days is the issue of immigration. Many individuals in the federal government claim the enforcement of the Naturalization

Clause falls under the jurisdiction of the national government. We will explore why the Founding Fathers intended for the sovereign, autonomous and independent states to enforce the Naturalization Clause.

Thomas Jefferson and James Madison taught us to reject a federal Naturalization act of Congress in 1798 known as the Alien and Sedition Act. Sovereign states nullified this act by not cooperating with federal officials and thus allowing us to keep the "Principles of '98" alive in America today.

Some jurists on the high court understood the writings of Jefferson and Madison and truly showed their teachings in their opinion and dissent briefs of the courts.

There are other people on the bench who don't quite seem to understand the rules of federalism. They've tried to rewrite their own form of federalism. Their own creation was in the form of totalitarianism. As Justice Robert H. Jackson tried to impose totalitarian views against federalism, members of today's courts have tried to impose their own personal beliefs and not the beliefs of our Founding Fathers. The federal government, from the executive branch, national Congress and Supreme Court have imposed federal government control against the sovereign state. Through its enforcement of the Naturalization clause, the federal government, has taken liberty out of the hands of the states and placed it into the claws of the federal government.

I will reveal how the federal government in recent years has ignored the rules of federalism. I will also show you how it applied its own rules and ignored the will of the Constitutional Framers took it upon themselves to craft them at the Constitutional Convention of 1787.

ONE

STATE SOVEREIGNTY AND LIFE

W HERE WE SEE ISSUES hit the high court that should be heard on the state level, because they are matters of the state, are the cases of abortion, homosexuality and same-sex marriage. This country was built to have individual autonomous state governments with an administrative central government. It was never the intention of the Founding Fathers to have a controlling central government. It was set up for administrative services, not a police state. Scalia always made quite clear in all his opinions and dissents the desire to institute the Tenth Amendment right and to leave these issues to the states, respectively, or to the people.

Scalia was a strict proponent of federalism and states' autonomy. With all the cases that came to the Supreme Court that he presided over, he examined each case and was very careful that the rulings did not trump state constitutions or exceed the central power. Scalia was indeed a man of life and supported the right to life of the unborn, as well as the mother's life. But I have seen that he was first and foremost a man of federalism.

"The States may, if they wish, permit abortion on demand, but the Constitution does not require them to do so. The permissibility of abortion, and the limitations upon it, are to be resolved like most important questions in our democracy: by citizens trying to persuade one another and then voting."

– Associate Justice Antonin Scalia

What I got out of this quote from Scalia was plain and simple. He did not say that he was pro-life or pro-choice. He stated that he was a states' sovereignty advocate. He wanted to let the states decide if they want to permit or prohibit abortion, but with the advice and consent of the people of that state. If the state legislatures of California, Oregon, New York, and Connecticut want to pass legislation that permits abortion-on-demand, that is the choice of those states, but most importantly the people of those states who elected those state legislators to be their voice in their respective state capitals. Now if the state legislatures of Colorado, Arizona, Alabama, and Florida want to pass legislative measures to prohibit abortion then so be it. The advice and consent are with the voice of those people since they elected their legislators.

We all know Scalia respected the rights of state sovereignty, but sometimes when the law is not too egregious and overstepping its boundaries onto states rights and that includes the abortion issue. In 1990, the Supreme Court heard a case involving [a] Minnesota law requiring minors to obtain parental consent before having an abortion. Scalia noted that at that time, the justices on the court had applied various legal standards (and even applied the same standards differently) to state abortion restriction, (Scalia's Court, Kevin A. Ring, 2004, 2016, page 92).

Scalia concluded, in his statement, "The random and unpredictable results of our consequently unchanneled individual views make it increasingly evident term after term that the tools for this job are not to be found in the lawyer's—and hence not in the judge's—work box. I continue to dissent from this enterprise of devising an abortion code, and from the illusion that we have authority to do so." (Scalia's Court, Kevin A. Ring, 2004, 2016, page 92-93).

Scalia concluded by saying that issues involving abortion should be handled at the state level to regulate lawfully the abortion questions. They should be resolved by legislatures, in which the majority of citizens could express their will through their elected (state) representatives, (Scalia's Court, Kevin A. Ring, 2004, 2016, page 93).

The Supreme Court is there to decide on federal issues that affect the country, while states, with their own autonomy and court systems, must decide their own fates. Having the federal court decide issues like abortion, affects not only that state but others, and is an encroachment of states' liberties.

Sadly, this ruling was decided in a 5-4 decision in favor of the Minnesota abortion law. Five justices did not decide to kick this dispute back to the states. Scalia dissented along with Justices Kennedy, Rehnquist, and White.

* * *

Another ruling over the abortion issue in which the high court totally disregarded states' autonomy and sided with the current precedent was the *Planned Parenthood SE v. Casey 1992* case.

"My views on this matter are unchanged from those I set forth in my separate opinions in *Webster v. Reproductive Health Services* and *Ohio v. Akron Center for Reproductive Health*. The states may, if they wish, permit abortion on demand, but the Constitution does not *require* them to do so. The permissibility of abortion, and the limitations upon it, are to be resolved like most important questions in our democracy: by citizens trying to persuade on another and then voting." (Scalia's Court, Kevin A. Ring, 2004, 2016, page 103, Scalia's dissent on Planned Parenthood SE PA v. Casey).

This author has asked the people who have agreed with the court's decision to point out where in the Constitution does it state, "Abortion is allowed and that no state should be allowed to prohibit it." The answer is that no such statement exists in this document that still governs our country. Whom would you rather rule this great land of ours, your voice in the state legislature or nine unelected lawyers who sit in a committee that is appointed by the chief executive?

I'll take the state legislature and the voice of the people over these nine unelected individuals. These nine lawyers are there to interpret correctly the law and to ensure that it fits appropriately within the Constitution. They are not there to reinvent it and mold it to their personal agenda. Scalia has always pointed out in his dissents and opinions, the need for a democratic voice by the state or respectively by the people on these issues.

"… the best the Court can do to explain how it is that the word "liberty" must be thought to include the right to destroy human fetuses is to rattle off a collection of adjectives that simply decorate a value judgment and conceal a political choice.", (Scalia's Court, Kevin A. Ring, 2004, 2016, page 107, Scalia's dissent on Planned Parenthood SE PA v. Casey).

The high court, in this case and other cases, sometimes loves to reinvent words and extend their vocabulary to fulfill their own personal agenda and to inflict it upon the rest of us by force.

In this court's opinion, the majority used the term *stare decisis* to achieve their objective. This term — which means the practice of adhering to precedent — was especially important in this case because the issue was divisive and because so many people had come to rely on the legality of abortion, (Scalia's Court, Kevin A. Ring, 2004, 2016, page 101-102).

The majority were so scared that this case would overrule a long-standing ruling known as *Roe v. Wade* that they decided to ignore states' autonomous rights and the will of life and still maintain that 1973 ruling on the books and declare this one out into the garbage. Scalia gave a convincing dissent upon the court's view on *stare decisis*, also known as "central holding."

"The Court's reliance upon stare decisis can best be described as contrived. It insists upon the necessity of adhering not to all of *Roe*, but only to what it calls "central holding." It seems to me that *stare decisis* ought to be applied even to the doctrine of stare decisis, and I confess never to have heard of this new, keep-what-you-want-and-throw-the-rest-version. I wonder whether, as applied of *Marbury v. Madison*, for example, the new version of *stare decisis* would be satisfied if we allowed courts to review the constitutionality of only those statutes that (like the one in *Marbury*) pertain to the jurisdiction of the courts." (Scalia's Court, Kevin A. Ring, 2004, 2016, page 114-115, Scalia's dissent on Planned Parenthood SE PA v. Casey).

This is the perfect example of how progressive jurists have applied, or in this case not applied, constitutional basis on the law being examined by the court. Most of the court's ruling was like cutting up a barbecue steak and saying, "This part is good, this part is bad." I am sorry to say but that is never how a jurist, a person of the law, is supposed to interpret the law. Either interpret as is or recuse yourself. I am going to show you a few excerpts and my opinions on the Opinion and Dissenting brief on *Planned Parenthood SE PA v. Casey*.

The majority opinion of the high court concluded that in "Part V-E that all of the statute's recordkeeping and reporting requirements, except that relating to spousal notice, are constitutional. The reporting provision relating to the reasons a married woman has not notified her husband that she intends to have an abortion must be invalidated because it places an undue burden on a woman's choice." (Opinion Brief on Planned Parenthood SE PA v. Casey).

It is a sad day for America that we take in the word of a bureaucrat over the right of its citizenry and families. I am not surprised, since the court ruling of *Wickard v. Filburn,* the court sought to give more power to the central government over the states and respectively to the people. The progressive movement has made their quest to destroy the American nuclear family and bring distortion and disharmony to the family circle. What kind of a nation have we become that a married woman cannot have a family discussion with her husband in a matter of her pregnancy because it is now invalidated and forbidden by a decree of the central power. How dare they, I ask! Who are these bureaucratic jurists interfering in the private lives of American families.

Then Chief Justice William Rehnquist, joined by Justices White, Scalia and Clarence Thomas concluded in their dissent the many reasons this ruling is unconstitutional.

"The Roe Court reached too far when it analogized the right to abort a fetus to the rights involved in *Pierce v. Society of Sisters, 268 U.S. 510, 69 L. Ed. 1070 , 45 S.*

Ct. 571; Meyer v. Nebraska, 262 U.S. 390, 67 L. Ed. 1042, 43 S. Ct. 625; Loving v. Virginia, 388 U.S. 1, 18 L. Ed. 2d 1010, 87 S. Ct. 1817; and _Griswold v. Connecticut, 381 U.S. 479, 14 L. Ed. 2d 510, 85 S. Ct. 1678,_ and thereby deemed the right to abortion to be "fundamental." None of these decisions endorsed an all-encompassing "right to privacy" as _Roe, supra at 152-153_, claimed. Because abortion involves the purposeful termination of potential life, the abortion decision must be recognized as _sui generis_, different kind from the rights protected in the earlier cases under the rubric of personal or family privacy and autonomy." (Dissenting Brief on Planned Parenthood SE PA v. Casey).

I am not familiar with the _Pierce v. Society of Sisters; Meyer v. Nebraska_ rulings but the ones that I am familiar with are _Loving v. Virginia and Griswold v. Connecticut._ With the ruling of _Loving_, it can most definitely apply as a violation of the Fourteenth Amendment's due process of the law and equal protection clause. It is sad, but I do not see how the legislator behind the FourteenthAmendment ever deemed to have applied the systematic slaughter of unborn babies while crafting his legislation. Before _Griswold_, the law in Connecticut was as stated that the use of contraception for conception between unmarried or married couples were forbidden to use. That law was set to be ruled within Connecticut state lines. If that law was deemed unfair to the residents of that state, then they should have gone to their state legislators and had them reform and/or repeal the law.

It was unnecessary for the high court to not only dictate how Connecticut residents live their lives, but also citizens elsewhere in the country.

"And the historical traditions of the American - - as evidenced by the English common law and by the American abortion statutes in existence both at the time of the Fourteenth Amendment's adoption and *Roe's* issuance - - do not support the view that the right to terminate one's pregnancy is "fundamental." (Dissenting Brief on Planned Parenthood SE PA v. Casey).

The dissenters of this brief are quite accurate. The Fourteenth Amendment was presented to Congress right after the Civil War. A war that was fought to end racial discrimination under the cruel terms of slavery. The proponents of the legislation were looking to pass a law to protect the rights of all Americans based on race. They were not looking to protect the rights of female citizens trying to get rid of a pregnancy. So, let's put this debate to an end, there is nothing in the Constitution, in all the amendments, that declares "the right to abort a fetus." It does not exist, never was written, and never was debated in Congress.

The correct analysis is that which is set forth by the plurality opinion in Webster, supra: A woman's interest in having an abortion is a form of liberty protected by the Due Process Clause, but states may regulate abortion procedures in ways rationally related to a legitimate state interest. P. 966." (Dissenting Brief on Planned Parenthood SE PA v. Casey).

In paraphrasing Scalia's words during an interview with TV commentator Piers Morgan, "Regardless if you think prohibiting abortion is good or bad, the Constitution does not say anything about it. It leaves it up to democratic choice, some states have prohibited, others have not, what *Roe v. Wade* stated is that no state can prohibit, and that simply is not in the Constitution." If the court ruling of 1973 made it clear that no state can prohibit it, fine, but it did not state that no state can regulate an abortion procedure. Is the central power now telling each state how to regulate on the issue of life? A state can pass any measure they see fit, if it does not go against the Constitution.

The dissenting opinion of the court concluded "that a woman's decision to abort her unborn child is not a constitutionally protected "liberty" because (1) the Constitution says absolutely nothing about it, and (2) the longstanding traditions of American society have permitted it to be legally proscribed. See e. g., <u>*Ohio v. Akron Center for Reproductive Health, 497 U.S. 502, 520, 111 L. Ed. 2d 405, 110 S. Ct. 2972*</u>. The Pennsylvania statute should be upheld in its entirety under rational basis test. Pp. 979-981." (Dissenting Brief on Planned Parenthood SE PA v. Casey).

The state law of Pennsylvania is quite clear. The state is not banning or prohibiting an abortion procedure, it is simply regulating it. Who is the central power to dictate something to the states when creating their own legislation? States can pass any legislative measure they see fit, if it is not contradictory to the Constitution, and there is nothing in it about abortion. Sadly, the majority in this court ruling behave like bureaucrat jurists and not true constitutional jurists.

* * *

Sadly, this court ruling was decided based on the heart and mind and not on the basis of the legal and constitutional mind. And in the year 2000, another court ruling as decided against states' autonomy and for central power control, *Sternberg v. Carhart*. This case ruling invalidated a state law, and this time it was from a Nebraska state law. The Nebraska state law was to prohibit the unprincipled, unethical and immoral medical procedure known as "partial- birth abortion." Again, the Supreme Court took up this and with my distinct displeasure, the court ruled against state law. And again, the Second Great Dissenter spoke his legal constitutional mind against this ruling in another powerful dissent.

"I am optimistic enough to believe that, one day, *Sternberg v. Carhart* will be assigned its rightful place in history of this Court's jurisprudence beside *Korematsu* and *Dred Scott*." (Scalia's Court, Kevin A. Ring, 2004, 2016, page 126, Scalia's dissent on Sternberg v. Carhart).

I also concur with this dissenting opening statement. This brutal murder of an almost born infant can be so rightfully compared to the unjust criminal prosecution and incarceration of Japanese-Americans as presented in *Korematsu* and to the unjust and now outlawed practice known as slavery as presented in *Dred Scott*.

"The notion that the Constitution of the United States, designed, among other things, "to establish Justice, insure domestic Tranquility, and secure the Blessings of Liberty to ourselves and our Posterity," prohibits the States from simply banning this visibly brutal means of eliminating our half-born posterity is quite simply absurd." (Scalia's Court, Kevin A. Ring, 2004, 2016, page 127, Scalia's dissent on Sternberg v. Carhart).

The notion that I have is that this high court has placed it upon themselves to behave as an Authoritarian Autocratic Central Committee and to tell the states and respectively their people the laws they must not pass (and pass). It is troubling how the high court has now become an attacker on states' autonomies. Even after the national Congress passed a partial-birth abortion ban in 2003, the court challenged the validity of this law. I do not agree with federal mandates like the one passed in 2003. The author of this article believes the states, and the people of those states, must choose the law as they see fit upon their state. The high court did uphold this law.

This land has truly become a central power governance body. Whether conservative or liberal, the United States of America has indeed lost the principles of federalism and the power to uphold state sovereignty in your own state.

In my opinion, Scalia always fought the good fight to stop abortion and he did not want to give one inch of that fight to the central power of government.

* * *

The last ruling on the life issue in America that I want to touch base on is one that I am truly disgusted with and leaves me asking how in the world the high court chose to uphold a Virginia law. Remember when I mentioned to you that a state can pass any legislative measure it seems fit to their constituents, as long as it does not contradict federal constitutional law. And quite frankly, the Virginia Sterilization Act of 1924 and the Virginia Racial Integrity Act of 1924 are two pieces of legislation that should have never reached the Virginia General Assembly, not only because they are disgraceful but because they are contradictory to the Constitution.

What is even more outrageous is that this case went all the way up to the Supreme Court of the United States and a majority of eight justices voted to uphold this Virginia legislative statute and crush down the entire system of federalism. This ruling was not only an attack on federalism but an attack on every single American citizen who has or has not a medical condition. Carrie Buck, the young lady that sued the State Colony for Epileptics and Feebleminded because they truly violated her equal justice under the law and violated her rights as an American female citizen.

"Carrie Buck is a feeble-minded white woman who was committed to the State Colony above mentioned in due form. She is the daughter of a feeble-minded mother in the same institution, and the mother of an illegitimate feeble-minded child." (Opinion Brief of Buck v. Bell, 1927 by Associate Justice Oliver Wendell Holmes).

In all my years reading Supreme Court opinion and dissenting briefs, I have never read a brief that would denigrate an American citizen. How can the central government force us to have differences between our citizenry based on the mental-health status of one of our own. The Supreme Court is a place where citizens can go to find equal justice under law regardless of race, color and mental challenges. What I found out about this legislative act in Virginia introduced is beyond horrifying.

"An Act of Virginia approved March 20, 1924 (Laws 1924, c. 394) recites that the health of the patient and the welfare of society may be promoted in certain cases by the sterilization of mental defectives, under careful safeguard, etc.; that the sterilization may be effected in males by vasectomy and in females by salpingectomy, without serious pain or substantial danger to life; that the Commonwealth is supporting in various institutions many defective persons who if now discharged would become *206 a menace but if incapable of procreating might be discharged with safety and become self-supporting with benefit to themselves and to society; and that experience has shown heredity plays an important part in the transmission of insanity, imbecility, etc. The statute then enacts that whenever the superintendent of certain institutions including the abovenamed State Colony shall be of opinion that it is for the best interest of the patients and of society that an inmate under his care should be sexually sterilized, he may have the operation performed upon any patient afflicted with hereditary forms insanity, imbecility, etc., on complying with the very careful provisions by which the act protects the patients from possible abuse." (Opinion Brief of Buck v. Bell, 1927 by Associate Justice Oliver Wendell Holmes).

In reading what this Virginia legislative act has been brought upon Virginia residents, and residents of other states that have passed similar legislation, is shameful and contradictory to federal constitutional law. Eight bureaucrat jurists have given authority to a sole bureaucrat to order the sexual sterilization of an American citizen just because of a mental disability. It is a similar ruling to when eight jurists gave permission to a Pennsylvania bureaucrat the right to decide a woman's "right" to terminate a pregnancy, *Planned Parenthood of SE PA v. Casey,* 1992. As I have said before, states can pass any legislative measure the state sees fit in accordance with the overwhelming majority of their constituents and not in contradiction to federal constitutional law. This Virginia statute is a pure contradiction of federal constitutional law, not only a violation of the Fourth, Sixth and Seventh Amendments, but a violation of the equal protection clause of the Fourteenth Amendment. But to have eight Supreme Court justices not take pity on possible American citizens who have been branded mentally-challenged is a disgrace. What is even more of a disgrace is what the majority of the high court would not mind doing to Americans diagnosed with a mental disability.

"It is better for all the world, if instead of waiting to execute degenerate offspring for crime, or to let them starve for their imbecility, society can prevent those who are manifestly unfit from continuing their kind. The principle that sustains compulsory vaccination is broad enough to cover cutting the Fallopian tubes. Jacobson v. Massachusetts, 197 U.S. 11, 25 S. Ct. 358, 49 L. Ed. 643, 3 Ann. Cas. 765. Three generations of imbeciles are enough." (Opinion Brief of Buck v. Bell, 1927 by Associate Justice Oliver Wendell Holmes).

"Three generations of imbeciles are enough." – Justice Oliver Wendell Holmes.

The central government is not here to tell the American citizenry how to kill our unborn, or our mentally-challenged family and friends, or tell us how much wheat to produce, or how to behave in the privacy in our bedroom. Maybe the eight jurists are the ones suffering from three generations of imbecility for having upheld this legislation.

Every time, I read these rulings and similar rulings, it makes me upset that we have allowed the central government to dictate what the law is without complete consideration of the Constitution and federalism. I have not seen writings from Scalia, but I believe he would agree with me that this ruling is a blatant violation of American federalism, just like *Planned Parenthood SE PA v. Casey*, 1992. A matter of life issue being handled by nine jurists, eight of whom sided with horror rather than federalism. Many Americans are unaware this court ruling took place, but I want to show them how dangerous the central government can be regardless of whether a left or right-wing administration is in power in Washington. I want people to read about Buck v. Bell and see it as wake-up call to stop supporting the continuing monstrosity of an overreaching central government.

In this court ruling, I dissent.

TWO

STATE SOVEREIGNTY AND
SAME-SEX MARRIAGE, HOMOSEXUALITY

THE HIGH COURT IS hearing cases that affect American family life that should be heard on the state level. Some of these cases involve homosexuality and same-sex marriage. This country was built to have individual autonomous state governments with an administrative central government. The Founding Fathers never intended for the central government to be so controlling. It was set up for administrative services, not a police state. Scalia always made it quite clear in his opinions and dissents the desire to institute the Tenth Amendment as it was intended and to leave these issues to the states, or respectively to the people.

As Scalia fought to preserve the Constitution from abortionists, he also fought to preserve it for family and states. Many people think Scalia was a rabid homophobe, but that could not be further from the truth. Being a state-sovereignty advocate does not make anyone a racist or homophobe. That is how this country was established. Yes, we have a central government, but the central power should only rely on diplomacy and defense, the other issues should be left to the states. The definition of marriage should be a state issue, plain and simple. Before Scalia took his judicial oath to the highest bench, he did not sit on a 1984 case. The highest court of the land voted to uphold a Georgia state law that punished sodomy. Writing for the majority was Justice White:

"The issue presented is whether the federal Constitution confers a fundamental right upon homosexuals to engage in sodomy and hence invalidates the laws of the many states that still make such conduct illegal and have done so for a very long time. The case also calls for some judgment about the limits of the Supreme Court's role in carrying out its constitutional mandate." (Opinion of Bowers v. Hardwick, Associate Justice Byron White, 1984).

Where in the federal Constitution does it state that homosexuality and sodomy are allowed or not allowed, and that federal law trumps the laws of the states? There is no such thing written in the original governing document of our republic. And furthermore, the Constitution must always respect the will of the state and respectively the will of the people. If the people of Georgia, Texas, and Illinois, for example, elect their state representatives to pass pro-sodomy or anti-sodomy legislation, then so be it. It is the will of the people of those states and it should not be the concern of the central government, the court, or the national Congress.

Sodomy was forbidden by laws of the original thirteen states when they ratified the Bill of Rights. In 1868, when the Fourteenth Amendment was ratified, all but five of the 37 states had criminal sodomy laws. Until 1961, all 50 states outlawed sodomy, and today, 24 states and the District of Columbia continue to provide criminal penalties for sodomy performed in private and between consenting adults (Opinion of Bowers v. Hardwick, Associate Justice Byron White, 1984).

Criminal sodomy statutes in effect in 1868:

- Alabama: Ala. Rev. Code S 3604 (1867)
- Arkansas: Ark. Stat. ch. 51, Art. IV. S 5 (1868)
- California: 1 Cal. Gen. Laws, para. 1450. S 48 (1865)
- Connecticut: Conn. Gen. Stat., Tit. 122. Ch. 7, S 124 (1866)
- Delaware: Del. Rev. Stat., ch. 131, S 7 (1893)
- Florida: Fla. Rev. Stat., div. 5S 2614 (passed 1868) (1892)
- Georgia: GA. Code SS 4286, 42874290 (1867)
- Illinois: IL. Rev. Stat., div. 5, SS 49, 50 (1845)
- Kansas: (Terr). Kan. Stat., ch. 53, S 7 (1855)
- Kentucky: 1 Ky. Rev. Stat., Crimes and Offences, S 5 (1860)
- Louisiana: La. Rev. Stat., ch. 28, Art IV. S 4 (1856)
- Maine: Me. Rev. Stat., Tit. XII., Ch. 160, S 4 (1840)
- Maryland: 1 Md. Code, Art. 30, S 201 (1860)
- Massachusetts: Mass. Gen. Stat., ch. 165, S 18 (1860)
- Michigan: Mich. Rev. Stat., Tit 30, ch. 158, S 16 (1846)
- Minnesota: Minn. Stat., ch. 96, S 13 (1859)
- Mississippi: Miss. Rev. Code, ch. 64, S LII, Art. 238 (1857)

- Missouri: Mo. Rev. Stat., ch. 50, Art. VIII, S 7 (1856)
- Nebraska: Neb. Rev. Stat., Crim. Code, ch. 4, S 47 (1866)
- Nevada: Nev. Comp. Laws, 1861-1900, Cri. Code, ch. 4, S 47 (1866)
- New Hampshire: N. H. Laws, Act. Of June 19, 1812, S 5, (1815)
- New Jersey: N. J. Rev. Stat., Tit. 8, ch. 1, S 9 (1847)
- New York: N. Y. Rev. Stat., pt. 4, ch. 1, Tit. 5, S. 20 (5th ed. 1859)
- North Carolina: N. C. Rev. Code, ch. 34, S 6 (1855)
- Oregon: Laws of Ore., Crimes – Against Morality, etc., ch. 7, S 655 (1874)
- Pennsylvania: Act of Mar. 31, 1860, S 32, Pub. L. 392, in 1 Digest of Statute Law of Pa. 1700-1903, p. 1011 (Purdon 1905).
- Rhode Island: R. I. Gen. Stat., ch. 232, S 12 (1872)
- South Carolina: Act of 1712, in 2 stat. at Large of S. C. 1682-1716, p. 493 (1837)
- Tennessee: Tenn. Code, ch. 8, Art. 1, S 4843 (1858)
- Texas: Tex. Rev. Stat., Tit. 10, ch 5, Art. 342 (1887) (passed 1860)
- Vermont: Acts and Laws of the State of Vt. (1779)
- Virginia: Va. Code, ch. 149, s 12 (1868)
- West Virginia: W. Va. Code, ch. 149, S 12 (1868)

(Opinion of Bowers v. Hardwick, Associate Justice Byron White, 1984)

The figure that Justice White gave that five states did not criminalize sodomy appears to be incorrect. I count four states: Indiana, Ohio, Iowa and Wisconsin.

This matter is a state issue, not a central power issue. If by 1868, there were four or five states that did not criminalize sodomy, then more states should follow suit or not follow suit. In those times, the central power left it up to the states. Did we ever see the federal government criminalize states that did not criminalize acts of sodomy or reward states that did? No, the central power knew its place and knew when not to interfere in matters that belong to the states.

There were two concurrences to this opinion, one from Chief Justice Warren E. Burger and Associate Justice Lewis F. Powell, Jr.

Burger also had the same sentiment in his concurrence opinion to White's opinion brief.

"This is essentially not a question of personal 'preferences' but rather of the legislative authority of the state. I find nothing in the Constitution depriving a state of the power to enact the statute challenged here." (Concurring Opinion of Bowers v. Hardwick, Chief Justice Warren Burger, 1984).

The Tenth Amendment to the Constitution clearly states that the power lies within the states and most respectively the people. State legislatures have the power because the majority of voters elected these legislators to pass such a measure. It is quite the same if, in the states of California, New York, Illinois, New Jersey, the majority elect representatives to enact measures that do not criminalize sodomy or homosexuality. In fact, California had a strict anti-sodomy state legislation and city ordinances up until the late 1970s until the people acted and reversed those decisions.

The concurrence opinion of Justice Powell does not raise the issue of state sovereignty. He raises the question to see if the Eighth Amendment was in clear violation. The Eighth Amendment states, "Excessive bail shall not be required, nor excessive fines imposed, nor cruel and unusual punishment inflicted." The Eighth Amendment is a protection that clearly means, "Let the punishment fit the crime." For example, in the fictional novel *Les Miserable* by Victor Hugo, character Jean Valjean suffered an excessive amount of years in prison for stealing a loaf of bread. It was unjust and cruel. The Founding Fathers wanted justice served, but properly. They wanted the punishment to fit the crime.

"This is not to suggest, however, that respondent may not be protected by the Eighth Amendment of the Constitution. The Georgia Statute at issue in this case, Ga. Code Ann. S 16-6-2 (1984), authorizes a court to imprison a person for up to 20 years for a single private, consensual act of sodomy." (Concurrence Opinion of Bowers v. Hardwick, Associate Justice Lewis Powell, 1984).

Of course, the respondent would be protected under the Eighth Amendment but for this type of statute, I believe this particular crime does not fit the punishment with accordance to the Eighth Amendment. In my opinion, it seems a tad severe, the type of punishment for the type of crime that the state legislature imposed onto the state onto the respondents if convicted or sentenced.

"In *Bowers v. Hardwick* however, respondent has not been tried, much less convicted and sentenced. Moreover, respondent has not raised the Eighth Amendment issue below. For these reasons this constitutional argument is not before us." (Concurrence Opinion of Bowers v. Hardwick, Associate Justice Lewis Powell, 1984).

The only reason Powell brought this issue on his concurrence was due to the dissent opinion of Associate Justice Harry Blackmun. He brings up three issues that the court should have taken under consideration -- the Eighth Amendment, Ninth Amendment, and the Equal Protection Clause of the Fourteenth Amendment. We know that the court was not going to listen to this case under the Eighth Amendment because the respondent was not even tried, convicted and sentenced. But still, what the highest court of the land should have done is to send a recommendation to the state of Georgia to review the current statute and to see if it did not violate the Eighth Amendment. Then comes the Equal Protection Clause of the Fourteenth Amendment. The progressive movement loves to twist and turn the verbiage of this amendment's language. I have said it before and continue saying it, the Fourteenth Amendment was written just after the Civil War to end slavery and discrimination of our citizens based on race. The United States of America did not fight a civil war based on the sexual preference of our citizens. So, the highest court had every right to refuse this issue. Now consider the Ninth Amendment that states, "The enumeration in the Constitution, of certain rights, shall not be construed to deny or disparage others retained by the people." Do those rights include sexual preference? No, the Ninth Amendment does not specify if same-sex or gender rights are included under this right. Sadly, the Constitution does not state anywhere that same sex is protected under those rights as stated in the Ninth Amendment. That is why this court has struck down this claim.

While Scalia was not on the bench when this case was heard, he did make his opinion known to the public. He said that a state is entitled to protect traditional sexual mores, which constituted a rational basis for regulating private sexual conduct (Scalia's Court, Kevin A. Ring, 2004, 2016, page 354).

Scalia truly believed that a state can pass whatever law they want to please their constituents and maintain the peace of that state with accordance with the majority of constituents that support this type of law. This was not the end of this debate; one more case came upon the highest court of the land and it sealed the fate of the 1984, *Bowers v. Hardwick* case.

In conclusion, in the opinion of the court and the concurrence opinion of the court that this issue belongs in the state legislature of Georgia or given in the form of a plebiscite to be decided by the residents of Georgia. It is a matter left to the states, not by the central power to fix.

* * *

The case that overruled *Bowers* was the 2003 *Lawrence v. Texas* ruling. The Texas state legislature, with the support of its constituents, gave them a majority to pass an anti-sodomy legislation. This court case was filed by a homosexual couple who were arrested and convicted for having sexual intercourse in the privacy of their home. The Supreme Court did not declare "homosexuality a fundamental right" but instead declared that the legislation was a violation of the right to privacy as stated in the 1965 court ruling of *Griswold v. Connecticut*. If the 1965 opinion stated that a judgment against an act in the bedroom was a violation of the "right to privacy," then how come it was never applied in the 1984 case. Scalia, joined by Rehnquist and Thomas, gave a memorable dissent in explaining how this judgement does not make "homosexual sodomy, a fundamental right" nor "a right to privacy." And Scalia shot down Justice O'Connor's claim that this law was a violation of the equal protection clause to the Fourteenth Amendment.

The opinion of the court by Kennedy, Stevens, Souter, Ginsburg, Breyer, and O'Connor that sealed the fate on *Bowers v. Hardwick*, stated: "In our tradition the State is not omnipresent in the home. And there are other spheres of our lives and existence, outside the home, where the State should not be a dominant presence." (Opinion of Lawrence v. Texas, 2003 by Associate Justice Anthony Kennedy).

Then who should be the omnipresent authority in the home? The central power? Kennedy begins his opinion as a dreamer rather than a constitutionalist. The states, or respectively the people, have the right to enact such laws that are not in contradiction with the federal Constitution. And before 2003 and 1984, and to this day, there is nothing dictating that homosexual sex or sodomy is protected under the federal Constitution regardless of current rulings. Kennedy continued the opinion by saying, "Freedom extends beyond spatial bounds. Liberty presumes an autonomy of self that includes freedom of thought, belief, expression, and certain intimate conduct. The instant case involves liberty of the person both in its spatial and more transcendent dimensions." (Opinion of Lawrence v. Texas, 2003 by Associate Justice Anthony Kennedy).

Parts of this opinion sound like a political poem rather than a legal precedent or true opinion brief. Kennedy stated that yes, this country has freedom and liberty based on the Bill of Rights in the Constitution. But he bypassed the Tenth Amendment right that gives the states, or respectively the people, the right to enact such laws. He was decreeing from on high an imaginary law that blocked states, or respectively the people, from dictating their own set of laws.

Kennedy brought into his opinion brief a presiding ruling with a similar case basis. The court ruled that *Romer v. Evans*, 1996, needed to be struck down because it violated the homosexual community's equal protection clause of the Fourteenth Amendment.

Scalia brought this issue of plebiscite referendums on this issue on another case involving same-sex relationships, 2013 *Windsor v. United States*. Scalia had always stated that these issues are better to be left to democratic choice either by the state or the people. The central court of the land struck down a state constitution amendment in Colorado which was basically a pro-family referendum vote. Just because the governor of that state, Roy Romer, and the Supreme Court did not like the outcome of a plebiscite vote, does not mean that they are the final voice and have the authority to bypass the Tenth Amendment.

Since the inception of the Tenth Amendment, citizens on all sides of the question of same-sex and sodomy have seen victories and they have seen defeats. There have been plebiscites, legislation, persuasion, and loud voices — in other words, a representative republic.

"Victories in one place for some, see North Carolina Const., Amdt. 1 (providing that "[m]arriage between one man and one woman is the only domestic legal union that shall be valid or recognized in this state") (approved by a popular vote, 61% to 39% on May 8, 2012), are offset victories in other places for others, see Maryland Question

6 (establishing "that Maryland's civil marriage laws allow gay and lesbian couples to obtain a civil marriage license") (approved by a popular vote, 52% to 48%, om November 6, 2012.). Compare Maine Question 1 (permitting "the state of Maine to issue marriage licenses to same-sex couples") (approved by a popular vote of 53% to 47%, on November 6, 2012) with Maine Question 1 (rejecting "the new law that lets same-sex couples marry"), (Scalia's Court, Kevin A. Ring, 2004, 2016, page 392, Justice Scalia dissent on Windsor v. US).

"We might have let the people decide," (Scalia's Court, Kevin A. Ring, 2004, 2016, page 393, Justice Scalia dissent on Windsor v. US).

In Maryland, they had a plebiscite to allow homosexual couples to obtain a marriage license. Did anybody challenge that? No. Because the state, or respectively the people, were the ones in charge of passing their own legislation. In what way, this nation has become tolerant on the issue issue on same-sex marriage but not tolerant to other forms of marriages.

We want the states, people and the central power to respect the laws/rules of federalism and let the people pass any legislative measure they see fit if it does not contradict with federal constitutional law. What would be contradictory to the federal Constitution is if Maryland passes this type of plebiscite, but it is for a whites-only same-sex marriage legislation.

Let's take a few excerpts from Scalia's dissent on *Lawrence v. Texas*, and see who was right, the majority opinion or the second Great Dissenter, Antonin Scalia.

Most of today's opinion has no relevance to its actual holding — that the Texas statute "furthers no legitimate state interest which can justify its application to petitioners under rational-basis review, (Scalia's Court, Kevin A. Ring, 2004, 2016, page 358, Scalia's dissent on Lawrence v. TX).

Will the majority opinion say the same statement if the states of California, Oregon, New York pass a legislative measure that supports sodomy and/or same-sex marriage?

It's whatever most of these states' constituents elect -- a majority legislative body to have their views represented by the distinguished legislative members.

"… nowhere does the Court's opinion declare that homosexual sodomy is a "fundamental right" under the Due Process Clause; nor does it subject the Texas law to the standard review that would be appropriate (strict scrutiny) if homosexual sodomy were a "fundamental right." (Scalia's Court, Kevin A. Ring, 2004, 2016, page 358, Scalia's dissent on Lawrence v. TX).

As usual, these majority opinions leave deep holes to later fill and cause more complications in future legislative matters and later judicial matters. If the majority opinions of these court cases would indeed think with their minds and the law and not with their hearts and emotions, then the law would be simplified and understood for it to be a nation of laws.

"… the court simply describes petitioners' conduct as "an exercise of their liberty"—which it undoubtedly is—and proceeds to apply an unheard-of form of rational-basis review that will have far-reaching implications beyond this case." (Scalia's Court, Kevin A. Ring, 2004, 2016, page 358, Scalia's dissent on Lawrence v. TX).

Justice O'Connor voiced her opinion that the Texas law was in violation of the equal protection clause of the Fourteenth Amendment. Scalia gave a true constitutional compelling argument that O'Connor was and is still wrong to this day.

"Finally, I turn to petitioners' equal-protection challenge which no Member of the Court save Justice O'Connor embraces: On its face [the Texas law] applies equally to all persons. Men and women, heterosexuals and homosexuals, are all subject to its prohibition of deviate sexual intercourse with someone of the same sex. To be sure, Section 21.06 does distinguish between the sexes insofar as concerns the partner whom the sexual acts are performed: men can violate the law with other men, and women only with other women." (Scalia's Court, Kevin A. Ring, 2004, 2016,, page 368, Scalia's dissent on Lawrence v. TX.) But this cannot itself be a denial of equal protection, since it is precisely the same distinction regarding partner that is drawn in state laws prohibiting marriage with someone of the same sex while permitting marriage with someone of the opposite sex." (Scalia's Court, Kevin A. Ring, 2004, 2016, page 370, Scalia's dissent on Lawrence v. TX).

What Scalia was trying to state is that every single Texas citizen is equal to the state law being disputed. Both men and women, heterosexual and homosexual, are subject to criminalization of this Texas statute and no one is equal and unequal under law.

It is so depressing when jurists, pundits and politicians do not know the basis of the law. Especially when jurists rewrite the law to fit their own agenda. I am talking about the completely and misguided interpretation of the race statute of the Equal Protection Clause of the Fourteenth Amendment.

"This objection is made, however, that the anti-miscegenation laws invalidated *in Loving v. Virginia (1967)*, similarly were applicable to whites and blacks alike, and only distinguished between the races insofar as the partner was concerned. In *Loving*, however, we correctly applied heightened scrutiny, rather than the usual rational-basis review, because the Virginia statute was 'designed to maintain White Supremacy.' No Purpose to discriminate against men and women as a class can be gleaned from the Texas law, so rational-basis review applies. That review is readily satisfied here by the same rational-basis that satisfied it in Bowers—society's belief that certain forms of sexual behavior are "immoral and unacceptable," (Scalia's Court, Kevin A. Ring, 2004, 2016, page 370, Scalia's dissent on Lawrence v. TX).

Jurists that have truly no disregard for how the law was written and should be interpreted. Those that do such things should not be allowed to be on any bench let alone the highest bench of the land. The purpose of the decision of *Loving v. Virginia* was to end the "racial" discrimination between races across the country. The *Loving* ruling was indeed more constitutional than *Lawrence v. Texas* and *Obergefell v. Hodges*. That court ruling was based on the racial equal protection clause of the Fourteenth Amendment which that was the intention of the legislator that presented that legislation to the Halls of Congress. No legislator to this day has presented legislation to give equal protection toward the homosexual community and the court is not a legislature. And Scalia always kept pointing out that if this legislation was passed by the legislature of a state that satisfied most society that wanted their voices heard in that legislative body then so be it. Will I argue if the state legislation favored the homosexual community? No.

"It is one thing for a society to elect change; it is another for a court of law to impose change by adjudging those who oppose it hostes humani generis, enemies of the human race," (Scalia's Court, Kevin A. Ring, 2004, 2016, page 388, Justice Scalia dissent on Windsor v. US).

Justice Thomas made a short but to the point dissenting opinion and joined with Scalia.

"If I were a member of the Texas Legislature, I would vote to repeal it," (Dissenting Opinion of Lawrence v. Texas, 2003 by Associate Justice Clarence Thomas).

What does Thomas mean by this statement? It clearly means that he wants to give this legislation back to Texas for review, reform or repeal. He and the other members of the

Supreme Court are not legislators, they are jurists. Their job is to interpret the debated law to see if this law is applied in federal court or needs to be returned to the state for review.

"Notwithstanding this, I recognize that as a member of this court I am not empowered to help petitioners and others similarly situated. My duty, rather, is to "decide cases 'agreeably to the Constitution and laws of the United States.'" *Id., at 530, 14 L Ed 2d 510, 85 S Ct 1678.* And, just like Justice Stewart, I "can find [neither in the Bill of Rights nor any other part of the [*606] Constitution a] general right to privacy," *ibid.*, or as the Court terms it today, the "liberty of the person both in its spatial and more transcendent dimensions," *ante*, at 156 L Ed 2d at 515," (Dissenting Opinion of Lawrence v. Texas, 2003 by Associate Justice Clarence Thomas).

Regrettably, there is nothing in the Bill of Rights or Constitution that these individuals were violated without due process of the law -- federal or state. I also stand in dissent with Scalia, Thomas and Potter Stewart.

THREE

ACROSS STATE LINES
AND COMMERCE

Article I, Section 8, Clause 3:[3]

> [The Congress shall have Power] To regulate Commerce with foreign Nations, and among the several States, and with the Indian Tribes;

THIS SMALL PHRASE IN the Constitution has caused a lot of dismay and chaos in an attempt to find out what the Founding Fathers were trying to say to our new nation and its autonomous states. People from the left and from the right have interpreted in their own ways what this truly means. On one side, they do not want Congress to control commerce and the other side wants absolute control.

In this article, I am going to run down a few major court rulings in which the jurists have interpreted this clause in their own way. Some have done a good job, and others have contributed a massive bureaucratic buildup that has caused nothing but disaster. Let's first talk about the most famous case that established the Commerce Clause for government expansion on public and private use of substances. I am talking about the Supreme Court ruling of *Wickard v. Filburn*, 1942.

Roscoe Filburn was an Ohio wheat farmer who grew wheat for personal consumption by his family. There was no evidence brought against him that he sold, publicized, marketized, or distributed his product to his neighbors, city, county, or across state lines. The entire wheat production at the Filburn farm was for complete and personal use. But the central power disagreed and fined him for growing too much wheat.

This case went all up to the Supreme Court of the United States. Sadly, at that time, the highest court of the land was filled with FDR judicial appointments who acted as if they were members of the Politburo rather than jurists.

"The general scheme of the Agricultural Adjustment Act of 1938 as related to wheat is to control the volume moving in interstate and foreign commerce in order to avoid surpluses and shortages and the consequent abnormally low or high wheat prices and obstructions to commerce," (Opinion Brief of Wickard v. Filburn by Associate Justice Robert H. Jackson).

Robert H. Jackson came to the highest court in 1941 with an attitude that government, specifically the central government, had to be in control. He did not regard anything pertaining to the laws of federalism or in particular to the Tenth Amendment. When I read this statement above from his brief, I said to myself, "Is the United States of America, a tsarist nation or a Soviet nation? 'As related to wheat is to control the volume?' Where the central power has the audacity to place control onto the states? Especially when a farmer is growing this product for personal consumption."

"On May 19, 1941, the Secretary of Agriculture made a radio address to the wheat farmers of the United States in which he advocated approval of the quotas and called attention to the pendency of the amendment of May 26, 1941, which had at that time been sent to Congress to the White House and pointed out its provision for an increase in the loans on wheat to 85 percent of parity. He (Secretary of Agriculture) made no mention of the fact that it also increased the penalty from 15 cents a bushel to one-half of the parity loan rate of about 98 cents, but stated 'Because of the uncertain world situation, we deliberately planted several million extra acres of wheat. Farmers should not be penalized because they have provided insurance against shortages of flood," (Opinion Brief of Wickard v. Filburn by Associate Justice Robert H. Jackson).

Again, were we living and are we still living under a totalitarian form of government? From 1929 through1946, the United States had been secretly trying to institute policies like the Union of Soviet Socialist Republics. Having members of the politburo institute quotas that were probably not in the legislative act passed by Congress. And establishing hidden penalties to everyday hardworking Americans. While the central power sought not to punish farmers with these so-called wheat penalties when they did not work as hard to increase the level of production. Just because these farmers gave them an "insurance promissory note" that if they do not grow an excessive amount of wheat, they should not be punished. There you have it, folks, the beginning to punish merit and reward laziness.

As for Filburn, who made no insurance claim nor had to because his wheat production was not for public sale, distribution and consumption, he was nevertheless penalized because he grew too much and broke an indeed unconstitutional act of Congress by growing more of his wheat than what the law allows.

"Appellee says that this is a regulation of production and consumption of wheat. Such activities are, he urges, beyond the reach of Congressional power under the Commerce Clause, since they are local in character, and their effects upon interstate commerce are at most 'indirect.' In answer the Government argues that the statute regulates neither production or consumption, but only marketing; and, in alternative, that if the Act does go beyond the regulation of marketing it is sustainable as a 'necessary and proper' implementation of the power of Congress over interstate commerce," (Opinion Brief of Wickard v. Filburn by Associate Justice Robert H. Jackson).

The appellee did produce and consume the product of wheat, but for personal use. He did not sell it, market it, or distribute it and for that Congress has no right to enforce the Commerce Clause for farmers like Filburn. Government says that this regulation is only to regulate the marketing of products such as wheat. Did Filburn hire advertisers on Madison Avenue, New York City to work on a wheat campaign in Ohio? "Buy Midwest Buckwheat from the Buckeye State!" If this farmer was producing and consuming this product for personal use, I doubt he would broadcast its sale all over Ohio or its neighboring states. A bureaucrat will find a way to punish the people and the consumer for their need to control. Even when their logic is going against the federalism founding principle of this republic, they will white wash it away.

Justice Jackson is a prime example of a bureaucratic jurist. He compared this case to other rulings in which the Supreme Court decided that Congress had the right to enforce the Commerce Clause.

One comparison that he made was the 1824 *Gibbons v. Ogden* case.

"… however, other cases called forth broader interpretations of the Common Clause destined to supersede the earlier ones, and to bring about the return to the principles first enunciated by Chief Justice Marshall in *Gibbons v. Ogden*," (Opinion Brief of Wickard v. Filburn by Associate Justice Robert H. Jackson).

The ruling of *Gibbons v. Ogden* was completely and utterly different to the one they were discussing in that brief. This court made it known that Congress has the right to regulate the Commerce Clause for navigational purposes for commerce. I am a state sovereignty advocate and the first thing I would ask Chief Justice Marshall was whether he believed that individual states cannot run their ports. If the port of New York harbor charges outrageous amounts for a tariff, then that commercial ship will unload their items in the ports of Philadelphia, Newark, Baltimore, Charleston, or Savannah.

I believe I've figured out what the Founding Fathers were trying to say about this clause. Congress has a right to regulate commerce, yes, but only regulate it when states have committed an offense or cannot get along with their neighboring states or foreign nations. As I have said again and again, the central government is to be an administrative power. The Founding Fathers picked the wrong word when they wrote this clause. Instead of the word "regulate", they should have picked this word:

> [The Congress shall have Power] To "administer" Commerce with foreign Nations, and among the several States, and with the Indian Tribes;

From the beginning of this nation, it was never the intention of the founders to create a regulatory central power. The central power was to administer that all states worked together with each other and with each foreign nation to provide good commerce and friendship. Chief

Justice John Marshall, Robert Jackson, Woodrow Wilson, progressive Republicans, progressive Democrats, FDR, and even our public officials of today, have failed to really see how this nation was established.

Another ruling Justice Jackson pointed out was that Congress had the right to regulate monopolies under the Commerce Clause in the ruling of *Swift and Co. v United States*, 1905.

As I have said before, bureaucrats and politicians will find a way to control the citizenry and consumers for their own personal indulgences.

Another idiotic statement that Jackson made was that certain states do not have a large supply of certain crops, and in this case it was wheat.

"On the other hand, in some New England states less than one percent of the crop is devoted to wheat, and the average harvest is less than five acres per farm," (Opinion Brief of Wickard v. Filburn by Associate Justice Robert H. Jackson).

What did he truly mean about this statement?

We all know that states in the New England will have a low percentage of wheat production. Iowa, Kansas, Nebraska, and other states in the Plains are land-locked states and they will have a low percentage of fish and seafood. Now because the New England states have a lower percentage of what states have a higher percentage of, such as wheat, does that mean that we must punish the wheat farmers? If there was to be a certain punishment to be made,

I believe the punishment would have come from the state governments and not the central government.

"Only when he threshed and thereby made it part of the bulk of wheat overhanging the market did he become subject to penalty," (Opinion Brief of Wickard v. Filburn by Associate Justice Robert H. Jackson).

"To deny him this is not to deny him due process of the law," (Opinion Brief of Wickard v. Filburn by Associate Justice Robert H. Jackson).

When I and other constitutional scholars read this unanimous ruling brief, the first thing that at least comes to my mind, and hopefully to other Americans, is that nine politburo bureaucrat jurists established what the law was and enforced a law that was yet unconstitutional. This law, this incident and this ruling took place just after Soviet dictator Joseph Stalin sent in his troops to arrest, imprison and confiscate the land of many wheat farmers in the Russian farmland. I am glad that Justice Jackson did not ask the Department of Justice to arrest and imprison Roscoe Filburn and other American farmers. I guess that is somewhat how we differ from communist Soviet Union. But this ruling is like something that came out of the Soviet Union Dumas.

More rulings came after this one in which the high court ruled in favor of the Commerce Clause that Congress has the authority to "regulate," not "administer." At least the next ruling that I am about to discuss, the background of this case is somewhat to blame in involving the central government and other states.

I have always been a supporter of states to obtain, pass, and enforce their own laws that don't conflict with the Constitution. The whole reason that states have this right is to remain autonomous and not regulated by the central government. I have an issue when the central government acts to become an authoritarian centrist, but I have a bigger concern when the state welcomes the central government and other states to share their laws.

* * *

In 1996, California voters passed Proposition 215, now codified as the Compassionate Use Act of 1996. The proposition was designed to ensure that "seriously ill" residents of the state have access to marijuana for medical purposes, and to encourage federal and state Governments to take steps toward ensuring the safe and affordable distribution of the drug to patients in need." (Opinion Brief of Gonzales v. Raich, 2005 by Associate Justice John Paul Stevens).

I have to say that California disappoints me in ways that I cannot describe. California has forgotten how to preserve its rights as a state and instead has become a smaller version of a centralized (central form) of government.

What California does with their own laws is not the concern of the other states or the federal government. But when its leaders involve the federal government and other states to help, it is a recipe for disaster.

When multiple states decided to nullify the federal law of the Fugitive Slave Act, the state of Pennsylvania did not mention that it welcomes the support of the state of Delaware to help it enforce the law. There are other ways to encourage other states to pass similar laws and requesting assistance is not one of them.

"Shortly after taking office in 1969, President Nixon declared a national 'war on drugs.' As the first campaign of that war, Congress set out to enact legislation that would consolidate various drug laws on the books into a comprehensive statute, provide meaningful regulation over legitimate sources of drugs to prevent diversion into illegal channels, and strengthen law enforcement tools against the traffic in illicit drugs. That effort culminated in the passage of the Comprehensive Drug Abuse Prevention and Control Act of 1970, 84 Stat. 1236." (Opinion Brief of Gonzales v. Raich, 2005 by Associate Justice John Paul Stevens).

This was not, however, Congress' first attempt to regulate drugs in the national marketplace. Rather, as early as 1906, Congress enacted federal legislation "imposing labeling regulations on medications and prohibiting the manufacture or shipment of any adulterated or misbranded drug traveling in interstate commerce." (Opinion Brief of Gonzales v. Raich, 2005 by Associate Justice John Paul Stevens).

Marijuana itself was not significantly regulated by the federal government until 1937 when accounts of marijuana's addictive qualities and physiological effects, paired with dissatisfaction with enforcement at state and local levels, prompted Congress to pass the Marihuana Act, 50 Stat. 551 (repealed in 1970). Like the Harrison Act [1914 Opium & Coca Trade Restriction Act], the Marihuana Act did not outlaw the possession or sale of marijuana outright. (Opinion Brief of Gonzales v. Raich, 2005 by Associate Justice John Paul Stevens).

The central government of the United States has made it in their quest to act and to outlaw all forms of substances in the lives of the American citizenry. First, it was the constitutional Eighteenth Amendment that outlawed the sale, possession, production and distribution of liquor ... later repealed by the Twenty-First Amendment. Now it's the total unconstitutional prohibition of drugs. Whether they enacted laws in 1914, 1937 and 1970, the national Congress has failed to grasp that it states nothing in the Constitution that the central government has the right to outlaw any of these substances.

The liquor prohibition was indeed passed by a legal form, but it was still going against the principle of our American republic. But Congress passing these laws with no constitutional basis in order, makes these laws null and void and states have the absolute right to file a nullification legislation against them.

When I see a central government overreaching its power in unconstitutional laws onto the states, more respectively the people, it blows my mind. But what really frustrates me is when a state does not know to behave and act in the federalism republic that is America. Specifically, when I see a state with good, intellectual people, such as California, acting with pure ignorance to the rule of law and federalism.

For a state to ask for the help and support of other states and from the central government when proposing legislation, whether via legislation or plebiscite, is beyond comprehension. Especially when the central government has made it clear in their intentions that they will enforce their (unconstitutional) drug prohibition laws against the states.

"A state is not here to seek an alliance with the central government."

As James Madison, Father of the Constitution, put, "A refusal to cooperate with union officials."

Now I know why Scalia voted to side with the liberal wing of the Supreme Court, which I will explain in a little bit.

The opinion brief of Justice John Paul Stevens is a reassurance that the central government has the power and the states do not have that right and he is blatantly wrong.

"Then in 1970, after a declaration of the national "war on drugs," federal drug policy underwent a significant transformation. A number of noteworthy events precipitated this policy shift. First, in *Leary v. United States*, 395 U.S. 6, 89 S. Ct. 1532, 23 L.Ed.2d 57 (1969), this court held certain provisions of the Marihuana Tax Act and other narcotics legislation unconstitutional. Second, at the end of his term, President Johnson fundamentally reorganized the federal drug control agencies ... Congress [then] enacted the comprehensive Drug Abuse Prevention and Control Act." (Opinion Brief of Gonzales v. Raich, 2005 by Associate Justice John Paul Stevens).

Even after the Supreme Court ruled certain provisions of the Marihuana Act and other legislations unconstitutional, that should have been a clear sign for Congress to reexamine future laws regarding these types of substances when it comes to federal constitutional law. But that is asking too much for the national legislators when they now crave more central government control.

And if these national legislators want to impose control onto the states and respectively the people. Then it is up to the state and respectively the people, to reject these unconstitutional acts of Congress by way of nullification and non-cooperation. The way that California proposed their plebiscite legislation by asking for federal and other states' cooperation is completely insane and does not align itself with the rules of federalism.

"I agree with the Court's holding that the Controlled Substances Act (CSA) may validly be applied to the respondents' cultivation, distribution and possession of marijuana for personal, medicinal use. I write separately because my understanding of the doctrinal foundation on which that holding rests is, if not inconsistent with that of the court, at least more nuanced." (Concurrence Brief of Gonzales v. Raich, 2005 by Associate Justice Antonin Scalia).

I always wondered why Scalia voted in favor of the Commerce Clause of the central power and not with the dissenters. I finally had closure when I read his concurrence opinion to the court and I was satisfied. His concurrence opinion voted in favor of the Commerce Clause but gave a clear picture of what state sovereignty and the rules of federalism mean to this republic.

"As the Court said in the *Shreveport R. Co.*, the Necessary and Proper Clause does not give "Congress… the authority to regulate the internal commerce of a State, as such," but it does allow Congress "to take all measures necessary or appropriate to." 234 U.S., at 353, 34 S. Ct. 833; see also *Jones & Laughlin Steel Corp.*, U.S., at 38, 57 S.Ct. 615 (the logic of the *Shreveport Rate Cases* is not limited to instrumentalities of commerce.)." (Concurrence Brief of Gonzales v. Raich, 2005 by Associate Justice Antonin Scalia).

"As Lopez itself states, and the Court affirms today, Congress may regulate noneconomic intrastate activities only where the failure to do so "could… undercut" its regulation of interstate commerce. See *Lopez, supra*, at 561, 115 S. Ct. 1624; ante at 2206, 2210. This is not a power that threatens to obliterate the line between "what is truly national and what is truly local." *Lopez, supra*, at 561, 115 S. Ct. 1624. (Concurrence Brief of Gonzales v. Raich, 2005 by Associate Justice Antonin Scalia).

What Scalia is stating here is quite simple to interpret. In one case, he is saying that the law does not give Congress the right to place authority to regulate the inside commerce of a state, but it does give them power to take immediate actions to do so. I think especially when the state offers in their legislation a welcome mat for the central government to enter, a central government that is not friendly to the legalization of these substances, is a recipe for disaster and more central government intrusion onto state sovereignty. So, I now see why Scalia voted with the liberal base and not with the dissenters and not for central government control but for a better explanation of how the rules of federalism must be applied. Whether California wants to follow the rules of federalism like other states do, it is how this republic was established.

"Finally, neither respondents nor the dissenters suggest any violation of state sovereignty of the sort that would render this regulation "inappropriate," *id.,* at 421-except to argue that the CSA regulates an area typically left to state regulation... At bottom, respondents' *42 state-sovereignty argument reduces to the contention that federal regulation of the activities permitted by California's Compassionate Use Act is not sufficiently necessary to be "necessary and proper" to Congress's regulation of the interstate market..."

(Concurrence Brief of Gonzales v. Raich, 2005 by Associate Justice Antonin Scalia).

When I read this last paragraph of Scalia's concurrence brief, I understood from my interpretation that Antonin Scalia was a man of federalism and a state-sovereignty activist whether it supports or opposes the idea and cause of states' rights. How can this legislation from California be considered an attack on state sovereignty when California itself in its wisdom wrote in the plebiscite legislation to invite the central government to help enforce it? California invited the central government and other states that have similar anti-drug legislation in place to help them in their quest for marijuana legalization. California has always believed now that anything coming out of Sacramento should be taken seriously by other states and the central government. With all respect to the state government of Sacramento, this federalism republic does not revolve around them. It also does not revolve around the central government either. It revolves around every single state capital to choose their own legislation with the popular support of its citizens, legislation that is not contradicting federal constitutional law and most importantly that it does not form alliances with the central government. I strongly believe that even James Madison, a strong proponent of federalism and state sovereignty, if sitting on the high court today, would side with the opinion. Not for central government control, but because this California legislation contradicts the Tenth

Amendment, the nullification process and state sovereignty. And to end this discussion, I side with Scalia and on the side of state sovereignty.

In this case ruling, I must agree with Scalia and not with most of the court or the dissenters. Even though the dissenters want to lower the power of the Commerce Clause and that is great, it leaves a black hole that the states cannot seek to form alliances with a central government, especially when that central government has unconstitutional acts of Congress.

"Respondents Diane Monson and Angel Raich use marijuana that has never been bought or sold, that has never crossed state lines, and that has had no demonstrable effect on the national market for marijuana. If Congress can regulate *58 this under the Commerce Clause, then it can regulate virtually, anything-and the Federal Government is no longer one of the enumerated powers." (Dissenting Brief of Gonzales v. Raich, 2005 by Associate Justice Clarence Thomas).

In some cases, Clarence Thomas is right to defend the principles of state autonomy, but he is also wrong in the principles of American federalism. Indeed, the respondents were indeed not crossing state lines to produce, market, sell, and distribute marijuana. That being said, every state can pass any legislation as long as it does not contradict with federal constitutional law or federal law. But they do not have to do it. The state law has given a green-card permission for an alliance between the state of California, other states and the federal government. The California state plebiscite states, "… and to encourage Federal and State Governments to take steps toward ensuring the safe and affordable distribution of the drug to patients in need."

This state law completely contradicts the whole process of the Tenth Amendment and the state's allowance to disavow federal drug law by way of nullification. So, in the end, this law is indeed asking its California residents to cross state lines to do business for marijuana sales. Why would you seek an alliance from the central government, when that government has made unconstitutional acts of Congress against these substances. It is the duty of each state, to not cooperate with federal officials and that includes the Drug Enforcement Agency (DEA).

"We enforce the 'outer limits' of Congress' Commerce Clause authority not for their own sake, but to protect historic spheres of state sovereignty from excessive federal encroachment and thereby to maintain the distribution of power fundamental to our federalist system of government." (Dissenting Brief of Gonzales v. Raich, 2005 by Associate Justice Sandra Day O'Connor).

How can you, the Highest Court of the Land protect the historic spheres of state sovereignty when the state itself is seeking help from other states and the central government? The Founding Fathers only wrote it in one way, indefinite power by the states and refusal to cooperate with the central power. You can't have it both ways and get away with it.

"Today's decision allows Congress to regulate intrastate activity without check, so long as there is some implication by legislative design that regulating intrastate activity **2223 is essential (and the Court appears to equate "essential" with "necessary") to the intrastate regulatory scheme." (Dissenting Brief of Gonzales v. Raich, 2005 by Associate Justice Sandra Day O'Connor).

The California plebiscite legislation is opening a floodgate of problems that provides Congress the reason to enforce the Commerce Clause in California. Again, if this plebiscite would have never ushered the word, "encourage" for the central government and other state governments to assist them in their legislation, then Congress indeed has no power. But they are welcoming federal officials with open arms to enforce unconstitutional federal acts.

"The Court suggests that _Wickard_, which we have identified as "perhaps the most far reaching example of the Commerce Clause authority over intrastate activity," Lopez, supra, at 560, 115 S. Ct. 1624, established federal regulatory power over any home consumption of a commodity for which a national market exists." (Dissenting Brief of Gonzales v. Raich, 2005 by Associate Justice Sandra Day O'Connor).

The court may find some similarities between _Wickard_ and this case but in Scalia's concurrence brief, he does not mention a similarity or the opposite. And that is because these two cases are not one and the same. In _Wickard_, farmer Filburn was not encouraging his fellow neighboring states and central government to partake in his wheat business.

He was producing and consuming wheat for his household. It was the central government with the interpretation of the Supreme Court that this case ruling is unconstitutional. While *Raich*, the state of California was encouraging her fellow citizens to partake encouragement to invite other states and even the central government in enforcing a law that in the eyes of the central government is not supposed to be there. If California would have supported a law that nullified the federal drug laws and was not going to help enforce the CSA, then maybe Scalia would have sided with Thomas and O'Connor. That was not the case and to this day, Antonin Scalia is a man of true federalism principles.

We saw in one case ruling where the central government forced its citizens how to conduct business in the wheat and farm business and in that case, the farmer was not seeking partnerships with the central power or states. We saw in another case ruling where one state completely disavow the idea of federalism and states' rights and the court with its infinite wisdom of Scalia, struck down a California law that wanted to change our states rights and federalism republic way of life. And now I am going to show you a case ruling, where very similar to *Wickard v. Filburn*, the high court acted like bureaucratic jurists and not constitutional jurists. In conclusion, I side with Scalia and the rules and laws of state sovereignty and federalism.

* * *

The Supreme Court yet once again behaved like nine bureaucrats. They did not behave as constitutional jurists to preserve, protect and maintain the laws passed by Congress and determine what laws were appropriate to be in accordance with the Constitution. On June 25, 2015, five jurists decided to act like legislators and dictate how the law was to be enforced. They decided to force a way of life upon the American citizenry without their knowledge and representation.

"Second, the Act generally requires each person to maintain insurance coverage or make payment to the Internal Revenue Service. And third, the Act gives tax credits to certain people to make insurance more affordable." (Opinion Brief of King v. Burwell, 2015 by Chief Justice John Roberts).

By reading how Chief Justice John Roberts describes this act of Congress, it is blatantly unconstitutional. This has been an argument even before Congress voted for the Affordable Care Act, whereas Congress truly has the authority to "require" or "force" its citizens to buy and maintain health insurance. It's not the first time that the Internal Revenue Service has promoted and rewarded laziness while punishing and penalizing hard work. This is what happens when the republic becomes a lazy empire of incompetence. When Caesar triumphed in Gaul, the Romans who supported the republic were not pleased because Caesar started giving the winnings of Rome to the people. That promoted discontent between the hard-working people of Rome and the ordinary people of Rome. This is what is currently happening in our American republic right now.

"In addition to those reforms, the Act requires the creation of an "Exchange" in each —basically, a marketplace that allows people to compare and purchase insurance plans. The Act gives each State the opportunity to establish its own Exchange, but provides that the Federal Government will establish the Exchange if the State does not." (Opinion Brief of King v. Burwell, 2015 by Chief Justice John Roberts).

If the Compassionate Use Act of 1996 in California, in my eyes and Scalia's eyes, showed no legal weight for federalism, then this Act shares this same weightlessness for federalism. Again, the central government has the audacity, but not the authority, to dictate policy onto the states in how to set up their state government. And if that state government wishes not to cooperate with federal officials, the central government can still use those funds in that non-cooperative state, but it is a waste of federal tax funds. It would be in the best interest of the central government to focus their resources in a state that would be more cooperative with the act of Congress.

I believe the issue is that the central government wants control of the citizenry's health and they would do anything to bypass the Constitution and the laws of federalism for that control. Health insurance is not a commodity, no matter how these anti-constitutionalists want to create this picture. Neither wheat or health insurance is a commodity, but the central government has made it so. For what? For control.

Roberts and most bureaucrat jurists argue how other states have established market-share healthcare plans. I have no issue where states, respectively the majority of those residents, want to create their own legislation for their own market-share healthcare plans. Just as they do not use federal tax dollars for their plans and keep it between their own state lines.

"… in 1993, the State of Washington reformed its individual insurance market by adopting the guaranteed issue and community rating requirements." "…also in 1993, New York adopted the guaranteed issue and community rating requirements." "In 1996, Massachusetts adopted the guaranteed issue and community rating requirements and experienced similar results. But in 2006, Massachusetts added two more reforms: The Commonwealth required individuals to buy insurance or pay a penalty, and it gave tax credits to certain individuals to ensure that they could afford the insurance they were required to buy." (Opinion Brief of King v. Burwell, 2015 by Chief Justice John Roberts).

I have always stated that states, respectively the people, can pass whatever legislation they deemed fit if it doesn't conflict and contradict with federal constitutional law. Again, they can pass whatever legislation they see fit. Who are we to judge what Massachusetts, New York or California do in their own state capitols just as long as they keep it within their state lines and show no encouragement of support from other states or from the central power.

But what I see with this act of Congress in being a problem to our federalism principles is that Congress cannot give power to the executive to force its states, respectively the people, to buy a product they do not want or establish offices where that state has stated that they will not cooperate with union officials.

"The IRS addressed the availability of tax credits by promulgating a rule that made them available on both State and Federal Exchanges. 77 Fed. Reg. 30378 (2012). As relevant here, the IRS Rule provides that a taxpayer is eligible for a tax credit if he enrolled in an insurance plan through "an exchange," 26 CFR Sec. 1.36B—2 (2013), which is defined as " an Exchange serving the individual market... regardless of whether the Exchange is established and operated by a State... or by HHS," 45 CFR Sec. 155.20 (2014). At this point, 16 states and the District of Columbia have established their own Exchanges; the other 34 states have elected to have HHS do so." (Opinion Brief of King v. Burwell, 2015 by Chief Justice John Roberts).

As I said before, it is not the first time that the Internal Revenue Service has gotten involved in dictating legislation onto its citizens, the first time was *Wickard v. Filburn*. If I had to agree with Scalia that the Compassionate Use Act of 1996 of California showed no federalism standing, this federal act of Congress entitled the Affordable Care Act, shows even less federalism standing. The central government can pass legislation but cannot force its states and citizens to go along with this legislation and likewise a state cannot encourage other states and the central government to help them enforce their law. It is not how our republic was established.

"After telling each State to establish an Exchange, Section 18031 provides that all Exchanges "shall make available qualified health plans to qualified individuals." (Opinion Brief of King v. Burwell, 2015 by Chief Justice John Roberts).

I have a big problem with Justice Robert Jackson unanimous court opinion of *Wickard v. Filburn*, and I have a bigger problem with this statement from Chief Justice Roberts: "After telling each State 'to establish.'" This is what happens when the central power has overreached their power boundaries and now truly believes it has the ultimate power over its states and respectively the people.

"The Court holds that when the Patient Protection and Affordable Care Act says [the] "Exchange established by the State or the Federal Government." That is of course absurd, and the Court's 21 pages of explanation make it no less so." (Dissenting Brief of King v. Burwell, 2015 by Associate Justice Antonin Scalia).

Even in his opening dissenting opinion, Scalia knew when an act of Congress or when a state does not behave in the federalism fashion of our republic. This is why to this day Scalia remains the only jurist on that court with a true understanding of American federalism principles.

"This case requires us to decide whether someone who buys insurance on an Exchange established by the Secretary gets tax credits. You would think the answer would be obvious—so obvious there would hardly be a need for the Supreme Court to hear a case about it. In order to receive *2497 any money under Sec. 36B, an individual must enroll in an insurance plan through an "Exchange established by the State." The Secretary of Health and Human Services is not a State. So an Exchange established by the Secretary is not an Exchange established by the State—which means people who buy health insurance through such an Exchange get no money under Sec. 36B." (Dissenting Brief of King v. Burwell, 2015 by Associate Justice Antonin Scalia).

The audacity of the central government knows no bounds. The states respectively are beholden to a central departmental agency, such as the Agriculture Department and now the Department of Health and Human Services. We are also beholden to the Department of Homeland Security by giving up certain national security liberties in the name of "national security." We the states, people, have lost our health liberty in the base of the word meaning "Exchanges established by the State."

"Words no longer have meaning if an Exchange that is *not* established by a State is "established by the State." It is hard to come up with a clearer way to limit tax credits to state Exchanges than to use words "established by the State." And it is hard to come up with a reason to include the words "by the State" other than the purpose of limiting credits to state Exchanges. "[T]he plain, obvious, and rational meaning of a statute is always to be preferred to any curious, narrow, hidden sense that nothing but the exigency of a hard case and the ingenuity and study of an acute and powerful intellect would discover." *Lynch v. Alworth—Stephens Co.,* 267 U.S. 364, 370, 45 S. Ct. 274, 69 L.Ed. 660 (1925) (internal quotation marks omitted). Under all the usual rules of interpretation, in short, the Government should lose the case. But normal rules of interpretation seem always to yield to the overriding principle of the present Court: The Affordable Care Act must be saved." (Dissenting Brief of King v. Burwell, 2015 by Associate Justice Antonin Scalia).

Since the beginning of the progressive movement, the Bolsheviks in Russia, left and right anarchists in the German Weimar Republic, Italy's constitutional monarchy republic, Austria, Great Britain, and the United States have always found a way to appeal to the masses to approach their progressive-socialist message in a hidden manner. Whether they called it "The New Freedom Agenda of 1912," "The New Deal Programs of 1932," "The Great Society of 1964," "The Silent Majority of 1968," "Employee Free Choice Act," "Affordable Care Act," and "Exchanges established by the State," -- they are all hidden central government agendas to control all states' autonomies and respectively the people.

"Today's interpretation is not merely unnatural; it is unheard of. Who would ever have dreamt that "Exchange established by the State *or the Federal Government*"? Little short of an express statutory definition could justify adopting this similar reading. Yet the only pertinent definition here provides that "State" means "each of the 50 States and the District of Columbia." 42 U.S.C Sec. 18024(d). Because the Secretary is neither one of the 50 states nor the District of Columbia, that definition positively contradicts the eccentric theory that an Exchange established by the Secretary has been established by the State." (Dissenting Brief of King v. Burwell, 2015 by Associate Justice Antonin Scalia).

I truly understand that when the legislator, non-profit or corporation was writing this legislation that they knew nothing of federalism. What they refer to "Exchanges established by the State," they do not mean the independent, autonomous and sovereign 50 states and the District of Columbia. They mean the national central "State" government. It is so easy to misconstrue and mislead the states and the people on these word meanings. But that is how these progressives love to twist and turn the meanings of words to appease the masses. In the end, the only thing that suffers is the true republic, truly being misrepresented by its representatives.

"Making matters worse, the reader of the whole Act will come across a number of provisions beyond Sec. 36B that refer to the establishment of Exchanges by States. Adopting the Court's interpretation means nullifying the term "by the State" not just once, but again and again throughout the Act. Consider for the moment only those parts of the Act that mention an "Exchange established by State" in connection with tax credits: The formula for calculating the amount of the tax credit, as already explained, twice mentions "an Exchange established by the State." 26 U.S.C Sec. 26B(b)(2)(A), (c)(2)(A)(i).

- The Act directs States to screen children for eligibility for "[tax credits] under section 36B" and for "any other assistance or subsidies available for coverage obtained through" and "Exchange established by the State." 42 U.S.C. Sec 1396w—3(b)(1)(B)—(C).

- The Act requires "an Exchange established by the State" to use a "secure electronic interface" to determine eligibility for (among other things) tax credits. Sec. 1396w—3(b)(2).

- The Act authorizes "an Exchange established by the State" to make arrangements *2499 under which other state agencies "determine whether a State resident is eligible for [tax credits] under Section 36B." Sec 1396w—3(b)(2).

- The Act directs States to operate Web sites that allow anyone "who is eligible to receive [tax credits] under section 36B" to compare insurance plans offered through

"an Exchange established by the State." Sec. 1396w—3(b)
(4).

- One of the Act's provisions addresses the enrollment
  of certain children in health plans "offered through an
  Exchange established by the State" and then discusses the
  eligibility of these children for tax credits. Sec. 1397ee(d)
  (3)(B).

"It is bad enough for a court to cross out "by the State"
once. But seven times?"(Dissenting Brief of King v. Burwell, 2015
by Associate Justice Antonin Scalia).

This legislation was created with one sole purpose and
that purpose is to have the central government, "The State,"
control everything. They truly did not mean the individual
and sovereign and independent 50 states and the District
of Columbia. By reading parts of the Affordable Care Act,
it is quite obvious that whoever wrote it wants full central
government control over states and citizens regardless of
how much it will cost Americans in each state. I read parts
of this dissenting brief -- that includes part of the legislation
-- and it truly sickens me that nobody knows the true and
real meaning of our American federalism principle. That
now we are truly beholden to a central power with total
disregard to the autonomous, independent and sovereign 50
states.

I love it when the majority of the court that truly has no
regard for our American federalism principles loves to make

predictions that will cause damage to our republic, but they hide it so well.

"Worst of all for the repute of today's decision, the Court's reasoning is largely self-defeating. The Court predicts that making tax credits unavailable in States that do not set up their own Exchanges would cause disastrous economic consequences there. If that is so, however wouldn't one expect States to react by setting up their own Exchanges?" (Dissenting Brief of King v. Burwell, 2015 by Associate Justice Antonin Scalia).

Every time the central government interfered across state lines into a sovereign state, you have had nothing but disastrous outcomes. Let each state form its own set of healthcare laws. I am seeking each individual state to pass its own healthcare law, whether left or right leaning of the law and with strict accordance and no contradiction to the federal Constitution. But not seeking an encouragement alliance or cooperation between states or the central government.

"And wouldn't that outcome satisfy two of the Act's goals rather than just one: enabling the Act's reforms to work *and* promoting state involvement in the Act's implementation? The Court protests that the very existence of a federal fallback shows that Congress expected that some States might fail to set up their own Exchanges." (Dissenting Brief of King v. Burwell, 2015 by Associate Justice Antonin Scalia).

There is the arrogance of the central government from the high court to the halls of Congress. The central government truly believes that the individual states, respectively the people, cannot lead or decide for themselves. I have not seen this act of arrogance since Justice Oliver Wendell Holmes delivered his opinion brief of *Buck v. Bell*, see Chapter One.

"The Act that Congress passed provides that every individual "shall" maintain insurance or else pay a "penalty." 26 U.S.C. Sec. 5000A. This Court, however, saw that the Commerce Clause does not authorize a federal mandate to buy health insurance. So, it rewrote the mandate-cum-penalty as a tax. 567 U.S., at, 132 S. Ct., 2583—2601 (principal opinion). This Court, however, saw that the Spending Clause does not authorize this coercive condition. So, it rewrote the law to withhold only the incremental funds associated with the Medicaid expansion. 567 U.S., at, 132S.Ct., at 2601—2608 (principal opinion). Having transformed two major parts of the law, the Court today has turned its attention to a third. The Act that Congress passed makes tax credits available only on an "Exchange established by the State." This Court, however, concludes that this limitation would prevent the rest of the Act from working as well as hoped. So it rewrites the law to make tax credits available everywhere. We should start calling this law SCOTUScare." (Dissenting Brief of King v. Burwell, 2015 by Associate Justice Antonin Scalia).

Imagine the audacity and arrogance of the high court to now rewrite a law passed by the national Congress. What is the point in having 535 voting members when 6 who don't represent the states, let alone the people, will create the law of the land. This court case should have been sent back to the national Congress for further debate to reach an understanding of reform or repeal.

"The somersaults of statutory interpretation they have performed ("penalty means tax, "further [Medicaid] payments to the State" means only incremental Medicaid payments to the State, "established by the State" means not established by the State) will be cited by litigants endlessly, to the confusion of honest jurisprudence. And the cases will publish forever the discouraging truth that the Supreme Court of the United States favors some laws over others, and is prepared to do whatever it takes to uphold and assist its favorites. I dissent." (Dissenting Brief of King v. Burwell, 2015 by Associate Justice Antonin Scalia).

I also dissent along with Scalia and his fellow jurists on this great knowledge of American federalism court opinion. The court in itsever-progressive wisdom distorts the language in how a piece of legislation is presented. Now we know that whenever anyone means "Anything established by the State" they do not mean the federalism principle of individual states but by the central government. The Supreme Court is not an elected legislative body and so they have no authority to rewrite the law to please themselves or anyone else. Their job is to interpret the law and see if it contradicts or supports the federal Constitution in the principles of federalism. And if the law is contradictory, then they must send it back to Congress for further debate to reach an agreement of reform or repeal. I truly dissent in this court case in the true spirit of maintaining the principles of American federalism and state sovereignty.

FOUR

ACROSS STATE LINES
AND IMMIGRATION

Article 1, Section 8 of the United States Constitution:
"[T]o establish an uniform Rule of Naturalization."

On the issue of immigration, the Constitution may appear vague to the untrained eye. But in the eyes of legal experts and scholars, it is not vague, in fact, it is quite simple to comprehend. The uniform code of the

> **"B**uild the Wall" chant is all right and fine, to state if the chant is being represented at the state level but not on the national level.

American immigration system has been established under our principled governing document, The Constitution. It states in the Constitution, that Congress is "[T]o establish," not "[T]o enforce an uniform code of naturalization." The national Congress has already done its job by establishing it. Now in my opinion, it is the job of each individual state to enforce the Naturalization Clause with its own legislation.

The "Build the Wall" chant is all right and perfectly fine to chant. But the chant should be represented at the state level and not on the national level. If the state of Texas wants to build a wall to enforce the American immigration code, then it should be able to build its own wall with state funds and not via-federal government funding. The wall is an infrastructure structure that benefits the citizens of a city, county, and state. Each state is responsible for their borders, whether it borders another nation, has sea borders or landlocked. So, if Texas wants to enforce its borders as it is its right and duty to do so, then it should come out of the state budget and not from the federal budget. If the state of Kansas, a land-locked state, seeks to enforce the Clause and wants to build a wall along its border, then again, it is that state's Constitutional and sovereign duty to do so.

* * *

You will read a Supreme Court opinion about the first immigration enforcement policy enacted by the federal government. Prior to that opinion, the sole responsibility to enforce the Naturalization Clause rested in the hands of the sovereign states. Today, many Americans believe that because we are called "The United States of America," the states are under the control of a central (federal) government entity.

Despite the misinformation peddled by lawmakers and the media, nothing could be further from the truth. Yes, we are indeed "The United States of America." But only because this nation was to be established with autonomous state governments with a guiding principle known as the federal Constitution. But from the start, the Constitutional framers of this republic never intended to create a centralized government as it was and still is in Great Britain. Every state is responsible for enforcing all aspects of the Constitution and that includes the Naturalization Clause. In this federalism republic, no such power of naturalization has been granted to the United States.

The federal government, regardless of which political party is in power, has taken the reins to enforce the Naturalization Clause. The federal Congress and the federal executive branch have increased the levels of immigration enforcement. They have systematically taken away these duties from the sovereign states themselves. You will read in these rulings where the federal government has given itself discretionary power to enforce the Clause against the states and respectively, the people. Until recently, the federal government has given back this power to the states.

* * *

"When an alien has been found to be unlawfully present in the United States and a final order of removal has been entered, the government ordinarily secures the alien's "removal period," during which time the alien normally is held in custody. A special statute authorizes further detention if the Government fails to remove the alien during the 90 days. It says:

> "An alien ordered [1] removed who is inadmissible. . . [2] [or] removable [as a result of violations of criminal law, or reasons of security or foreign policy] or [3] who has been determined by the Attorney General to be a risk to the community or unlikely to comply with the order of removal, may be detained beyond the removal period and, if released, shall be subject to [certain] terms of supervision …." 8 U.S.C. Section 1231(a)(6) (1994 ed., Supp. V). (Opinion Brief of Associate Justice Stephen Breyer on Zadvydas v. Davis, et., al, 2001).

"In these cases, we must decide whether this post-removal-period statute authorizes the Attorney General to detain a *removable* alien indefinitely beyond the removal period or only for a period *reasonably necessary* to secure the alien's removal. We deal here with aliens who were admitted to the United States but subsequently ordered removed. Aliens who have not yet gained initial admission to this country present a very different question. See *Infra*, at 693-694." (Opinion Brief of Associate Justice Stephen Breyer on Zadvydas v. Davis, et., al, 2001).

This is a perfect example of a rogue, arrogant, and overreaching federal government. The federal Congress creates an (unconstitutional) immigration enforcement law that informs citizens that federal authorities can arrest, arraign and oversee the 90-day deportation process. So, now this court is examining if it's all right for the federal executive branch to exceed more than the required by law 90-day removal process to remove a deportable legal or illegal undocumented person from the nation.

In the words of James Madison, "the federal government executive branch does not have the power to deport/exile aliens."

That power lies with the sovereign states themselves to deport any legal or illegal alien.

"Based on our conclusion that indefinite detention of aliens in the former category would raise serious Constitutional concerns, we construe the statute to contain an implicit "reasonable time" limitation, the application of which is subject to federal-court review." (Opinion Brief of Associate Justice Stephen Breyer on Zadvydas v. Davis, et., al, 2001).

The indefinite detention of aliens not only raised constitutional concerns, but also concerns about the rules of federalism being broken. These applications of indefinite or definite detentions must be applied and enforced by state government review, not federal government review.

"The post-removal-period detention statute is one of the related set of statutes and regulations that govern detention during and after removal proceedings. While the removal proceedings are in progress, most aliens may be released on bond or paroled. 66 Stat. 204, as added and amended, 110 Stat. 3009-585, 8 U.S.C. Sub-Section(a)(2), (c) (1994 ed.,

Supp. V). After entry of a final removal order and during the 90-day removal period, however, aliens must be held in custody. Section 1231(a)(2). Subsequently, as the post-removal period statute provides, the Government "may" continue to detain that alien under supervision. Section 1231(a)(6)." (Opinion Brief of Associate Justice Stephen Breyer on Zadvydas v. Davis, et., al, 2001).

The law that Congress passed is quite clear — if the 90-day removal proceedings deadline has passed, then the suspect must be allowed to be free under supervision. This is what happens when a rogue, overpowering and arrogant federal government changes the rules of federalism to fit its own agenda and principles.

"In its view, the Government would never succeed in its efforts to remove Zadvydas from the United States, leading to his permanent confinement, contrary to the Constitution." *Id.*, at 1027. (Opinion Brief of Associate Justice Stephen Breyer on Zadvydas v. Davis, et., al, 2001).

In my view, the federal government will do what it pleases, whenever they please against the will of the citizens, residents and legal, illegal aliens of this country. We must find a way to make our efforts known to allow states to retake their power away from the federal government.

"The second case is that of Kim Ho Ma. Ma was born in Cambodia in 1977. When he was two, his family fled, taking him to refugee camps in Thailand and the Philippines and eventually to the United States, where he has lived as a resident alien since the age of seven. In 1995, at age 17, Ma was involved in a gang-related shooting, convicted of manslaughter, and sentenced to 38-months imprisonment. He served two years, after which he was released into INS custody. In light of his conviction of an "aggravated felony," Ma was ordered removed. See 8 U.S.C. Sub-Section 1101(a)(43)(F) (defining certain violent crimes as aggravated felonies), 1227(a)(2)(A)(iii) (1994 ed., Supp. IV) (aliens convicted of aggravated felonies are deportable). The 90-day removal period expired in early 1999, but the INS continued to keep Ma in custody, because in light of his former gang membership, the nature of his crime, and his planned participation in a prison hunger strike, it was "unable to conclude that Mr. Ma would remain nonviolent and not violate the conditions of release." (Opinion Brief of Associate Justice Stephen Breyer on Zadvydas v. Davis, et., al, 2001).

"The Ninth Circuit affirmed Ma's release. *Kim Ho Ma v. Reno*, 208 F 3d 815 (2000). It concluded, based in part on Constitutional concerns, that the statute did not authorize detention for more than a "reasonable time" beyond the 90-day period authorized for removal. *Id.*, at 818. And, given the lack of repatriation agreement with Cambodia, that time had expired upon passage of the 90n days. *Id.*, at 830-831." (Opinion Brief of Associate Justice Stephen Breyer on Zadvydas v. Davis, et., al, 2001).

The crimes that were brought against Ma were the same crimes against Zadvydas, a state offense. Ma and Zadvydas were both found guilty of their crimes and served their time. There was no need for them to be handed over to the Department of Justice/INS. And to make matters worse, the INS agency found that Ma, a legal resident, could be removed from the nation. They found this legal alien resident removable because of his alleged association with gang members.

This is another example of a completely rogue and arrogant federal government. And what's worse is that the Ninth Circuit Court of Appeals is just as bad as the highest court of the land. The jurists completely ignored the rules of federalism and should have given these cases back to the appropriate state governments to legislate or interpret.

"And in 1961 Congress replaced district court APA review with initial *deportation order review in courts of appeals.* The 1961 Act specified that federal habeas corpus courts were also available to hear statutory and Constitutional challenges to *deportation* (and exclusion) *orders.* See 8 U.S.C. Sub-Section 1105a(a)(10), (b) (repealed 1996). These statutory changes left habeas untouched as the basic method for obtaining review of continued *custody after* deportation order had become final. More recently, Congress has enacted several statutory provisions that limit the circumstances in which judicial review of deportations decisions is available. But none applies here. One provision, 8 U.S.C. Section 1231(h) (1994 ed., Supp. V), simply forbids courts to construe *that section* "to create any. . .procedural right or benefit that is legally enforceable"; it does not deprive an alien of the right to rely on 28 U.S.C. Section 2241 to challenge detention that is without statutory authority. Another provision, 8 U.S.C. Section 1252(a)(2)(B)(ii) (1994 ed., Supp. V), says that "no court shall have jurisdiction to review decisions "specified . . . to be in the discretion of the Attorney General." We conclude that Section 2241 habeas corpus proceedings remain available as a forum for statutory and Constitutional challenges to post-removal-period detention. And we turn to the merits of the alien's claims." (Opinion Brief of Associate Justice Stephen Breyer on Zadvydas v. Davis, et., al, 2001).

The federal Congress has given too much power to the federal Executive Branch. The federal court has affirmed this abusive power of the federal Executive Branch. All federal branches of government have stolen this power from the sovereign states.

"The post-removal period detention statute applies to certain categories of aliens who have been ordered removed, namely, inadmissible aliens, criminal aliens, aliens who have violated their nonimmigrant status conditions, and aliens removable for certain national security or foreign relations reasons, as well as any alien "who has been determined by the Attorney General to be a risk to the community or unlikely to comply with the order of removal," 8 U.S.C. Section 1231(a)(6) (1994 ed., Supp. V); see also 8 CFR Section 241.4(a)(2001). It says that an alien who falls into one of these categories "may be detained beyond the removal period and, if released, shall be subject to [certain] terms of supervision." 8 U.S.C. Section 1231(a)(6) (1994 ed., Supp. V.)." (Opinion Brief of Associate Justice Stephen Breyer on Zadvydas v. Davis, et., al, 2001).

What right does the federal government have to decide these categories and where do they get the gall to set these categorical policies?

"The Government argues that the statute means what it literally says. It sets no 'limit on the length of time beyond the removal period that an alien who falls within one of the Section 1231(a)(6) categories may be detained.' Hence, "whether to continue to detain such an alien and, if so, in what circumstances and for how long" is up to the Attorney General, not up to the courts. *Ibid.*" [I]t is a cardinal principle" of statutory interpretation, however, that when an Act of Congress raises "a serious doubt" as to its Constitutionality, "this Court will first ascertain whether a construction of the statute is fairly possible by which the question may be avoided." (Opinion Brief of Associate Justice Stephen Breyer on Zadvydas v. Davis, et., al, 2001).

It is a known federalism, constitutional cardinal principle that when an act of Congress raises "a serious doubt" as to its constitutionality and validity. It is the job and duty of the sovereign states to question its validity, nullify and refuse cooperation. It is mainly the job of the highest court of the land to question the validity of the act, but it must also respect the rules of federalism among the sovereign states.

I am deeply disappointed in this Court and in past ones because of how their rulings disrespect the rules of federalism.

"I join in Part I of JUSTICE KENNEDY's dissent, which establishes the Attorney General's clear statutory authority to detain criminal aliens with no specified time limit. I write separately because I do not believe that, as JUSTICE KENNEDY suggests in Part II of his opinion, there may be some situations in which the courts can order release. I believe that in both *Zadvydas v. Davis*, No. 99-7791, and *Ashcroft v. Ma*, No. 00-38, a "careful description" of the substantive right claimed, *Reno v. Flores,* 507 U.S. 292, 302 (1993), suffices categorically to refute its existence. A criminal alien under final order of removal who allegedly will not be accepted by any other country in the reasonably foreseeable future claims a Constitutional right of supervised release into the United States. This claim can be packaged as freedom from "physical restraint" or freedom from "indefinite detention", *ante*, at 689,690, but it is at bottom a claimed right of release into this country by an individual who *concededly* has no legal right to be here. There is no such Constitutional right." (Dissenting Brief of Associate Justice Antonin Scalia on Zadvydas v. Davis, et., al, 2001).

I join in JUSTICE SCALIA's dissent in his first sentence statement but I disagree with his continuing statements. I do not think we need to give clear statutory and absolute power to the attorney general or anybody else in the

federal government. I take issue with how criminal aliens
are detained for an unrestricted amount of time. When a
criminal or non-criminal alien is being held by the federal
government, it is completely unconstitutional. This is where
I disagreed with JUSTICE SCALIA and the ruling court
opinion on this matter and quite frankly on the current
situation over immigration today.

"Like a criminal alien under final order of removal, an
inadmissible alien at the border has no right to be in the
United States." (Dissenting Brief of Associate Justice Antonin Scalia
on Zadvydas v. Davis, et., al, 2001).

Under a federalism republic such as the United States,
whether a criminal under final order of removal, or an
inadmissible alien at the border or any port of entry has the
right to be in the United States should be decided only by
the sovereign states themselves. Prior to 1875, the sovereign
states sought to enforce the Naturalization Clause without
the consultation of the federal government.

"*The Chinese Exclusion Case*, 130 U.S. 581, 603
(1889). *In Shaughnessy v. United States ex rel. Mezei*, 345
U.S. 206 (1953), we upheld potentially indefinite of such
an inadmissible alien whom the Government was unable
to return anywhere else. We said that "we [did] not think
that respondent's continued exclusion deprives him of any
statutory or Constitutional right." *Id.*, at 215. While four
Members of the Court thought that Mezei deserved greater
procedural protections (the Attorney General had refused

to divulge any information as to why Mezei was detained, id., at 209), no Justice asserted that Mezei had a substantive Constitutional right to release into this country. And Justice Jackson's dissent, joined by Justice Frankfurter, affirmatively asserted the opposite, with no contradiction from the Court: "Due Process does not invest any alien with a right to enter the United States, *nor confer on those admitted the right to remain against the national will.* Nothing in the Constitution requires admission or sufferance of aliens hostile to our scheme of government." *Id.*, at 222-223 (emphasis added). Insofar, as a claimed legal right to release into this country is concerned, an alien under final removal stands on an equal footing with an inadmissible alien at the threshold of entry: He has no such right." (Dissenting Brief of Associate Justice Antonin Scalia on Zadvydas v. Davis, et., al, 2001).

"This Court has suggested, however, that the Constitution may well preclude granting "an administrative body the unreviewable authority to make determinations implicating fundamental rights." *Superintendent, Mass. Correctional Institution at Walpole v. Hill,* 472 U.S. 445, 450 (1985) (O'Connor, J); see also *Crowell,* 285 U.S., at 87 (Brandeis, J., dissenting) ("[U]nder certain circumstances, the Constitutional requirement of due process is a requirement of judicial process"). The Constitution demands greater procedural protection even for property. See South Carolina v. Regan, 465 U.S. 367, 393, (1984) (O'Connor, J., concurring in judgment); Phillips v. Commissioner,

283 U.S. 589, 595-597 (1931) (Brandeis, J.). The serious
Constitutional problem arising out of a statute, that, in these
circumstances, permits an indefinite, perhaps permanent,
deprivation of human liberty without any such protection
is obvious." (Opinion Brief of Associate Justice Stephen Breyer on
Zadvydas v. Davis, et., al, 2001).

This is correct in that the Constitution not just grants,
but demands, a greater procedural protection for all citizens'
lives, including property. But that procedural protection is
given to the states to enforce. Not once did Justice Jackson,
or now Justice Breyer, mention the rules of federalism or the
autonomous authority each sovereign state has to enforce
the immigration clause. Jackson and Breyer are plainly
focusing on giving this enforcement (immigration) duty to
the federal government while ignoring the will of the rules
of federalism.

"The Government argues that, from a Constitutional
perspective, alien status itself can justify indefinite
detention, and points to *Shaughnessy v. United States ex rel.
Mezei*, 345 U.S. 206 (1953), as support. That case involved
a once lawfully admitted alien who left the United States,
returned after a trip abroad, was refused admission, and was
left on Ellis Island, indefinitely detained there because the
Government could not find another country to accept him.
The Court held that Mezei's detention did not violate the
Constitution. *Id.*, at 215-216." (Opinion Brief of Associate Justice
Stephen Breyer on Zadvydas v. Davis, et., al, 2001).

I discuss this case because since 1953, and even before 1953, this has been a problem of the federal government. This has been my biggest issue of a rogue and arrogant federal government, taking away the Constitutional duty from the sovereign states.

"His presence on Ellis Island did not count as entry into the United States. Hence, he was "treated," for Constitutional purposes, "as if stopped at the border." Id., at 213, 215. And that made all the difference." (Opinion Brief of Associate Justice Stephen Breyer on Zadvydas v. Davis, et., al, 2001).

When the federal government denies the entry of the residents of their sovereign state, we have lost the very freedom we received from the framers of the Constitution. Either at a border land of entry, seaport port of entry, or airport port of entry, it is not the official duty of the federal government to be the official doorman of each sovereign state.

"In light of this critical distinction between *Mezei* and the present cases, Mezei does not offer the Government significant support, and we need not consider the alien's claims that subsequent developments have undermined *Mezei's* legal authority. (Opinion Brief of Associate Justice Stephen Breyer on Zadvydas v. Davis, et., al, 2001).

"*Mezei* thus stands unexplained and undistinguished by the Court's opinion. We are offered no justification why an alien under a valid and final order of removal— which has *totally extinguished* whatever right to presence in this country he possessed—has any greater due process right to be released into the country than an alien at the border seeking entry. Congress undoubtedly thought that both groups of aliens—inadmissible aliens at the threshold and criminal aliens under final order of removal—could be Constitutionally detained on the same terms, since it provided the authority to detain both groups in the very same statutory provision, see 8 U.S.C. Section 1231(a)(6). Because I believe Mezei controls these cases, and, like the Court, I also see no reason to reconsider Mezei, I find no Constitutional impediment to the discretion Congress gave to the Attorney General. JUSTICE KENNEDY's dissent explains the clarity of the detention provision, and I see no obstacle to following the statute's meaning." (Dissenting Brief of Associate Justice Antonin Scalia on Zadvydas v. Davis, et., al, 2001).

Mezei, Zadvydas, and Kim Ho Ha all shared one thing in common. They were all legal residents of their sovereign state, within the borders of their own state. We do not know why Mezei was detained because Congress gave the federal executive branch unlimited discretionary power to not share any information of this person's detainment. That right there, is a violation of our Constitutional Bill of Rights. As far the other

> The National Congress giving unlimited immigration enforcement power to the National Executive Branch and then being confirmed by the National Court is an attack on our rules of federalism.

two residents, they were legal alien residents and they indeed committed an illegal infraction in their respective sovereign states and they were prosecuted. Why the federal Department of Justice ordered their arrest, excessive detainment and final order of removal is unclear. But, yet again, Congress gave unlimited power to the federal executive branch.

"…, the Constitution permits detention that is indefinite and potentially permanent." (Opinion Brief of Associate Justice Stephen Breyer on Zadvydas v. Davis, et., al, 2001).

The Constitution does permit detention that is indefinite, but only within the confines of the enforcement policy of each of the sovereign and independent states. It does not grant the federal government permission for any such immigration enforcement.

"The Court expressly declines to apply or overrule Mezei, ante, at 694, but attempts to distinguish it—or, I should rather say, to obscure it in a legal fog. First, the Court claims that "[t]he distinction between an alien who has effected an entry into the United States and one who has never entered runs throughout immigration law." *Ante*, at 693. True enough, but only where that distinction makes perfect sense: with regard to the question of what *procedures* are necessary to prevent entry, as opposed to what *procedures* are necessary to eject a person already in the United States." (Dissenting Brief of Associate Justice Antonin Scalia on Zadvydas v. Davis, et., al, 2001).

The case of Mezei has a lot of significance in detailing how much power the federal executive branch can obtain and ignore the will of state sovereignty. From what I learned from this story, he (Mezei) re-entered the United States after a visit to his native Hungary and he was denied entry by federal immigration authorities. He was held indeterminately on Ellis Island and he obtained no chance to invoke his due-process rights.

First, whether you are a temporary worker, permanent alien resident, or a citizen, you have rights. No one can take away those rights without due process of the law. And for the chief enforcer of this federalism republic to have an arrogant and rogue attitude, and not share with the Court the reason behind this man's arrest and detention, it illustrates just how out of control the federal government has become — then and now.

> **A** jurist not willing to defend the rules of federalism is no defender of sovereignty.

I expect Justice Jackson to be nothing less than a Constitutional jurist. He wrote the dissent of the Mezei case and yet sided with the opinion of the court. Talk about a flip-flopper. Either you stand for federalism or you stand for totalitarianism, but you cannot stand for both.

> "Due Process does not invest any alien with a right to enter the United States, *nor confer on those admitted the right to remain against the national will.* Nothing in the Constitution requires admission or sufferance of aliens

> hostile to our scheme of government."([supposed] Dissenting Opinion of Associate Justice Robert Jackson, Shaughnessy v. United States ex rel. Mezei, 1953).

"Due Process does not invest any alien with a right to enter the United State …." The federal government is not here to invest its time and resources in enforcing the Naturalization Clause. Again, it is the sovereign states that have a Constitutional right and duty to invest their time and resources on the due process of an alien entering their sovereign borders. Honestly, this statement from Justice Jackson is rogue, arrogant and demanding that the federal power supersedes the sovereignty of the states. Frankly, I am not surprised by this statement made by Justice Jackson. The jurist that wrote the opinion of *Wickard v. Filburn*. A jurist not willing to defend the rules of federalism is no defender of sovereignty and liberty.

If I do not quite believe and trust Justice Jackson, why would I believe and trust Justice Breyer on his court opinion of *Zadvydas v. Davis*.

"A statute permitting indefinite detention of an alien would raise a serious Constitutional problem. The Fifth Amendment's Due Process Clause forbids the Government to "depriv[e]" any person … of … liberty … without due process of law." Freedom from imprisonment—from government custody, detention, or other forms of physical restraint—lies at the heart of the liberty that Clause protects. See *Foucha v. Louisiana*, 504 U.S. 71, 80 (1992). And this Court has said that government detention violates that Clause unless the detention is ordered in a criminal proceeding with adequate procedural protections, see *United States v. Salerno*, 481 U.S. 739, 746 (1987), or in certain special and "narrow" nonpunitive "circumstances," *Foucha supra*, at 80, where a special justification, such as harm-threatening mental illness, outweighs the "individual's Constitutionally protected interest in avoiding physical restraint." *Kansas v. Hendricks*, 521 U.S. 346, 356 (1997). (Opinion Brief of Associate Justice Stephen Breyer on Zadvydas v. Davis, et., al, 2001).

"The proceedings at issue here are civil, not criminal, and we assume that they are nonpunitive in purpose and effect. There is no sufficiently strong special justification here for indefinite civil detention—at least as administered under this statute. The statute, says the government, has two regulatory goals: "ensuring the appearance of aliens at future immigration proceedings" and "[p]reventing danger to the community." Brief for respondents in No. 99-7791, p. 24. But by definition the first justification—preventing flight— is weak or nonexistent where removal seems a remote possibility at best." (Opinion Brief of Associate Justice Stephen Breyer on Zadvydas v. Davis, et., al, 2001).

The Due Process Clause is a right bestowed by anybody paying a tribute to their sovereign state. It is a right best enforced by the individual sovereign state and not by the federal government. The only duty of the federal government is to administer that enforcement. If for some reason, these states are denying any sort of due process toward a citizen, legal alien, and temporary worker, then it is the job of the

> **F**ederal constitutional immigration law has so much weight than Federal immigration law.

federal government to let them know of their actions and remind them of their duties. Not by forcing the state or enforcing it on their own.

"The Government also points to the statute's history. That history catalogs a series of changes, from an initial period (before 1952) when lower courts had interpreted statutory silence, Immigration Act of 1917, ch. 29, Sub-Section 19, 20, 39 Stat. 889, 890, to mean that deportation-related detention must end within a reasonable time, Spector v. Landon, (CA9 1954) (collecting cases); United States ex rel. Doukas v. Riley (CA7 1947); *United States ex rel. Ross v. Wallis*, (CA2 1922), to a period (from the early 1950's through the late 1980's) when the status permitted, but did not require, post-deportation order detention for up to six months, Immigration and Nationality Act of 1952, (1982 ed.; to more recent statutes that have at times mandated and at other times permitted the post-deportation-order detention of aliens falling into certain categories such as aggravated felons, Anti-Drug Abuse Act of 1988....(mandating detention); Immigration Act of 1990;.... (permitting release under certain circumstances); Miscellaneous and Technical Immigration and Naturalization Amendments of 1991, section 306(a)(4), 105 Stat. 1751, 8 U.S.C. Section 1252(a) (2)(B) (same)." (Opinion Brief of Associate Justice Stephen Breyer on Zadvydas v. Davis, et., al, 2001).

"In early 1996, Congress explicitly expanded the group of aliens subject to mandatory detention, eliminating provisions that permitted release of criminal aliens who had at once been lawfully admitted to the United States. Antiterrorism and Effective Death Penalty Act of 1996, Section 439(c), 110 Stat. 1277. And later that year Congress enacted the present law, which liberalizes pre-existing law by shortening the removal period from six months to 90 days, mandates detention of certain criminal aliens during the removal proceedings and for subsequent 90-day removal period, and adds the post-removal-period provision here at issue. Illegal Immigration Reform and Immigration Responsibility Act of 1996, Div. C, Sub-Section 303, 305, 110 Stat. 3009-585, 3009-598 to 3009-599; 8 U.S.C. Sub-Section 1226(c), 1231(a) (1994 ed., Supp. V)". (Opinion Brief of Associate Justice Stephen Breyer on Zadvydas v. Davis, et., al, 2001).

Whatever statute the national Congress passes, it must be aligned with the Constitution. These past and present immigration statutes passed by the national congress, does not align with the constitution.

From the unconstitutional immigration enforcement acts passed and signed during the Woodrow Wilson administration to the Ronald Reagan administration, all share the same overreach and force from the federal government.

> **T**he national government has truly become more arrogant than when it first enacted its first federal immigration statute of 1875.

In 1996, the national Congress passed a more lenient but still unconstitutional measure liberating the detention process from six months to ninety days. Now, the esteemed members of the Supreme Court are stating that the federal executive branch, with the utmost discretion from the attorney general can arrest, detain and deport any alien, legal or illegal, residing in any of the sovereign states for 90 days. The national government has truly become more rogue and arrogant now than when it first enacted its first federal immigration statute in 1875.

"The Government seems to argue that, even under our interpretation of the statute, a federal habeas court would have to accept the Government's view about whether the implicit statutory limitation is satisfied in a particular case, conducting little or no independent review of the matter. In our view, that is not so. Whether a set of particular circumstances amounts to detention within, or beyond, a period reasonably necessary to secure removal is determinative of whether the detention is, or is not, pursuant to statutory authority. The basic federal habeas corpus statute grants the federal courts authority to answer that question. See 28 U.S.C. Section 2241(c)(3) (granting courts authority to determine whether detention is "in violation of the . . . laws . . . of the United States"). In doing so the Courts carry out what this namely, "to relieve detention by executive authorities without judicial trial." Brown v. Allen, 344 U.S. 443, 533 (1953) (Jackson, J., concurring in result)." (Opinion Brief of Associate Justice Stephen Breyer on Zadvydas v. Davis, et., al, 2001).

Justice Breyer keeps quoting a concurring quote from Justice Robert Jackson and again does not surprise me at all. To summarize his quote, Justice Jackson is stating that the courts are relieved from any cases involving aliens, whether citizen or not, that have been detained by the federal government. Justice Jackson is advocating for the federal government to disavow our citizens' or aliens' rights.

"We recognize, as the Government points out, that review must take appropriate account of the greater immigration related expertise of the Executive Branch, of the serious administrative needs and concerns inherent in the necessarily extensive INS efforts to enforce this complex statute, and the Nation's need to "speak with one voice" in immigration matters." (Opinion Brief of Associate Justice Stephen Breyer on Zadvydas v. Davis, et., al, 2001).

"And they consequently require courts to listen with care when the Government's foreign policy judgments, including, for example, the status of repatriation negotiations, are at issue, and to grant the Government appropriate leeway when its judgments rest upon foreign policy expertise." (Opinion Brief of Associate Justice Stephen Breyer on Zadvydas v. Davis, et., al, 2001).

"To speak with one voice" in immigration matters exemplifies the sheer arrogance of the federal government. If this republic was intended to have one voice dictate all policy-making decisions, including the naturalization enforcement. Then we would never have separated from England. This country had 13 different voices speaking all at once with one goal in mind, the rules of federalism. The rules of federalism which is dictated in the national Constitution. Now it has 50 different voices, but the principle remains the same.

The arrogant federal government has always wanted to obtain for central autonomy control to appease the mob with hints of patriotism. From the claim to "Protect the Homeland" with more security that violates our Bill of Rights or protecting the so-called "national sovereignty" from foreign invaders. In this republic, there is no such thing called "national sovereignty." We have a federal government that administers, not regulates our "state sovereignty." It is the states that protect our sovereignty and borders to keep these United States safe and united.

"While an argument can be made for confining any presumption to 90 days, we doubt that when Congress shortened the removal period to 90 days in 1996 it believed that all reasonably foreseeable removals could be accomplished in that time. We do have reason to believe, however, that Congress previously doubted the Constitutionality of detention for more than six months. See Juris. Statement in United States v. Witkovich, O.T. 1956, No. 295, pp. 8-9." (Opinion Brief of Associate Justice Stephen Breyer on Zadvydas v. Davis, et., al, 2001).

"Consequently, for the sake of uniform administration in the federal courts, we recognize that period. After this 6-month period, once the alien provides good reason to believe that there is no significant likelihood of removal in the reasonably foreseeable future, the Government must respond with evidence sufficient to rebut that showing. And for detention to remain reasonable, as the period of prior post-removal grows, what counts as the "reasonably foreseeable future" conversely would have to shrink. This 6-month presumption, of course, does not mean that every alien not removed must be released after six months. To the contrary, an alien may be held in confinement until it has been determined that there is no significant likelihood of removal in the reasonably foreseeable future." (Opinion Brief of Associate Justice Stephen Breyer on Zadvydas v. Davis, et., al, 2001).

Since the turn of the Twentieth century, the national Congress has never understood the repercussions of its involvement and the involvement of the federal executive branch in enforcing the Naturalization Clause. Whether it be the six months or a 90-days removal of an alien by the federal government, it holds no Constitutional value. We the states, are not beholden to a central power, it is the other way around. And these past and current national court jurists must comprehend these rules. These rules of federalism must always be applied whether they like it or not.

I foremost respectfully one-hundred percent dissent with this opinion of this court ruling of *Zadvydas v. Davis* because it is a clear assault and invasion of our rules of federalism and autonomy of each state. The federal government has absolutely no authority in enforcing any aspect of the Naturalization Clause regarding the detention and removal of aliens. Let the states alone apprehend, prosecute, detain and remove any alien residing in a sovereign state, which they do have and have always had the full authority to do. And so, I dissent in full.

* * *

"Under the Immigration and Nationality Act [of 1965], 8 U.S.C. Section 1226(c), "[t]he Attorney General shall take into custody any alien who" is removable from this country because he has been convicted of one of a specified set of crimes, including an "aggravated felony." (Syllabus of Demore, District Director, San Francisco District of Immigration and Naturalization Service, v. Kim, 2003).

* * *

This act of Congress is the first attack on our rules of federalism and state sovereignty. The Supreme Court has used this act of Congress to justify the actions of the federal government in becoming overly aggressive and overpowering. After September 11, 2001, we have seen the national Congress take the reins in full force of passing enforcement legislation on the Naturalization Clause.

I am going to discuss a 2003 case ruling that is another attack on our rules of federalism. This case is just another sheer example of an arrogant federal government. The state of California was doing a fine job of handling the documented and undocumented alien situation within its borders. But then the federal government intervened in the immigration matters of the sovereign state of California.

"In July 1996, he [the respondent] was convicted of first-degree burglary in state court in California and, in April 1997, he was convicted of a second crime, "petty theft with priors". The Immigration and Naturalization Service (INS) charged respondent with being deportable from the United States in light of these convictions, and detained him pending his removal hearing. We hold that Congress, justifiably concerned that deportable criminal aliens who are not detained continue to engage in crime and fail to appear for their removal hearings in large numbers, may be require that persons such as respondent be detained for the brief period necessary for their removal proceedings. Respondent does not dispute the validity of his prior convictions, which were obtained following the full procedural protections our criminal justice offers. Respondent also did not dispute the INS' conclusion that he is subject to mandatory detention under Section 1226(c). Respondent instead filed a habeas corpus action pursuant to 28 U.S.C Section 2241 in the United States District Court for the Northern District of California challenging the Constitutionality of Section 1226(c) itself. He argued that this detention under Section 1226(c) violated due process because INS had made no determination that he posed either a danger to society or a flight risk. *Id.*, at 31a, 33a." (Opinion Brief of Demore, District Director, San Francisco District of Immigration and Naturalization Service, v. Kim, Chief Justice William D. Rehnquist, 2003).

The young man, who was of legal status, was already apprehended and brought to justice by state authorities. So why did the federal government have to intervene? If he were a documented or an undocumented alien, the enforcement still remains the responsibility of each sovereign state.

In my opinion, the respondent should have challenged the conclusion of INS because of the way in which he was detained by an obtrusive federal government. That is a big piece of the puzzle in examining how the federal government behaves against the Constitution and the will of the states. The respondent being a lawful permanent legal resident did not argue his convictions by the state court of California.

I hereby challenge Section 1226(c) of the Immigration and Nationality Act of 1965 because it is an unconstitutional section of this congressional act. It shares no validity to what the framers of the Constitution envisioned while writing the Naturalization Clause.

The Supreme Court has sanctioned this unconstitutional activity and affirmed the power of the national Congress and national executive branch to continue their arrogance against the rules of federalism.

"In this country, Congress did not pass the first law regulating immigration till 1875. See 18 Stat 477. In the late 19th century, as statutory controls on immigration tightened, the number of challenges brought by aliens to Government deportation or exclusion decisions also increased. See *St. Cyr*, supra, at 305-306. Because federal immigration laws from 1891 until 1952 made no express provision for judicial review, what limited review existed took the form of petitions for writs of habeas corpus. See, e.g., *Ekiu v. United States*, 142 U.S. 651 (1892); Fong Yue Ting v. United States, supra; *The Japanese Immigrant Case*, 189 U.S. 86 (1903); *Chin Yow v. United States*, 208 U.S. 8 (1908); *Kwock Jan Fat v. White*, 253 U.S. 454 (1920); *Ng Fung Ho v. White*, 259 U.S. 276 (1922). Though the Court was willing to entertain these habeas challenges to Government exclusion and deportation decisions, in no case did the Court question the right of immigration officials to temporarily detain aliens while exclusion or deportation proceedings was ongoing. By the mid-20th century, the number of aliens in deportation proceedings being released on parole rose considerably. See, e.g., Carlson v. Landon, 342 U.S., at 538, n. 31. Nonetheless, until 1952 habeas corpus petitions remained the only means by which deportation orders could be challenged. Under this regime, an alien who had been paroled but wished to challenge a final deportation order had to place himself in government custody before filing a habeas petition challenging the order. Given this, it is not surprising that the Court was not faced with numerous habeas claims brought by aliens seeking release from detention pending deportation." (Dissenting Brief of Demore, District Director, San Francisco District of Immigration and Naturalization Service, v. Kim, Associate Justice Sandra Day O'Connor, 2003).

"So far as I am aware, not until 1952 did we entertain such a challenge. See *Carlson v. Landon, supra*. And there, we reaffirmed the power of Congress to order temporary detention of aliens during removal proceedings." (Dissenting Brief of Demore, District Director, San Francisco District of Immigration and Naturalization Service, v. Kim, Associate Justice Sandra Day O'Connor, 2003).

I have one big issue with these statements from Justice O'Connor. The Supreme Court reaffirmed the power of Congress to review again an unconstitutional act of Congress. Justice O'Connor is one of the few Reagan appointees who never understood how to apply the rules of federalism. Since 1875, the federal government has taken the responsibility of immigration enforcement away from the sovereign states and placed it into the hands of the national government. What the national court should have done in 1952, was to reaffirm the power of the sovereign states and order them to revisit, in their 48 state legislatures, their own immigration enforcement measures.

Not in 1875, 1922, 1952, 2001, 2003, 2012, and through today, has the responsibility rested on the federal government to enforce any aspect of the Naturalization Clause. From Justice Jackson to Justice O'Connor to Justice Breyer to Justice Kennedy, the need to remind them kindly, the wise words from the Father of the Constitution. "There is nothing in the Constitution that grants the federal executive branch the right to arrest, imprison and exile aliens," James Madison.

It is still wrong for the National Court to advise the Congress to revise a law which contradicts the Constitution.

The federal government needs to lay off this illusion that they are here to enforce the clause onto the states — whether to arrest, imprison, detain, deport or exile aliens. And so, I respectfully dissent to the opinion of this court ruling. I still stand fully with the rules of federalism and the sovereignty of each state.

* * *

In 2010, the sovereign state of Arizona tested the waters of the rules of federalism to see if it could escape the grasp of an overpowering federal government. The state legislature of Arizona passed a statewide immigration enforcement measure to stop the flow of aliens from entering their borders. Just because the state of Arizona shares a border with a sovereign nation, does not mean that they cannot enact an immigration enforcement statute. The state of Kansas which borders no nation, can do the same to protect their borders.

All fifty states within the union of these United States of America have the power pass an immigration enforcement measure as long as it does not contradict the Naturalization Clause. Now, if a state does contradict the clause itself, then it is the duty of the federal government to administer the affected issue and advise the state to enforce the clause. What the federal government must never do is take it upon themselves to regulate or enforce the clause.

After the state of Arizona passed and began to enforce this measure, the federal government, under President Barack Obama, placed an injunction by the federal Department of Justice.

What the federal government administration under Obama and the current federal government administration under President Donald Trump are doing regarding the immigration enforcement situation remains unconstitutional. One administration cannot claim it

> **A** state is not here to create an alliance with the central government.

has a duty to enforce the clause and then institute a lax enforcement policy. While the other administration cannot also claim this duty and institute a strong enforcement policy.

You will read below about the state of Arizona enforcing the Naturalization Clause as is their Constitutional duty. But what the state of Arizona did wrong was to find a cooperation alliance with the federal government. States are not here to cooperate with the federal government. If federal immigration laws passed since 1875 are to be deemed unconstitutional. In other words, a state is not here to create an alliance with the central government, even if that law of the United States is unconstitutional.

"Section 3 makes failure to comply with federal alien-registration requirements a state misdemeanor; Section 5 (C) makes it a misdemeanor for an unauthorized alien to seek or engage in work in the state; Section 6 authorizes state and local officers to arrest without a warrant a person 'the officer has probable cause to believe… has committed any public offense that makes the person removable from the United States; and Section 2(B) requires officers conducting a stop, detention, or arrest to make efforts, in some circumstances, to verify the person's immigration status with the Federal Government." (Syllabus of Arizona, ET AL., Petitioners v. United States, SB1070 legislation, 2012).

The state immigration law of Arizona is a plain enforcement law. It is not creating a new uniform code of the

American Naturalization code. In my simple Constitutional scholar mind, I see a few things that are right and wrong with the Arizona immigration enforcement law and I shall explain my opinion.

"(a) Section 3 intrudes on the field of alien registration, a field in which Congress has left no room for States to regulate." (Syllabus of Arizona, ET AL., Petitioners v. United States, SB1070 legislation, 2012).

The Bill of Rights applies to United States citizens and legal residents that have a legal status in the United States of America. Unauthorized people that enter this country illegally, they do not share the same rights and privileges of our laws and Constitution of the United States. But if an individual is apprehended, the local and state authorities must respect that person's rights until their status is verified. This enforcement right lies within the states.

I want to discuss the main issue that relates to the Naturalization Clause given it by the "sovereignty" of the states in this united republic. This whole issue is a test to see how modern-day Americans see this country: Do they see it with individual sovereign states with an administrative federal/central government? Or do they see it as a regulating and enforcing federal/central government over non-autonomous states?

This is another case in which Justice Antonin Scalia and second case of Justice Alito both show their true stance on state sovereignty. There are few items where I agree and disagree with them, but to be clear, I still dissent in the Opinion of the Court made by Associate Justice Anthony Kennedy. I am going to explain how this republic was formed to have the states be the driving enforcement force on immigration.

"The United States is an indivisible "Union of sovereign States." "Hinderlider v. La Plata River & Cherry Creek Ditch Co., 304 U.S. 92, 104 (1938). Today's opinion, approving virtually all of the Ninth Circuit's injunction against enforcement of the four challenged provisions of Arizona's law, deprives States of what most would consider the defining characteristic of sovereignty: the power to exclude from the sovereign's territory people who have no right to be there. Neither the Constitution itself nor even any law passed by Congress supports this result. I dissent." (Concurring and Dissenting Opinion of Associate Justice Antonin Scalia on Arizona, ET AL., Petitioners v. United States, 2012).

Justice Scalia could not have said it better than me. "The United States is an indivisible "Union of sovereign States." This is what the rules of federalism are all about and what people fail to comprehend and neglect. This republic was built so individual, autonomous and sovereign states could create and follow their own laws/rules that are in accordance with the federal Constitution. The federal government's role is to settle any disputes as an administrator to make sure this "A More Perfect Union" works together.

Below you shall see that the Immigration and Naturalization Clause in the Constitution is a clause passed by Congress and that it sets the boundaries of who regulates and who enforces the clause. In my opinion, it is the federal government that is here to confirm that the regulation is set in place for the states. Contrary

> ... It is the states that have broad, undoubted power over the subject of immigration and the status of aliens.

to popular belief, from the opinion of the court written by Associate Justice Anthony Kennedy.

"The Government of the United States has broad, undoubted power over the subject of immigration and the status of aliens." (Opinion of Anthony Kennedy on Arizona, ET AL., Petitioners v. United States, 2012).

In reading this statement, American citizens have allowed themselves to become too dependent on the federal government. Prior to and after Justice Kennedy's retirement, the High Court has seen a staggering number of activist justices who preach total federal government autonomy. It's the FDR Court all over again.

As you will see in Justice Scalia's and Justice Alito's concurrence and dissenting opinion, it is the states that have broad power over the subject of immigration and the status of aliens.

"As a sovereign, Arizona has the inherent power to exclude persons from its territory, subject only to those

limitations expressed in the Constitution or Constitutionally imposed by Congress. The power to exclude has long
been recognized as inherent in sovereignty. There is no
doubt that "before the adoption of the Constitution of
the United States" each state had the authority to "prevent
[itself] from being burdened by an influx of persons". *Mayor
of New York v. Miln*, 11 Pet. 102, 132—133 (1837). And
the Constitution did not strip the States of that authority.
To the contrary, two of the Constitution's provisions were
designed to enable the States to prevent "the intrusion of
obnoxious aliens through other states." Letter from James
Madison to Edmund Randolph (Aug. 27, 1782), in 1
The Writings of James Madison 226 (1900); accord, The
Federalist No. 42, pp. 269-271 (C. Rossiter ed. 1961) (J.
Madison). The Articles of Confederation had provided
that "the free inhabitants of each of these States, paupers,
vagabonds and fugitives from justice excepted, shall be
entitled to all privileges and immunities of free citizens in
the several States." Articles of Confederation, Art IV. This
meant that an unwelcome alien could obtain all the rights of
a citizen of one State simply by first becoming an *inhabitant*
of another. To remedy this, the Constitution's Privileges
and Immunities Clause provided that "[t]he Citizens of
each State shall be entitled to all privileges and Immunities
of Citizens in the several States." Art. IV, Section 2, cl. 1
(emphasis added). But if one State had particularly lax
citizenship standards, it might serve as a gateway for entry

of "obnoxious aliens" into other States. This problem was solved "by authorizing the general government to establish a uniform rule of naturalization power was given to Congress not to abrogate States' power to exclude those they did not want, but to vindicate it. (Concurring and Dissenting Opinion of Associate Justice Antonin Scalia on Arizona, ET AL., Petitioners v. United States, 2012).

Since the beginning of this republic with its first Constitution, The Articles of Confederation, Congress gave the power to the states to enforce the immigration situation and determine who should enter and not enter each state. It's always been the sovereign states themselves that regulate and enforce this issue and still the idea has not changed. Regardless of what the federal government claims.

Justice Scalia touches on the very first nullification acts by two states against the intrusive federal government on the issue of Naturalization and Immigration. I believe every American must learn how the "Principles of '98," first established a defiant rule against an unconstitutional action led by the federal government.

"In fact, the controversy surrounding the Alien and Sedition Acts involved a debate over whether, under the Constitution, the States had *exclusive* authority to enact such immigration laws. Criticism of the Sedition Act has become a prominent feature of our First Amendment jurisprudence, see, e.g., *New York Times Co., v. Sullivan*, (1964), but one of the Alien Acts also aroused controversy at the time:

"Be it enacted by the Senate and House of Representatives of the United States of America in Congress assembled, That it shall be lawful for the President of the United States at any time during the continuance of this act, to order all such aliens as he shall judge dangerous to the peace and safety of the United States, or shall have reasonable grounds to suspect are concerned in any treasonable or secret machinations against the government thereof, to depart out of territory of the United States ...." An Act concerning Aliens, 1 Stat. 570, 570-571.

The Kentucky and Virginia Resolutions, written in denunciation of these Acts, insisted that the power to exclude unwanted aliens rested solely in the States." (Concurring and Dissenting Opinion of Associate Justice Antonin Scalia on Arizona, ET AL., Petitioners v. United States, 2012).

The Alien and Sedition Acts were written by men who once had allegiances to the British Crown. They still wanted to impose "One-Man-Rule" onto the sovereign states themselves.

Thomas Jefferson wrote the nullifying act of Kentucky while James Madison wrote the Virginia Nullifying Act against The Alien and Sedition Acts. The Kentucky and Virginia resolutions were the first acts of refusal to cooperate with the federal government. Leave it to Madison and Jefferson to lead the charge for state sovereignty.

"Jefferson's Kentucky Resolutions insisted "that alien friends are under the jurisdiction and protection of the laws of the state wherein they are [and] that no power over them has been delegated to the United States, nor prohibited to the individual states, distinct from their power over citizens." Kentucky Resolutions of 1798, reprinted in J. Powell, Languages of Power: A Sourcebook of Early American Constitutional History 131 (1991)." (Concurring and Dissenting Opinion of Associate Justice Antonin Scalia on Arizona, ET AL., Petitioners v. United States, 2012).

"Madison's Virginia Resolutions likewise contended that the Alien Act purported to give the President "A power nowhere delegated to the federal government." Virginia's Resolutions of 1798, reprinted in Powell supra, at 134 (emphasis omitted). Notably, moreover, the Federalist proponents of the Act defended it primarily on the ground that "[t]he removal of aliens is the usual preliminary of hostility" and could therefore be justified in exercise of the Federal Government's war powers. Massachusetts Resolutions in reply to Virginia, reprinted in Powell, *supra*, at 136." (Concurring and Dissenting Opinion of Associate

> **M**adison's and Jefferson's response against The Alien and Sedition Acts speaks high volumes with tremendous respect that I have for both gentlemen of Virginia as well as true Americans.

Justice Antonin Scalia on Arizona, ET AL., Petitioners v. United States, 2012).

Madison's and Jefferson's responses against The Alien and Sedition Acts are why I have tremendous respect for both gentlemen of Virginia, as well as true Americans. Jefferson nails down that the state powers are unlimited. While Madison points out the enumerated powers given to the federal government, the executive branch.

While these two resolutions decided to nullify this act of Congress, other states decided to cooperate with the federal government. The state of Massachusetts, the home state of John Adams, decided to support the federal executive power. I still think it's wrong to support a law that has no constitutional backing but that is how the rules of federalism were established.

"In Mayor of New York v. Miln, [1837], this Court considered a New York statute that required the commander of any ship arriving in New York from abroad to disclose "the name, place of birth, and the last legal settlement, age, and occupation . . . of all passengers . . . with the intention of proceeding to the said city." 11 Pet., at 130-131. After the discussing the sovereign authority to regulate the entrance of foreigners described by the De Vattel, the Court said:

> "The power . . . of New York to pass this law having undeniably existed at the formation of the Constitution, the simply inquiry is, whether by that

instrument it was taken from the states, and granted
to Congress; for if it were not, it yet remains with
them." *Id.*, at 132.

And the Court held that it remains, *Id.*, at 139.

(Concurring and Dissenting Opinion of Associate Justice Antonin
Scalia on Arizona, ET AL., Petitioners v. United States, 2012).

This is the beauty of our federalism republic where
states are responsible for their borders within the United
States. But most importantly, states follow what is written
in the Constitution. And it clearly states that the federal
government has no authority in these areas of enforcement
to our visiting or residing aliens.

"One would conclude from the foregoing that after
the adoption of the Constitution there was some doubt
about the power of the Federal Government to control
immigration, but no doubt about the power of the States to
do so. Since the founding era (but not immediately), doubt
about the Federal Government's power has disappeared.
Indeed, primary responsibility for immigration policy
has shifted from the States to the Federal Government.
Congress exercised its power "[t]o establish an uniform rule
of Naturalization," Art. I, Section 8, cl. 4, very early on,
see An Act to establish an uniform Rule of Naturalization,
1 Stat. 103. But with the fleeting exception of the Alien
Act, Congress did not enact any legislation regulating
immigration for the better part of a century." (Concurring and

Dissenting Opinion of Associate Justice Antonin Scalia on Arizona, ET AL., Petitioners v. United States, 2012).

"This authority rests, in part, on the National Government's constitutional power to "establish an uniform Rule of Naturalization," U.S. Const., Art I, Section 8, cl. 4, and its inherent power as sovereign control and conduct relations with foreign nations, see Toll v. supra, at 10 (citing United States v. Curtiss Wright Export Corp., 299 U.S. 304, 318, (1936)." (Opinion of Anthony Kennedy on Arizona, ET AL., Petitioners v. United States, 2012).

> The Naturalization Clause has no mention of the federal government "[t]o enforce an uniform Rule of Naturalization". It just states to "establish" one.

Two complete differences of opinion in defining the rules of federalism that govern our American republic. The framers of the Constitution just decided "To establish an uniform Rule of Naturalization" code for the United States and the need for the states to enforce that code. This clause is setting the foundation whereby the sovereign and independent states are obliged to enforce the clause. The Naturalization Clause has no mention of the federal government "[t]o enforce an uniform Rule of Naturalization". It just states to "establish" one.

"In 1862, Congress passed "An Act to prohibit the 'Coolie Trade' by American Citizens in American vessels," which prohibited "procuring [Chinese nationals] . . . to be disposed of, or sold or transferred, for any term of years or for any time whatever, as servants or apprentices, or to be held to service or labor." 12 Stat. 340. Then, in 1875, Congress amended that act to bar admission to Chinese, Japanese, and other Asian immigrants who had "entered into contract or agreement for a term of service within the United States, for lewd and immoral purposes." An Act supplementary to the Acts in relation to immigration, ch. 14, 18 Stat. 477. And in 1882, Congress enacted the first general immigration statute. See An Act to regulate immigration, 22 Stat. 214. Of course, it hardly bears mention that Federal immigration law is now extensive. (Concurring and Dissenting Opinion of Associate Justice Antonin Scalia on Arizona, ET AL., Petitioners v. United States, 2012).

"I accept that as a valid exercise of federal power—not because of the Naturalization Clause (it has no necessary connection to citizenship) but because it is an inherent attribute of sovereignty no less for the United States than for the States. As this Court has said, it is an "'accepted maxim of international law, that every sovereign nation has the power, as inherent in sovereignty, and essential to within its dominions.'" Fong Yue Ting v. United States, 149 U.S. 698, 705 (1893) (quoting Ekiu v. United States, 142 U.S. 651, 659 (1892). That is why there was no need to set forth control of immigration as one of the enumerated powers of Congress, although an acknowledgement of that power (as well as of the States' similar power, subject to federal abridgement) was contained in Art I, Section 9, which provided that "[t]he Migration or Importation of such Persons as any of the States now existing shall think proper to admit, shall not be prohibited by the Congress prior to the Year one thousand eight hundred and eight . . ." (Concurring and Dissenting Opinion of Associate Justice Antonin Scalia on Arizona, ET AL., Petitioners v. United States, 2012).

I cannot consent to this concurring paragraph from Justice Scalia. Justice Scalia gives examples of federal immigration regulatory legislation during a troubled time in America. There was a Civil War going on and it was unconstitutional for the federal Congress to install these types of harsh federal immigration enforcement laws. From 1861 to 1865, the United States was on strict martial law and so all dictated policy arose from the nation's capital, and not from each of the state capitals. In the end, even in troubled times or in peace time, the rules of federalism must be applied above anything else.

Justice Scalia makes a point that the United States is a nation like every other nation and so it had to protect its borders like any other nation. But I say to that statement that the United States is not like any other nation of Europe, Orient, Africa and Oceania. The United States of America is quite unique and different. And it is that difference and uniqueness that makes this nation stand out from the rest.

From the very beginning in 1776, America broke away from the very idea of a total centralized government that has plagued many European nations. Even after the Union won the Civil War, the federal government obtained a newly enumerated power: Equality. Everything else should have gone back to the sovereign states to enforce and that includes the Naturalization enforcement. I have a major concern in where the independent and sovereign states cry out every time, when they have a grievance or question. Especially when that grievance has no constitutional value and holding. In war time or peace time, Congress cannot behave in such an unconstitutional manner of grievance holding.

"Possibility (1) need not to be considered here: there is no federal law prohibiting the States' sovereign power to exclude (assuming federal authority to enact such a law). We are not talking here about a federal law prohibiting the States from regulating bubble-gum advertising, or even the construction of nuclear plants. We are talking about federal law going to the *core* of state sovereignty: the power to exclude. Like elimination of the States' other inherent sovereign power, immunity from suit, elimination of the States' sovereign power to exclude requires that "Congress . . . unequivocally expres[s] its intent to abrogate," Seminole Tribe of Fla v. Florida, 517 U.S. 44, 55 (1996)." (Concurring and Dissenting Opinion of Associate Justice Antonin Scalia on Arizona, ET AL., Petitioners v. United States, 2012).

"Nor can federal power over illegal immigration be deemed exclusive because of what the Court's opinion solicitously calls "foreign countries['] concern[s] about the status, safety, and security of their nationals in the United States," ante, at 3. The Constitution gives all those on our shores the protections of the Bill of Rights are not expanded for foreign nationals because of their countries' views (some countries, for example, have recently discovered the death penalty to be barbaric), neither are the fundamental sovereign powers of the States abridged to accommodate foreign countries' views. Even in its international relations, the Federal Government must live with the inconvenient fact that it is a Union of independent States, who have their own sovereign powers." (Concurring and Dissenting Opinion of Associate Justice Antonin Scalia on Arizona, ET AL., Petitioners v. United States, 2012).

From these paragraphs, Justice Scalia clearly states that the states have strong sovereign powers over the federal government. Even in cases of international affairs, if a crime is committed by a foreign national in one of our independent and autonomous sovereign states, state law must take precedent over federal criminal law. Kidnapping is a federal criminal offense, thanks to the intrusive work of totalitarian Federal Bureau of Investigation Director J. Edgar Hoover. Some state sovereignty advocates would still consider that if any crime is being committed within a sovereign state, it is the duty for the state to bring justice, and not the federal government.

SECTION 2B OF S.B. 1070

The next paragraphs that I am going to discuss involve whether Arizona state law conflicts, or better said, contradicts federal constitutional immigration law. We shall see who is correct in this debate of immigration enforcement, the individual sovereign state of Arizona or the federal government.

"Section 2(B) of S.B. 1070 requires state officers to make a "reasonable attempt . . . to determine the immigration status" of any person they stop, detain, or arrest on some other legitimate basis if "reasonable suspicion exists that the person is an alien and is unlawfully present in the United States." Ariz. Rev. Stat. Ann. Section 11-1051(B) (West 2012). The law also provides that "[a]ny person who is arrested shall have the person's immigration status determined before the person is released." *Ibid.* The accepted way to perform these status checks is to contact ICE, which maintains a database of immigration records. (Opinion of Anthony Kennedy on Arizona, ET AL., Petitioners v. United States, 2012).

"What this case comes down to, then, is whether the Arizona law conflicts with federal immigration law—whether it excludes those whom federal law would admit, or admits those whom federal law would exclude. It does not purport to do so. It applies only to aliens who neither possess a privilege to be present under federal law not have been removed pursuant to the Federal Government's inherent authority. I proceed to consider the challenged provisions in detail." (Concurring and Dissenting Opinion of Associate Justice Antonin Scalia on Arizona, ET AL., Petitioners v. United States, 2012).

Section 2(B)
"For any lawful stop, detention or arrest made by a law enforcement official . . . in the enforcement of any other law or ordinance of a country, city, or town or this state where reasonable suspicion exists that the person is an alien and is unlawfully present in the United States, a reasonable attempt shall be made, when practicable, to determine the immigration status of the person, except if the determination may hinder or obstruct an investigation. Any person who is arrested shall have the person's immigration status determined before the person is released...." S.B. 1070, Section 2(B), as amended, Ariz. Rev. Stat. Ann. Section 11-1051(B)(West 2012).

"The Government has conceded that "even before Section 2 was enacted, state and local officers had state law authority to inquire of DHS [the Department of Homeland Security] about a suspect's unlawful status and otherwise cooperate with federal immigration officers." . . . . The Government's conflict-pre-emption claim calls on us "to determine whether, *under the circumstances of this particular case*, [the State's] law stands as an obstacle to the accomplishment and execution of the full purposes and objectives of Congress." *Hines v. Davidowitz* 312 U.S. 52, 67 (1941) (emphasis added. And on its face, Section 2(B) merely tells state officials that they are authorized to do something that they were, by the Government's concession, already authorized to do." (Concurring and Dissenting Opinion of Associate Justice Antonin Scalia on Arizona, ET AL., Petitioners v. United States, 2012).

In reading these two paragraphs from the two opinions, we see the logic in where the sovereign states have no need to cooperate with the federal government and enforce the code by themselves.

Justice Kennedy places the idea in the minds of the American citizenry that the sovereign states *must* cooperate with the federal immigration bureaucracy known as the Department of Homeland Security (DHS). While Justice Scalia is not disputing the fact of Justice Kennedy's logic that states must assist with the federal government. Justice Scalia adds that states can offer any assistance but not required to cooperate with the federal government on any issue, including immigration.

"Consultation between federal and state officials is an important feature of the immigration system. Congress has made clear that no formal agreement or special training needs to be in place for state officers to "communicate with the [Federal Government] regarding the immigration status of any individual, including reporting knowledge that a particular alien is not lawfully present in the United States." 8 U.S.C. Section 1357(g)(10)(A). And Congress has obligated ICE to respond to any request made by state officials for

verification of a person's citizenship or immigration status."
(Opinion of Anthony Kennedy on Arizona, ET AL., Petitioners v. United
States, 2012).

Justice Kennedy stated that Congress never authorized
any specific training or agreement between the federal
government and state officials. Again, I am not surprised
how the federal government, this time the branch that is
supposed to correctly interpret our principled document,
can lie and show contempt for the truth. Section 287(g),
a proposed agreement between the federal immigration
authorities with state and local authorities, is here to advise
them on immigration-related issues like how to apprehend
suspects who may have an undocumented alien status. This
section was added by section 133 of the Illegal Immigration
Reform and Immigrant Responsibility Act of 1996.

The non-profit organization known as Judicial Watch
in Washington, D.C. made complaints against many state
and local governments and argued they were not enforcing
Section 287(g) with the federal government. State and local
authorities not cooperating with the federal government
and the constant harassment from Judicial Watch was
completely uncalled for and unconstitutional.

One thing that states and local communities cannot do
is contradict and show conflict with federal constitutional
immigration law.

As those states and local communities plainly contradict
federal constitutional immigration law, Judicial Watch found

contradiction in forcing these states and local communities to cooperate with the federal government under the pretext of the 1996 Illegal Immigration Reform and Immigrant Responsibility Act. Judicial Watch is showing contradiction just as Justice Kennedy stated it.

"Of course, on this pre-enforcement record there is no reason to assume that Arizona officials will ignore federal immigration policy (unless it to be the questionable policy of not wanting to identify illegal aliens who have committed offenses that make them removable). As Arizona points out, federal law expressly provides that state officers may "cooperate with the Attorney General in the identification, apprehension, detention, or removal of aliens not lawfully present in the United States," 8 U.S.C. Section 1357(g)(10) (B); prior federal approval. It is consistent with the Arizona statute, and with the "cooperat[ive]" system that Congress has created, for state officials to arrest a removable alien, contact federal immigration authorities, and follow their lead on what to do next." (Concurring and Dissenting Opinion of Associate Justice Antonin Scalia on Arizona, ET AL., Petitioners v. United States, 2012).

If you read part of Justice Kennedy's opinion, he quotes a memorandum from 2011 from a bureaucrat appointed by the previous federal executive administration stating that the federal government will enforce all forms of immigration law across the republic. While the previous administration enforced it their way, the current administration is enforcing it their way.

When the policy changes every day, every month, every year, every four years, or every eight years from one administration to another, it becomes a revolving door of immigration enforcement chaos. Therefore, we must let the sovereign states enforce the clause as clearly stated in the Constitution.

"But that is not the most important point. The most important point is that, as we have discussed, Arizona is entitled to have "its own immigration policy"—including a more rigorous enforcement policy—so long as that does not conflict with federal law. The Court says, as though the point is utterly dispositive, that "it is not a crime for a removable alien to remain present in the United States," ante, 15. It is not a federal crime, to be sure. But there is no reason Arizona cannot make it a state crime for a removable alien (or any illegal alien, for that matter) to remain present in Arizona." (Concurring and Dissenting Opinion of Associate Justice Antonin Scalia on Arizona, ET AL., Petitioners v. United States, 2012).

"The government complains that state officials might not heed "federal priorities."' Indeed they might not, particularly if those priorities include willful blindness or deliberate inattention to the presence of removable aliens in Arizona. The State's whole complaint—the reason this law was passed and this case has arisen—is that the citizens of Arizona believe federal priorities are too lax. The State has the sovereign power to protect its borders more rigorously if it wishes, absent any valid federal prohibition. The

Executive's policy choice of lax federal enforcement does not constitute such a prohibition." (Concurring and Dissenting Opinion of Associate Justice Antonin Scalia on Arizona, ET AL., Petitioners v. United States, 2012).

I am not disputing that the independent, sovereign and autonomous states have a right to enact and enforce their own immigration policies, just as it does not contradict with the federal Constitution. When states defy and contradict the Naturalization Clause, then it only makes the federal government defy the rules of federalism and invade that sovereign state or states. And when states do not defy the Naturalization Clause, the federal government punishes them.

> **I** am not disputing that the independent, sovereign and autonomous States have a right to enact and enforce their own immigration policy just as it does not contradict with the federal Constitution.

Justice Scalia does state and does not dispute that the sovereign state of Arizona and other sovereign states have a sovereign and constitutional power to protect their borders and to enact and enforce their own laws in accordance with the Naturalization Clause. Justice

> **T**he requirement of states to fully cooperate with the federal power is as non-existent as the pretext that the "National Government has significant power to regulate immigration".

Scalia forgot to point out neither a lax enforcement policy nor a strong enforcement policy from the federal executive government branch constitutes any prohibition for the states to enforce their own laws. A lax or strong enforcement policy from the federal government should not even exist.

That is where I have somewhat of a difference of opinion with Justice Scalia — the idea of the cooperation between the states and federal government. The states and citizens have become too dependent on the national government. And so, Justice Scalia presents in his concurrence/dissent opinion the "idea of cooperation between the States and federal government." States can cooperate but are not required to, although how can they cooperate with a federal government policy that quite frankly does not exist and keeps changing. The requirement of states to fully cooperate with the federal power is as non-existent as the pretext that the "National Government has significant power to regulate immigration." States are here to not cooperate or seek advice or consultation with the federal government. States are here to refuse cooperation with the federal government if that federal law is deemed unconstitutional. I especially see nothing constitutional about the Illegal Immigration Reform and Immigrant Responsibility Act of 1996. So, states have the right to nullify this current law.

Section 6

"A peace officer, without a warrant, may arrest a person if the officer has probable cause to believe . . . [t]he person to be arrested has committed any public offense that makes the person removable from the United States." S.B. 1070, Section6(A)(5), Ariz. Rev. Stat. Ann. Section 13-3883(A)(5)(West Supp. 2011).

"Three limits are built into state provision. First, a detainee is presumed not to be an alien unlawfully present in the United States if he or she provides a valid Arizona driver's license or similar identification. Second, officers "may not consider race, color or national origin . . . except to the extent permitted by the United States [and] Arizona Constitution[s]." Ibid. Third, the provisions be "implemented in a manner consistent with federal law regulating immigration, protecting civil rights of all persons respecting the privileges and immunities of United States Citizens." Section 11—105(L) (West 2012). (Opinion of Anthony Kennedy on Arizona, ET AL., Petitioners v. United States, 2012).

The Highest Court found in its opinion that there is a violation of a Fourth Amendment violation in Section 6 of S.B. 1070. Let's examine their opinion in how they claim that holding a possible undocumented alien, neither a legal resident or U.S. citizen can take notice of a possible Fourth Amendment violation. I have mixed feelings about both opinions of the Court regarding this section of warrantless arrests. The Opinion of the Court is basing it to be unconstitutional on pure emotions.

"Section 6 attempts to provide state officers even greater authority to arrest aliens on the basis of possible removability than Congress has given to trained federal immigration officers. Under state law, officers who believe an alien is removable by reason of some "public offense" would have the power to conduct an arrest on the basis regardless of whether a federal warrant has issued or the alien is like to escape." (Opinion of Anthony Kennedy on Arizona, ET AL., Petitioners v. United States, 2012).

"The result could be unnecessary harassment of some aliens (for instance, a veteran, college student, or someone assisting with a criminal investigation) whom federal officials determine should not be removed." (Opinion of Anthony Kennedy on Arizona, ET AL., Petitioners v. United States, 2012).

With the beginning of this paragraph, I fear Justice Kennedy is operating under emotions in mind rather than with the Constitution in mind. Local, state and federal officers can pull over and question but must tread carefully while interrogating a possible suspect if indeed that individual has committed a "public offense."

The law is not supposed to see any color, ethnicity or national origin when interrogating a possible suspect, that is just common sense. So, for Justice Kennedy to bring up those emotions is wrong.

"This is not the system Congress created. Federal law specifies limited circumstances in which state officers may perform the functions of an immigration officer. A principal example is when the Attorney General has granted that authority to specific officers in a formal agreement with a state or local government. See Section 1357(g)(1); see also Section 1103(a)(10) (authority may be extended in the event of an "imminent mass of influx of aliens off the coast of the United States"); Section 1252c (authority to arrest in specific circumstance after consultation with the Federal Government); Section 1324(c) (authority to arrest for bringing in and harboring certain aliens). Officers covered by these agreements are subject to the Attorney General's direction and supervision. Section 1357(g)(3). There are significant complexities involved in enforcing federal immigration law, including the determination whether a person is removable. See *Padilla v. Kentucky*, 559 U.S. ___, ___--___ (2010) (ALITO, J., concurring in judgment) (slip op., at 4—7). As a result, the agreements reached with the Attorney General must contain written certification that officers have received adequate training to carry out the duties of an immigration officer. See Section 1357(g)(2); cf. 8 CFR Sub-Section 287.5(c) (arrest power contingent on training), 287.1(g) (defining the training)." (Opinion of Anthony Kennedy on Arizona, ET AL., Petitioners v. United States, 2012).

Justice Kennedy is wrong. This is the system that Congress created. But both sets of governments are contradicting the Constitution. All these federal laws that Congress established are a direct violation to the Naturalization Clause. I indeed quote James Madison and his famous Virginia Resolution against The Alien and Sedition Acts. 'There is nothing in the Constitution that grants the federal executive branch, the right to arrest, imprison and exile aliens.' For Justice Kennedy to go against the words of the Father of the Constitution is beyond disturbing. That he will permit the attorney general, a bureaucrat from a federal executive branch, to dictate and enforce immigration policy onto the states is truly tyrannical.

By authorizing state officers to decide whether an alien should be detained for being removable, Section 6 violates the principle that the removal process is entrusted to the discretion of the Federal Government. See e.g., Reno v. American-Arab Anti-Discrimination Comm., 252 U.S. 471, 483-484 (1999); see also Brief for Former INS Commissioners 8-13." (Opinion of Anthony Kennedy on Arizona, ET AL., Petitioners v. United States, 2012).

Truly, how arrogant the federal government has become —from the executive branch to the legislative branch leading up to the branch that we have entrusted to interpret correctly our constitution. "Section 6 violates the principle that the removal process is entrusted to the discretion of the Federal Government." What principle is that? The only principle that the federal government has is that "It has established a uniform code of Naturalization." The states' principle is to enforce that uniform code.

"In defense of Section 6, Arizona notes a federal statute permitting state officers to "cooperate with the Attorney

General in the identification, apprehension, detention, or removal of aliens not lawfully present in the United States." 8 U.S.C. Section 1357(g)(10)(B). There may be some ambiguity as to what constitutes cooperation under federal law; but no coherent understanding of the term would incorporate the unilateral decision of state officers to arrest an alien for being removable absent any request, approval, or other instruction from the Federal Government. The Department of Homeland Security gives examples of what would constitute cooperation under federal law. These include situations where States participate in a joint task force with federal officers, provide operational support in executing a warrant, or allow federal immigration officials to gain access to detainees held in state facilities. See Dept. of Homeland Security, Guidance on State and Local Government's Assistance in Immigration Enforcement and Related Matters 13—14 (2011), online at http://www.dhs.gov/files/resources/immigration.shtm (all Internet materials as visited June 21, 2012, and available in Clerk of Court's case file)." (Opinion of Anthony Kennedy on Arizona, ET AL., Petitioners v. United States, 2012).

"As Arizona points out, federal law expressly provides that state officers may "cooperate with the Attorney General in the identification, apprehension, detention, or removal of aliens not lawfully present in the United States," 8 U.S.C. Section 1357(g)(10)(B); and "cooperation" requires neither identical efforts nor prior federal approval.

It is consistent with the Arizona statute, and with the "cooperat[ive]" system that Congress has created, for state officials to arrest a removable alien, contact federal immigration authorities, and follow their lead on what to do next. The most important point is that, as we have discussed, Arizona is *entitled* to have "its own immigration policy"—including a more rigorous enforcement policy— so long as that does not conflict with federal law. The Court says, as though the point is utterly dispositive, that "it is not a crime for a removable alien to remain present in the United States," ante, at 15. It is not a federal crime, to be sure. But there is no reason Arizona cannot make it a state crime for a removable alien (or any illegal alien, for that matter) to remain present in Arizona." (Concurring and Dissenting Opinion of Associate Justice Antonin Scalia on Arizona, ET AL., Petitioners v. United States, 2012).

"Section 6 of S.B. 1070 authorizes Arizona law enforcement officers to make warrantless arrests when there is probable cause to believe that an arrestee has committed a public offense that renders him removable under federal immigration law. States, as sovereigns, have inherent authority to conduct arrests for violations of federal law, unless and until Congress removes that authority. See *United States v. Di Re*, 332 U.S. 581, 589 (1948) (holding that state law determines the validity of a warrantless arrest for a violation of federal law "in absence of an applicable federal statute"). (Concurring and Dissenting Opinion of Associate

Justice Clarence Thomas on Arizona, ET AL., Petitioners v. United States, 2012).

Just because the federal government wants to contradict the national Constitution, it does not mean states have to as well. Federal, state and local authorities cannot work with their instinct and make warrantless arrests, just because they believe someone has committed a possible public offense. I am the first to always glorify the sacred autonomy of each sovereign state to enforce correctly the Constitution. The same goes for the federal government.

With the issue of the Fourth Amendment, regarding the stop, interrogate, take into custody, arrest and possible deportation … if that individual is without a doubt a legal alien, then it is a violation to the Fourth Amendment. But if that alien is an illegal alien residing in that state, then he must face the laws and penalties of that sovereign state, not the ones from the federal government.

"Congress has put in place a system in which state officers may not make warrantless arrests of aliens based on possible removability except in specific, limited circumstances." (Opinion of Anthony Kennedy on Arizona, ET AL., Petitioners v. United States, 2012).

"Before Section 6 was added, that statute already permitted arrests without a warrant for felonies, misdemeanors committed in the arresting officer's presence, petty offenses, and certain traffic related criminal violations. See Sub-Section 13-3883(A)(1)-(4)." (Concurring and

Dissenting Opinion of Associate Justice Samuel Alito on Arizona, ET AL., Petitioners v. United States, 2012).

Both statements, one made by Justice Kennedy and the other by Justice Alito are wrong. One blames the bad milk and the other blames the sickly cow that gave that bad milk. The framers placed the Fourth Amendment to give the American citizenry the rights and protections from a potentially oppressive and tyrannical regime whether in peace or war time. But from the very start of our republic, the federal government has found loopholes around the Fourth Amendment and instituted tyrannical policies. If the federal government found a loophole to arrest people without the proper documentation and states initiate these similar loopholes, both sectors of government are wrong in conflicting with federal constitutional immigration law.

"Finally, the Court tells us that Section 6 conflicts with federal law because it provides state and local officers with "even greater authority to arrest aliens on the basis of possible removability than Congress has given to trained federal immigration officers." *Ante*, at 16-17. The Court points to 8 U.S.C Section 1357 (a)(2), which empowers "authorized" officers and employees of ICE to make arrests without a federal warrant if "the alien so arrested is in the United States in violation of any [immigration] law or regulation and is likely to escape before a warrant can be obtained for his arrest." (Concurring and Dissenting Opinion of Associate Justice Samuel Alito on Arizona, ET AL., Petitioners v. United States, 2012).

"By granting warrantless arrest authority to *federal officers*, Congress has not manifested an unmistakable intent to strip *state and local officers* of their warrantless arrest authority under state law." (Concurring and Dissenting Opinion of Associate Justice Samuel Alito on Arizona, ET AL., Petitioners v. United States, 2012).

Neither the Federal Government nor individual state governments have the power to contradict the Fourth Amendment to our Constitution. Regardless of whether the person is legal or illegal. Authority figures have no idea if the individual is here in this country by legal or illegal means until he is questioned through the proper legal channels. The Constitution has not granted any authority of the federal government or the states to conduct warrantless arrests.

If I do not like the federal government to contradict the rules of federalism, I do not like the sovereign states to do the same.

I oppose Justice Kennedy's judgment regarding his Fourth Amendment take because he rules with emotions. I also oppose in Justice Alito's judgment because it resulted in pointing the finger and justifying the actions of the state of Arizona in response to the actions of a rogue and arrogant federal government.

Yes, the states have unlimited and numerous powers, more than the federal government. But the states cannot overreach those powers. There are limits and that limit is the Constitution.

Section 5(C)

"It is unlawful for a person who is unlawfully present in the United States and who is an unauthorized alien to knowingly apply for work, solicit work in a public place or perform work as an employee or independent contractor in this state." S.B. 1070, Section 5(C), as amended, Ariz. Rev. Stat. Ann. Section 13—2928(C)."

"Here, the Court rightly starts with *De Canas v. Bica*, 424 U.S. 351 (1976), which involved a California law providing that "[n]o employer shall knowingly employ an alien who is not entitled to lawful residence in the United States if such employment would have an adverse effect on lawful resident workers."" *Id.*, at 352 (quoting California Labor Code Ann. Section 2805(a)). This Court concluded that the California law was not pre-empted, as Congress had neither occupied the field of "regulation of employment of illegal aliens" nor expressed "the clear and manifest purpose" of displacing such state regulation. *Id.*, at 356-357 (internal quotation marks omitted). Thus, at the time, *De Canas* was decided, Section 5(C) would have indubitably lawful."
(Concurring and Dissenting Opinion of Associate Justice Antonin Scalia on Arizona, ET AL., Petitioners v. United States, 2012).

"The United States contends that the provision upsets the balance struck by the Immigration Reform and Control

Act of 1986 (IRCA) and must be preempted as an obstacle to the federal plan of regulation and control. When there was no comprehensive federal program regulating the employment of unauthorized aliens, this Court found that a State had authority to pass its own laws on the subject." (Opinion of Anthony Kennedy on Arizona, ET AL., Petitioners v. United States, 2012).

If the highest court of the land found a way to give states the right to regulate the issue of immigration back in 1976 of states prosecuting criminals, whether, legal or illegal, then this precedent should have still stood in 2012 through today. I will give this to Justice William Brennan, who when he gave his opinion on *De Canas v. Bica*, finally stood for state sovereignty over federal government. And Congress should have respected the wishes of the Supreme Court in protecting the sovereignty of the state of California and other states.

But every time, the High Court gave a shred of sovereignty to the states, the national Congress steps in and crushes every bit of federalism.

"Current federal law is substantially different from the regime that prevailed when *De Canas* was decided. Congress enacted IRCA as a comprehensive framework "combating the employment of illegal aliens." Hoffman Plastic Compounds, Inc., v. NLRB, 535 U.S. 137, 147 (2002). The law makes it illegal for employers to knowingly hire, recruit, refer, or continue to employ unauthorized workers. See 8 U.S.C. Sub-Section1324a(a)(1)(A), (a)(2). It also requires every employer to verify the employment authorization status of prospective employees." (Opinion of Anthony Kennedy on Arizona, ET AL., Petitioners v. United States, 2012).

"Section 5(C) of S.B. 1070 prohibits unlawfully present aliens from knowingly applying for, soliciting, or performing work in Arizona. Nothing in the text of the federal immigration laws prohibits States from imposing their own criminal penalties on such individuals. Federal law expressly pre-empts States from "imposing civil or criminal sanctions (other than through licensing and similar laws) upon *those who employ*, or recruit or refer for a fee for employment, unauthorized aliens." 8 U.S.C. Section 1324a(h)(2) (emphasis added). But it leaves States free to impose criminal sanctions on the employee themselves." (Concurring and Dissenting Opinion of Associate Justice Clarence Thomas on Arizona, ET AL., Petitioners v. United States, 2012).

In 1976, this court explained that the states have the power to create, pass and enforce any law that punishes the employer as well as the employee when they hire undocumented aliens. That all changed when the national Congress created the Immigration Reform and Control Act of 1986 (IRCA). This took away and diminished the power of the states.

"The Court now tells us that times have changed. Since *De Canas*, Congress has enacted "a comprehensive framework for combating the employment of illegal aliens," and even though aliens who seek or obtain unauthorized work are not subject to criminal sanctions, they can suffer civil penalties. *Ante*, at 12-13 (internal quotation marks omitted). Undoubtedly, federal regulation in this area is more pervasive today. But our task remains unchanged: to determine whether the federal scheme discloses a clear and manifest congressional intent to displace state law." (Concurring and Dissenting Opinion of Associate Justice Samuel Alito on Arizona, ET AL., Petitioners v. United States, 2012).

Federal constitutional immigration law is the same federal constitutional immigration law established before and after the ruling of *De Canas*. Federal law clearly IMPLIES there is to be no federal enforcement of the Naturalization Clause. The enforcement application is left up to the states.

This court could not confirm it because it had the backing of another unconstitutional act of Congress. After the 1976 ruling, the national Congress established IRCA and now set a new precedent in giving unlimited and unconstitutional power to the federal government. This would be the perfect time and for the states to nullify IRCA and refuse to cooperate with federal union officials.

Justice Alito is correct in this dissent paragraph. The national Congress since 1913 has always been trying to undermine and diminish the powers of the state by handing it over to the federal government. This includes the powers to regulate immigration. This 2012 ruling has shown a new precedent and is an attack to our rules of federalism. It truly increases the power of the federal government and establishes an even bigger precedent for future federal government executive branch administrations to proceed the same way.

I cannot stress enough the roles of federal and state governments on the issue of immigration. If this same court in 1976 gave the power to the states to enforce the employment status of their residents/citizens of their state, then it should be in the best interest for the rules of federalism.

But we have seen this before where the national Congress interjects their federal power grab onto the states and ignores the will of the rules of federalism. That is my discussion for the next issue of the Arizona state legislation of S.B. 1070.

Section 3

"In addition to any violation of federal law, a person is guilty of willful failure to complete or carry an alien registration document if the person is in violation of 8 [U.S.C.] Section1304(e) or Section1306(a)." S.B. 1070, Section3(A), as amended, Ariz Rev. Stat. Ann. Section13-1509(A)."

"It is beyond question that a State may make violation of federal law a violation of state law as well. We have held that to be even when the interest protected is a distinctively federal interest, such as protection of the dignity of the national flag, see Halter v. Nebraska, 205 U.S. 34 (1907), or protection of the Federal Government's ability to recruit soldiers, Gilbert v. Minnesota, 254 U.S. 325 (1920). [T]he State is not inhibited from making the national purposes its own purposes to the extent of exerting its police power to prevent its own citizens from obstructing the accomplishment of such purposes. Much more is that so when, as here, the State is protecting its own interest, the integrity of its borders. And we have said that explicitly with regard to illegal immigration: 'Despite the exclusive federal control of this Nation's borders, we cannot conclude that the States are without any power to deter the influx of persons entering the United States against federal law, and whose numbers might have a discernible impact on traditional concerns. Plyler v. Doe, 457 U.S. 202, 228, n. 23 (1982)." (Concurring and Dissenting Opinion of Associate Justice Antonin Scalia on Arizona, ET AL., Petitioners v. United States, 2012).

It is beyond question that a state may make a law in accordance to the Constitution without consulting federal law. States like Arizona have the sovereign duty to enforce the Naturalization Clause. We have concluded that the states have significant power to deter the influx of persons entering the United States for or against federal law, *Plyler v. Doe*, 1982.

This ruling in 1982, began to open the flood gates for federal (central) government autonomy forcing a one-size-fits-all immigration policy onto the states. This legislative statute passed the Texas State Legislature in 1975. It allowed this state to deny illegal alien students the right to attend public education with in-state tuition funds. Then other states like Texas followed suit. The opinion of this 1982 ruling made the claim that Texas was violating the Equal Protection Clause of the Fourteenth Amendment toward illegal alien students. In my opinion, this is bogus for two reasons. First, since these alien students have an illegal status within the United States and its territories, they honestly cannot share in the guarantees and liberties that the Bill of Rights and the 14th Amendment offers. Secondly, this goes to my whole argument, whereby the federal government cannot dictate by force how a state enforces the Naturalization Clause.

"The United States contends that this state enforcement mechanism intrudes on the field of alien registration, a field in which Congress has left no room for States to regulate. See Brief for United States 27, 31. The Court discussed federal alien-registration requirements in *Hines v. Davidowitz*, 312 U.S. 52. In 1940, as international conflict spread, Congress added to federal immigration law a "complete system for alien registration." Id., at 70. The new federal law struck a careful balance. It punished an alien's willful failure to register but did not require aliens to carry identification cards. The Court found that Congress intended the federal plan for registration to be a "single integrated and all-embracing system. *Id.*, at 74. Because this "complete scheme ... for the registration of aliens" touched on foreign relations, it did not allow the States to "curtail or complement" federal law or to "enforce additional or auxiliary regulations." *Id.*, 66-67.

As a consequence, the Court ruled that Pennsylvania could not enforce its own alien-registration program. (Opinion of Anthony Kennedy on Arizona, ET AL., Petitioners v. United States, 2012).

"Federal law now includes a requirement that aliens carry proof of registration. 8 U.S.C. Section1304(e). Aliens who remain in the country for more than 30 days must apply for registration and be fingerprinted." (Opinion of Anthony Kennedy on Arizona, ET AL., Petitioners v. United States, 2012).

First, I have big issues with this statement from Justice Kennedy. I am beyond disgusted that the national Congress established a national statute using the excuse of international conflicts occurring on the other side of Atlantic Ocean. Every time there is a crisis, the federal government takes it upon itself to create an executive order via the executive branch or a national statute passed by the national Congress. Both actions are extremely unconstitutional. But the fact of the matter is that the federal government has no right to initiate or enforce any aspect of the Naturalization Clause while denying it to the states.

The Commonwealth of Pennsylvania, as it is their duty as a sovereign state, passed a statute requiring any aliens living in the commonwealth to register with the state and obtain an alien registration document. Any self-respected state sovereign constitutional advocate would agree that the Keystone State acted in accordance with our rules of federalism. But not the Supreme Court or the national Congress.

"The Court's opinion relies upon *Hines v. Davidowitz supra*. Ante, 9-10. But that case did not, as the Court believes, establish a "field preemption" that implicitly eliminates the States' sovereign power to exclude those whom federal law excludes. It held that the States are not permitted to establish "additional or auxiliary" registration requirements for aliens. 312 U.S., at 66-67. But Section 3 does not establish additional or auxiliary registration requirements. It merely makes a violation of state law the very same failure to register and failure to carry evidence of registration that are violations of federal law. *Hines* does not prevent the State from relying on the federal registration system as "an available aid in the enforcement of a number of statutes of the state applicable to aliens whose constitutional validity has not been questioned." (Concurring and Dissenting Opinion of Associate Justice Antonin Scalia on Arizona, ET AL., Petitioners v. United States, 2012).

The Supreme court made the claim that the Pennsylvania statute was unconstitutional but not the federal law passed in 1940. Whatever *Hines* stated in 1941 to benefit a 1940 act of congress, it remains an unconstitutional ruling.

The state of Arizona had to comply with the unconstitutional ruling of *Hines* and established a new valid statute. But, to a state sovereign scholar, Section 3 was

> **T**he enforcement immigration policy must lie within each State to dictate it in accordance with the clause.

an attack on the sovereignty of the state of Arizona. The State of Arizona stated that it is not creating its own alien registration document, like Pennsylvania did at one point. They complied with federal law and made it their own state violation if an alien violated federal law.

I find it difficult to comprehend why a sovereign state would have the need to enforce a federal law when it has its own duties to enforce it on their own without complying with federal law. But, since 1941 the federal government has tied the hands of all states, including states sharing an international border. On one hand, the federal government has made it difficult for each sovereign state to create and enforce the laws as dictated by the Naturalization Clause. And on the other hand, the federal government is penalizing every sovereign state from passing its laws to be tough when an alien, whether legal or illegal, does not respect the law.

"Section 3 simply incorporates federal registration standards. Unlike the Court, I would not hold that Congress pre-empted the field of enforcing those standards. "[O]ur recent cases have frequently rejected field pre-emption in the absence of statutory language expressly requiring it." *Camps New Found/Owatonna, Inc. v. Town of Harrison*, 520 U.S. 564, 617, (1997) Thomas J., dissenting); see e.g., *New York State Dept., of Social Servs v. Dublino*, 413 U.S. 405, 415 (1973). Here, nothing in the text of the relevant federal statutes indicates that Congress created a "full set of standards governing alien registration," *ante*, at 10 (majority opinion), merely indicates that if intended the scheme to be capable of working on its own, not that it wanted to preclude the States from enforcing the federal standards. *Hines v. Davidowitz*, 312 U.S. 52 (1941), is not to the contrary. As JUSTICE SCALIA explains, *ante*, at 14, *Hines* at most holds that federal law pre-empts the States from creating additional registration requirements. But here, Arizona is merely seeking to enforce the very registration requirements that Congress created." (Concurring and Dissenting Opinion of Associate Justice Clarence Thomas on Arizona, ET AL., Petitioners v. United States, 2012).

I have major issues with Section 3 of S.B. 1070 and the court ruling of *Hines*. As I explained above, this Supreme Court ruling of 1941 was unconstitutional and must be overturned. Regarding Section 3, states are here to comply with the federal Constitution, not with federal law.

These acts of Congress that the high court mentions that federal law supersedes state laws is plainly unconstitutional. Even when states do comply with these acts, the federal government finds a way to intercede. States should focus on their own enforcement and away from the cutches of the federal government.

"What I do fear—and what Arizona and the States that support it fear—is that "federal policies" of nonenforcement will leave the States helpless before those evil effects of illegal immigration that the Court's opinion dutifully recites in its prologue (ante, at 6) but leaves unremedied in its disposition." (Concurring and Dissenting Opinion of Associate Justice Antonin Scalia on Arizona, ET AL., Petitioners v. United States, 2012).

In this republic, we cannot have a lax or non-existent immigration-enforcement policy. The enforcement immigration policy *must* lie within each state to dictate it.

"The National Government has significant power to regulate immigration." (Opinion of Anthony Kennedy on Arizona, ET AL., Petitioners v. United States, 2012).

Let's take this sentence from Justice Kennedy's words on who should control the immigration enforcement of our republic. It is typical of the pure arrogance and self-contempt that the federal government has shown toward the rules of federalism and state sovereignty. This has set an immense precedent to undermine the states' sovereign power under the Constitution. The federal government's arrogance continues to this day.

"With power comes responsibility, and the sound exercise of national power over immigration depends on the Nation's meeting its responsibility to base its laws on a political will informed by searching, thoughtful, rational civic discourse. Arizona may have understandable frustrations with the problems cause by illegal immigration while the process continues, but the State may not pursue policies that undermine federal law." (Opinion of Anthony Kennedy on Arizona, ET AL., Petitioners v. United States, 2012).

With power comes responsibility. Whose power? The last time I checked, the Constitution and Naturalization

Clause established by Congress intend to let the states enforce their borders within this republic.

Lastly, it frustrates the state of Arizona, and quite frankly the other states in this not so perfect union, to be told how to enforce the rules of federalism within their borders. As I have said before, either a lax enforcement policy or a strong enforcement would frustrate anybody in state power just because it is not the constitutional duty of the federal government to enforce any aspect of the clause.

"The United States has established that Sections 3, 5(C), and 6 of S.B. 1070 are preempted. It was improper, however, to enjoin Section 2(B) before the state courts had an opportunity to construe it and without some showing that enforcement of that provision in fact conflicts with federal immigration law and its objectives." (Opinion of Anthony Kennedy on Arizona, ET AL., Petitioners v. United States, 2012).

I want you to remember this immortal, fateful phrase that gives more power to the states: "The powers dictated to the states are numerous and indefinite, while the powers of the federal government are few and defined."

I respectfully dissent with this opinion of the court because it truly undermines the rules of federalism and our complete power of and for state sovereignty.

"Under the Supremacy Clause, pre-emptive effect is to be given to congressionally enacted laws, not to judicially divined legislative purposes. See *Wyeth, supra*, at

604 (THOMAS, J., concurring in judgment). Thus, even assuming the existence of some tension between Arizona's law and the supposed "purposes and objectives" of Congress, I would not hold that any of the provisions of the Arizona law at issue here are pre-empted on that basis." (Concurring and Dissenting Opinion of Associate Justice Clarence Thomas on Arizona, ET AL., Petitioners v. United States, 2012).

"As if often the case, discussion of the dry legalities that are the proper object of our attention suppresses the very human realities that gave rise to the suit. Arizona bears the brunt of the country's illegal immigration problem. Its citizens feel themselves under siege by large numbers of illegal immigrants who invade their property, strain their social services, and even place their lives in jeopardy. Federal officials have been unable to remedy the problem, and indeed have recently shown that they are unwilling to do so." (Concurring and Dissenting Opinion of Associate Justice Antonin Scalia on Arizona, ET AL., Petitioners v. United States, 2012).

"Arizona has moved to protect its sovereignty—not in contradiction of federal law, but in complete compliance with it. The laws under challenge here do not extend or revise federal immigration restrictions, but merely enforce those restrictions effectively. If securing its territory in this fashion is not within the power of Arizona, we should cease referring to it as a sovereign State. I dissent." (Concurring and Dissenting Opinion of Associate Justice Antonin Scalia on Arizona, ET AL., Petitioners v. United States, 2012).

Many people are perplexed by the true meaning of the Supremacy Clause. This is how I read the Supremacy Clause of the federal constitution: all laws passed by the federal government, if deemed constitutional passed by congress and interpreted by the highest court of the land, is the supreme law of the land. But the said law must not be a contradiction to the Constitution in order to remain supreme, as also Justice Clarence Thomas states.

The 1940 national Congress enforcement measure on immigration, the *Hines* decision, is based on no constitutional precedent. As the state of New York established naturalization guidelines when entering their cities within their borders and the borders of the United States, Pennsylvania has that right as well.

I have two major issues with the Opinion of the Court by Justice Kennedy and Dissenting Opinions by Justices Scalia, Thomas and Alito.

The first one is the usage of warrantless arrests. If the state of Arizona or any other state wants to remain autonomous and sovereign, then they must abide by and not contradict the federal Constitution. Once the local, state and federal law enforcement authorities start to contradict the Constitution regarding the Fourth Amendment, there will be mistrust and confusion as to the citizens' rights.

Following federal immigration law is not the same as following federal constitutional law.

We must never forget that "We the States, respectively the people, have more power than the federal government," and we must keep reminding the government that we won't lose that power.

The second and last issue I have with these opinions, and especially with how the state of Arizona constructed this legislation, is that it truly showed no one-hundred percent state sovereignty and autonomy. Following federal immigration law is not the same as following federal constitutional law. Federal immigration law is passed down by legislators who truly have no grasp to the meaning of the Constitution and the clear picture of the rules of federalism.

But that is not what troubles me with S.B. 1070. It is the idea that if a state is supposed to remain a completely autonomous and sovereign stage, then why do states have to abide by federal immigration law. Their official duty is to enforce their law with no contradiction to the national Constitution. States are advised, but not obligated, to comply with federal law if it is an unlawful act.

In reading sections of S.B. 1070, I tend to disagree that it shows no clear path to and of state sovereignty and autonomy.

One federal government executive administration institute a lax or non-existent enforcement policy while future ones offer strong enforcement policies leaving the states unable to understand who enforces the clause.

I still stand with the dissenters of this ruling because first, I will always stand with state sovereignty over federal government autonomy, but I still see no clear grasp of self-governing autonomy. While I stand in dissent with this Opinion of the Court, I will never stand with a rogue and arrogant federal government to claim more power.

* * *

Since the passing of Associate Justice Antonin Scalia on February 13, 2016, the High Court has been without its strongest possible advocate for state sovereignty. The Supreme Court lost a sole voice for the sovereignty of each state and true follower of our rules of federalism. The Naturalization Clause belongs in the enforcement hands of the states themselves. Not in the clutches of the federal government. And the late Associate Justice Antonin Scalia knew that. To some extent Justice Thomas and Justice Alito are good constitutional jurists who have also applied the rules of federalism as their late colleague once did.

We now come to the tip of the iceberg of a federal immigration measure that was not passed by Congress. It was passed by an executive decree by President Trump. We will examine if executive decrees are valid in federal government immigration enforcement just as if they were passed as legislation by the national Congress. Is this an abuse of a continuing rogue and arrogant federal government during peace time or war time? We shall see in the Opinion and Dissent of *Trump v. Hawaii, (2018)*.

* * *

"Under the Immigration and Nationality Act [of 1965], foreign nationals seeking entry into the United States undergo a vetting process to ensure that they satisfy the numerous requirements for admission. The Act also vests the President with authority to restrict the entry of aliens whenever he finds that their entry "would be detrimental to the interests of the United States." 8 U.S.C. Section 1182(f). Relying on that delegation, the President concluded that it was necessary to impose entry restrictions on nationals of countries that do not share adequate information for an informed entry determination., or that otherwise present national security risks. Presidential Proclamation No. 9645, 82 Fed. Reg. 45161 (2017) (Proclamation)." (Opinion Brief of Donald J. Trump, President of the United States, Et At., Petitioners v. Hawaii by Chief Justice John Roberts, 2018).

It is peculiar and sad that today's American conservative movement behind the Republican Party praised the Immigration and Nationality Act of 1965. This act was proposed by a member of Congress of liberal and unconstitutional standards that sought to increase the size of the federal government. While decreasing in size the sovereignty of each autonomous state. This congressional member was Rep. Emanuel Celler of the State of New York. And this legislative measure was signed into law by none other than President Lyndon B. Johnson. A man who truly had no federalism scruples and increased dramatically the size of the federal government.

This congressional act gives ultimate power to the federal executive branch whether it be the attorney general or president, a special discretionary and ultimate power over the enforcement of the Naturalization Clause. And I am not surprised that the federal high court grants this power to succeed. Well, they did grant this unconstitutional power grab to another "Tyrant-In-Chief" back in 1944, why not continue it by granting it to another in 2018.

"We now decide whether the President had authority under the Act to issue the Proclamation, and whether the entry policy violates the Establishment Clause of the First Amendment. Shortly after taking office, President Trump signed Executive Order No. 13769, Protecting the Nation From Foreign Terrorist Entry Into the United States. 82 Fed. Reg. 8977 (2017) (EO-1). EO-1 directed the Secretary of Homeland Security to conduct a review to examine the adequacy of information provided by foreign governments about their nationals seeking to enter the United States." (Opinion Brief of Donald J. Trump, President of the United States, Et At., Petitioners v. Hawaii by Chief Justice John Roberts, 2018).

We now decide whether this president or past presidents have had the authority under the act to violate the rules of federalism and initiate an invasion of state sovereignty. This act and executive orders do not only violate the Bill of Rights but violates the very existing rules of federalism that govern our American republic.

Shortly after Julius Caesar crossed the Rubicon and proclaimed himself Imperator, he issued unholy decrees against the Roman Republic. Well, this president, like Caesar, casts unholy measures against the American Republic. I see nothing constitutional about executive orders portraying to be legislative measures — especially on immigration.

"Pending that review, the order suspended for 90 days the entry of foreign nationals from seven countries—Iran, Iraq, Libya, Somalia, Sudan, and Yemen—that had been previously identified by Congress or prior administrations as posing heightened terrorism risks. Section 3(c). The District for the Western District of Washington entered a temporary restraining order blocking the entry restrictions and the Court of Appeals for the Ninth Circuit denied the Government's request to stay that order. *Washington v. Trump*, 847 F. 3d 1151 (2017) (*per curiam*)." (Opinion Brief of Donald J. Trump, President of the United States, Et At., Petitioners v. Hawaii by Chief Justice John Roberts, 2018).

What James Madison meant when addressing the sovereign states that refuse to cooperate with federal union officials, wasn't that the courts nullify any sort of federal government measures. He also did not definitely mean that federal courts join in with state courts in defiance of a federal government enforcement measure.

This nation has become a nation of lawyers, rather than a nation of constitutional laws. People today misrepresent the nation's constitutional principles with their own personal or special interest agenda. This republic has let the federal government run rogue and arrogant and forcibly take away the rightly powers from the autonomous and sovereign States.

"In response, the President revoked EO-1, replacing it with Executive Order No. 13780, which again directed a worldwide review. 82 Fed. Reg. 13209 (2017) (EO-2)... EO-2 also temporarily restricted the entry (with case-by-case waivers) of foreign nationals from six of the countries covered by EO-1: Iran, Libya, Somalia, Sudan, Syria, and Yemen. Sub-Section 2(c), 3(a). The order explained that those countries had been selected because each "is a state sponsor of terrorism, has been significantly compromised by terrorist organizations, or contains active conflict zones." Section 1(d). The entry restriction was to stay in effect for 90 days, pending completion of the worldwide review." (Opinion Brief of Donald J. Trump, President of the United States, Et At., Petitioners v. Hawaii by Chief Justice John Roberts, 2018).

This is what happens when we, members of the American republic, give too much power to the chief executive. But it does not surprise me, because we the states, respectively the people, have let go of that power and now we are beholden to federal government control of that power. One day, the chief executive issues one decree and then the next day issues another one. Of course, this creates disharmony and chaos among our federalism republic. Laws are made by the legislative process, not by the executive process.

"The District Courts for the Districts of Maryland and Hawaii entered nationwide preliminary injunctions barring enforcement of entry suspension, and the respective Court of Appeals upheld those injunctions, albeit on different grounds. International Refugee Assistance Project (IRAP) v. Trump, 857 F. 3d 554 (CA4 2017); *Hawaii v. Trump*, 859 F. 3d 741 (CA9 2017) (*per curiam*). This Court granted certiorari and stayed the injunctions—allowing the entry suspension to go into effect—with respect to foreign nationals who lacked a "credible claim of a bona fide relationship" with a person or entity in the United States. The temporary restrictions in EO-2 expired before this Court took any action, and we vacated the lower court decisions as moot." (Opinion Brief of Donald J. Trump, President of the United States, Et At., Petitioners v. Hawaii by Chief Justice John Roberts, 2018).

In Justice Thomas' Concurring Opinion to the Court, he mentions the unconstitutionality of lower courts permitting preliminary injunctions. I do tend to agree with Justice Thomas on this, but I disagree with this statement that he made on executive power within the realm of immigration:

> **A**s wonderful this republic is, we come to realize that even with our great admiration, comes great disappointment.

"Nor could it, since the President has inherent authority to exclude aliens from the country." (Concurring Brief of Donald J. Trump, President of the United States, Et At., Petitioners v. Hawaii by Associate Justice Clarence Thomas, 2018).

As I was sad and disappointed in the late Justice Scalia's comment on executive power in his concurring opinion of *Zadvydas v. Davis*. I am slightly disappointed and disillusioned with this statement from Justice Thomas. As wonderful as this republic is, we come to realize that even with our great admiration, comes great disappointment. But we can agree and disagree and remain at ease with one another.

I again truly do not believe that such power of naturalization has been granted to the United States, especially to the federal executive branch.

It is the sovereign states who enforce every aspect of the Bill of Rights within the Constitution, not the federal government.

I understand Justice Thomas' concerns with the dissenting opinion of this ruling. I cannot seem to understand how Justice Thomas supports this ruling by disavowing our rules of federalism.

"The plaintiffs cannot raise any other First Amendment claim, since the alleged religious discrimination in this case was directed at aliens abroad." (Concurring Brief of Donald J. Trump, President of the United States, Et At., Petitioners v. Hawaii by Associate Justice Clarence Thomas, 2018).

National Executive Decrees not only have an effect outside of the nation but inside as well. That is the danger of a one-man rule in ruling with executive decrees. Our American federalism republic was never intended to have a one-man rule. The intention was to have a one-thousand men rule to keep in line the one-man rule while the nine-member high court kept in line the one-thousand men rule.

Let's return to discuss this matter of lower federal and state courts creating injunctions against a federal government policy whether by legislative or executive means.

"Injunctions that prohibit the Executive Branch from applying a law or policy against anyone — often called "universal" or "nationwide" injunctions — have become increasingly common. District courts, including the one here, have begun imposing universal injunctions without considering their authority to grant such a sweeping relief. These injunctions are beginning to take a toll on the federal court system —preventing legal questions from percolating through the federal courts, encouraging forum shopping, and making every case a national emergency for the courts and for the executive branch. I am skeptical that district courts have the authority to enter universal injunctions. These injunctions did not emerge until a century and half later after the founding. And they appear to be inconsistent with longstanding limits on equitable relief and the power of Article III courts. If their popularity continues, this Court must address their legality." (Concurring Brief of Donald J. Trump,

President of the United States, Et At., Petitioners v. Hawaii by Associate Justice Clarence Thomas, 2018).

If Justice Thomas is skeptical of lower federal courts taking the rein of establishing a non-existent precedent, then I am skeptical of the highest court of the land granting excessive power to the federal government executive branch. It is not the job of any lower court or high court of the federal government to dictate immigration enforcement policy.

While Justice Thomas criticizes and brings forth an argument, the court system cannot seek to legislate from the bench.

"The scope of the federal courts' equitable authority under the Constitution was a point of contention at the founding, and the "more limited construction" of that power prevailed. *Id.*, at 126. The founding generation viewed equity "with suspicion." *Id.*, at 128." Several anti-Federalists criticized the Constitution's extension of the federal judicial power to "Case[s] in … Equity," Art. III, Section 2, as "givi[ng] the judge a discretionary power." Letters from The Federalist Farmer No, XV (Jan 18, 1788), in 2 The Complete Anti-Federalist 315, 322 (H. Storing, ed. 1981). That discretionary power, the anti-Federalists alleged, would allow courts to "explain the constitution according to the reasoning spirit of it, without being confined to the words of the letter." Essays of Brutus No. XI (Jan. 31, 1788), in *id.*, at 417, 419-420." (Concurring Brief of Donald J. Trump, President of the United States, Et At., Petitioners v. Hawaii by Associate Justice Clarence Thomas, 2018).

Their boundaries are quite simple, to interpret the enacted law whether it is constitutional or not constitutional. The power of injunctions, to be perfectly clear is not to be executed by the court. In my humble constitutional opinion, the theory of injunctions works as the theory of nullification. But it is the duty of each state's assembly to refuse to cooperate with the federal government regardless of an Act of Congress or Executive Decree. The courts are not there to interject their opinions as legislative measures, that is the job of the state legislature.

"'The Federalists' explanation was consistent with how equity worked in 18th-century England. English courts of equity applied established rules not only when they decided the merits, but also when they fashioned remedies." (Concurring Brief of Donald J. Trump, President of the United States, Et At., Petitioners v. Hawaii by Associate Justice Clarence Thomas, 2018).

We are not England. We became independent from Great Britain. Lower courts and federal courts granting and disavowing permissions for injunctions is not in the best interest to keep maintaining this lawful American republic. What is in the best interest, is for the states to grant nullification policies and refuse to cooperate with the federal government.

"In short, whether the authority comes from a statute or the Constitution, district courts' authority to provide equitable relief is meaningfully constrained. This authority must comply with longstanding principles of equity that predate this country's founding." (Concurring Brief of Donald J. Trump, President of the United States, Et At., Petitioners v. Hawaii by Associate Justice Clarence Thomas, 2018).

"Universal injunctions do not seem to comply with those principles. These injunctions are a recent development, emerging for the first time in the 1960s and dramatically increasing in popularity only very recently. And they appear to conflict with several traditional rules of equity, as well as the original understanding of the judicial role." (Concurring Brief of Donald J. Trump, President of the United States, Et At., Petitioners v. Hawaii by Associate Justice Clarence Thomas, 2018).

Courts interactions with legislative measures do not comply with how this republic was founded. This nation has become a nation of lazy sheep dwellers. It is the job of the state legislature of that respective sovereign state to tackle the unconstitutionality of a federal immigration law or executive decree.

We have let the court system dictate legislative policy for too long, whether it be for or against the enforcement of the immigration clause.

"This Court has long respected these traditional limits on equity and judicial power." (Concurring Brief of Donald J. Trump, President of the United States, Et At., Petitioners v. Hawaii by Associate Justice Clarence Thomas, 2018).

"Courts can review the constitutionality of an act only when "a justiciable issue" requires it to decide whether to "disregard an unconstitutional enactment." *Id.*, at 488. If the statute is unconstitutional, then courts enjoin "not the execution of the statute, but the acts of the official." *Ibid.* Courts cannot issue an injunction based on a mere allegation "that officials of the executive department of the government are executing and will execute an act of Congress asserted to be unconstitutional." *Ibid.* "To do so would not be not to decide a judicial controversy." *Id.*, at 488-489." (Concurring Brief of Donald J. Trump, President of the United States, Et At., Petitioners v. Hawaii by Associate Justice Clarence Thomas, 2018).

"In sum, universal injunctions are legally and historically dubious. If the federal courts continue to issue them, this Court is dutybound to adjudicate their authority to do so." (Concurring Brief of Donald J. Trump, President of the United States, Et At., Petitioners v. Hawaii by Associate Justice Clarence Thomas, 2018).

This court and past courts have long not respected the rules of federalism, nor the independent and sovereign states. Whether it was in 1875, with the national Congress' first immigration measure, the 2001 Patriot Act, or the executive decrees by past and present chief executives. The federal government has not respected this republic's sovereign standing principle and traditions. And when you have the courts give a free pass to the federal government to enforce the Naturalization Clause, that is a slap in the face to these traditions and principles.

In summary, universal injunctions by federal and state courts are indeed legally and historically dubious. Just as the federal government trying to enforce a clause that is not within their power is also dubious. It is not the duty of the high court to adjudicate these powers. Their duty is to seize these injunctions and give it back to the sovereign states to adjudicate their powers of enforcement on the Naturalization Clause.

It is ironic that Justice Breyer is not siding with the federal government in enforcing of the Naturalization Clause. He has done so in the past. And now he is seeing the dangers of this invasion, or is he? Or does he just have contempt for the current chief executive and not hatred toward a continuation of a federal government so intrusive to the sovereign states' borders?

He has sided multiple times with the federal government on the enforcement issue of the Naturalization Clause. Justice Breyer has granted the federal executive branch the sole discretion and authority to enforce the stated clause. He has never had any regard for the rules of federalism, so why start now.

"The question before us is whether Proclamation No. 9645 is lawful. If its promulgation or content was significantly affected by religious animus against Muslims, it would violate the relevant statute or the First Amendment itself." (Dissenting Brief of Donald J. Trump, President of the United States, Et At., Petitioners v. Hawaii by Associate Justice Stephen Breyer, 2018).

"In my view, the Proclamation's elaborate system of exemptions and waivers can and should be help us answer this question. That system provides for case-by-case consideration of persons who may qualify for visas despite the Proclamation's general ban. Those persons include lawful permanent residents, asylum seekers, refugees, students, children, and numerous others... The Solicitor General askes us to consider the Proclamation "as" it is "written" and "as" it is "applied," waivers and exemptions included. Tr., of Oral Arg., 38. He warned us against considering the Proclamation's lawfulness "on the hypothetical situation that [the Proclamation] is what it isn't," *ibid.*, while telling us that its waiver and exemption provisions mean what they say: The Proclamation does not exclude individuals from the United States "if they meet the criteria" for a waiver or exemption. *Id.*, at 33." (Dissenting Brief of Donald J. Trump, President of the United States, Et At., Petitioners v. Hawaii by Associate Justice Stephen Breyer, 2018).

In my view, this proclamation is just another intrusive action by the federal government to empower itself against the will of the sovereign states. Whether the proclamation was the 1965 Immigration and Nationality Act passed by Congress or an executive decree by the federal executive, it remains unconstitutional. And what's worse is that the federal government is creating a class of privilege exemption among the residents of the different states. If you are a United States citizen, whether by birth or naturalized, a permanent alien or legal worker, the federal government cannot install waivers and exemptions upon your citizenry.

By the federal government creating waivers and exemptions, they are indeed in violation of the Equal Protection Clause of the Fourteenth Amendment, not only the First. The federal government or any other entity cannot give privilege to one person and not the other. Neither the sovereign states can create waivers and exemptions, they are here to enforce the naturalization clause. Justice Breyer in his dissenting brief of *Trump v. Hawaii*, is not showing an allegiance to the rules of federalism. His only allegiance is to the special interests in attacking the current federal government. Chief Justice Roberts has not been an ally to the rules of federalism either.

"On the one hand, if the Government is applying the exemption and waiver provisions as written, then its argument for the Proclamation's lawfulness is strengthened." (Dissenting Brief of Donald J. Trump, President of the United States, Et At., Petitioners v. Hawaii by Associate Justice Stephen Breyer, 2018).

As I have always stated, you give the federal government an inch of power, they will take a mile of power. The constitutional framers never intended for the federal government to obtain this enormous amount of power by taking it away from the sovereign states. Now Justice Breyer is stating that if this national government proclamation goes into effect with all its power, it will continue to strengthen. Why didn't he think of this when he wrote the Opinion Brief of *Zadvydas v. Davis* or joined to support the sovereign state of Arizona? Justice Breyer has never shown any interest in less federal government control.

"Plaintiffs argue that the Proclamation is not a valid exercise of the President's authority under the INA. In their view, Section1182(f) confers only a residual power to temporarily halt the entry of a discrete group of aliens engaged

> **T**o further allow the executive branch of the federal government to gain such unnecessary power on Naturalization is both tyrannical and abhorrent.

in harmful conduct. They also assert that the Proclamation violates another provision of rhe INA—8 U.S.C. Section 1152(a)(1)(A)—because it discriminates on the basis of nationality in the issuance of immigrant visas." (Opinion Brief of Donald J. Trump, President of the United States, Et At., Petitioners v. Hawaii by Chief Justice John Roberts, 2018).

"By its plain language, Section 1182(f) grants the President broad discretion to suspend the entry of aliens into the United States. The President lawfully exercised that discretion based on the findings—following a worldwide, multi-agency review—that entry of the covered aliens would be detrimental to the national interest." (Opinion Brief of Donald J. Trump, President of the United States, Et At., Petitioners v. Hawaii by Chief Justice John Roberts, 2018).

The text of Section 1182(f) states:

"Whenever the President finds that the entry of any aliens or of any class of aliens into the United States would be detrimental to the interests of the United States, he may by proclamation, and for such period as he shall deem necessary, suspend the entry of all aliens or any class of aliens as immigrants or nonimmigrants, or impose on the entry of aliens any restrictions he may deem to be appropriate." (Opinion Brief of Donald J. Trump, President of the United States, Et At., Petitioners v. Hawaii by Chief Justice John Roberts, 2018).

I argue that not only is this proclamation not valid under the INA (Immigration and Nationality Act), but it's also not valid under the rules of federalism. To further allow the executive branch of the federal government to gain such unnecessary power on naturalization is both tyrannical and abhorrent. Then what was the entire point of the Virginia and Kentucky Resolutions of 1798. The federal chief executive is not the head constable of the nation, to impose such policies onto the sovereign states. And the federal executive branch cannot command the sergeants of each federal bureaucracy to impose these acts onto the states themselves. This discretionary power lies with each autonomous state.

"The Proclamation falls well within this comprehensive delegation. The sole prerequisite set forth in Section1182(f) is that the President "find[]" that the entry of the covered aliens "Would be detrimental to the interests of the United States." (Opinion Brief of Donald J. Trump, President of the United States, Et At., Petitioners v. Hawaii by Chief Justice John Roberts, 2018).

Would be detrimental to the interests of the United States? Whose interests would indeed be detrimental? The last time I read the Constitution and studied the rules of federalism. It was clear to me; it is in the best interests of each state to enforce the Naturalization and indeed detrimental to the republic. And if those states refuse to comply, then it is in the best interest of the federal government to administer and advise the state to comply. But it has never been in the best interest of the nation for the federal government to enforce the clause on their own.

I love to hate it when the federal government finds an action to justify another action to please the current federal executive branch administration. Just because past presidents have issued similar proclamations or legislations as President Trump issued, does not make it rightly so and constitutionally so. Both Jefferson and Madison made it clear to President Adams by signing the Alien and Sedition Act would be an attack on our Constitution and rules of federalism. That refusal documentation was the Principles of 1798. Whether in the federal executive branch, national

Congress and high court, they need to abide to the best interests of the Constitution and not to their own personal indulgences, nor special interest needs.

"The 12-page Proclamation—which thoroughly describes the process, agency evaluations, and recommendations underlying the President's chosen restrictions—is more detailed than any prior order a President has issued under Section 1182(f). Contrast Presidential Proclamation No. 6958, 3 CFR 133 (1996) (President Clinton) (explaining in one sentence why suspending entry members of the Sudanese government and armed forces "is in the foreign policy interests of the United States"); Presidential Proclamation No. 4865, 3 CFR 50-51 (1981) (President Reagan) (explaining in five sentences why measures to curtail "the continuing illegal migration by sea of large numbers of undocumented aliens into southeastern United States" are "necessary")." (Opinion Brief of Donald J. Trump, President of the United States, Et At., Petitioners v. Hawaii by Chief Justice John Roberts, 2018).

"Section 1182(f) authorizes the President to suspend entry "for such period as he shall deem necessary". It follows that when a President suspends entry in response to a diplomatic dispute or policy concern, he may link the duration of these restrictions, implicitly or explicitly, to the resolution of the triggering condition. See, *e.g.*, Presidential Proclamation No. 5829, 3 CFR 88 (1988) (President Reagan) (suspending the entry of certain Panamanian nationals "until such time as... democracy has been restored in Panama"); Presidential Proclamation No. 8693, 3 CFR 86-87 (2011) (President Obama) (suspending the entry of individuals subject to a travel restriction under United Nations Security Council resolutions "until such time as the Secretary of State determines that [the suspension] is no longer necessary"). In fact, not one of the 43 suspension orders issued prior to this litigation has specified a precise end date." (Opinion Brief of Donald J. Trump, President of the United States, Et At., Petitioners v. Hawaii by Chief Justice John Roberts, 2018).

In short, the language of Section 1182(f) is clear, and the Proclamation does not exceed any textual limit on the President's authority." (Opinion Brief of Donald J. Trump, President of the United States, Et At., Petitioners v. Hawaii by Chief Justice John Roberts, 2018).

The federal executive administrations, past, present and possibly for the future will likely be disloyal to the rules of federalism and intrusive to state sovereignty. Even President Reagan broke the rules of federalism and instructed his federal government to unconstitutionally enforce the Naturalization Clause. The Travel Ban Proclamation of President Trump, as well as past immigration enforcement proclamations of Presidents Carter, Reagan, Clinton, and Obama were all granted under the authority by an unconstitutional act of Congress passed in 1965, and signed by the most rogue and arrogant President in American political History. When I hear President Trump defend his proclamation actions, I hear him defending the biggest anti-federalism individual to ever be president, Lyndon Baines Johnson.

The Opinion of this Court continues and on to justify Trump's Proclamation action by naming more Proclamations of past Presidents. The federal government can justify all they want; they quite know that they are wrong. They are wrong because these Proclamations and the INA Act goes against the constitution and rules of federalism.

Whether President Obama created an Executive Proclamation to deny entry to Russian nationals, or President Clinton deny entry of people from Sudan, or President Reagan on Cuban nationals, it is not the job of the federal government to enforce something that it is clearly not in their bounds. And President Trump is not helping the situation but making it worse by continuing an arrogant and rogue federal government.

"More significantly, plaintiffs' argument about historical practice is a double-edged sword. The more ad hoc their account of executive action—to fit the history into their theory— the harder it becomes to see such a refined delegation in a statute that grants the President sweeping authority to decide

> **I** worry of more centrist ad hoc immigration enforcement policies proposed by the federal government in the present and the future.

whether to suspend entry, whose entry to suspend, and for how long." (Opinion Brief of Donald J. Trump, President of the United States, Et At., Petitioners v. Hawaii by Chief Justice John Roberts, 2018).

Well, the plaintiffs or the respondents are not to blame. The only ones to blame are the citizens and residents of each sovereign state who have allowed the federal government to go rogue. The continuation of unprecedented and unconstitutional ad hoc policies continues in our American republic. The federal government will continue to grow, not expand, into a more powerful and arrogant government and it won't end when President Trump leaves office because the next president will likely be the same or even more arrogant. The same unconstitutional actions will occur, and we will have more unconstitutional rulings dictating centrist policy onto the sovereignty of the state.

I worry about more centrist ad hoc immigration enforcement policies proposed by the federal government in the present and the future.

"We now turn to Plaintiffs' claim that the Proclamation was issued for the unconstitutional purpose of excluding Muslims. Because we have an obligation to assure ourselves of jurisdiction under Article III, we begin by addressing the question whether plaintiffs have standing to bring their constitutional challenge." (Opinion Brief of Donald J. Trump, President of the United States, Et At., Petitioners v. Hawaii by Chief Justice John Roberts, 2018).

"Plaintiffs first argue that they have standing on the ground that the Proclamation "establishes a disfavored faith" and violates "their own right to be free from federal [religious] establishments." Brief for Respondents 27-28 (emphasis added). They describe such injury as "spiritual and dignitary." *Id.*, at 29." (Opinion Brief of Donald J. Trump, President of the United States, Et At., Petitioners v. Hawaii by Chief Justice John Roberts, 2018).

"Our cases recognize that "[t]he clearest command of the Establishment Clause is that one religious denomination cannot be officially preferred over another." *Larson v. Valente*, 456 U.S. 228, 244 (1982). Plaintiffs believe that the Proclamation violates this prohibition by singling out Muslims for disfavored treatment. The entry suspension, they contend, operates as a "religious gerrymander," in part because most of the countries covered by the Proclamation have Muslim-majority populations." (Opinion Brief of Donald J. Trump, President of the United States, Et At., Petitioners v. Hawaii by Chief Justice John Roberts, 2018).

"One week after his inauguration, the President issued EO-1. In a television interview, one of the President's campaign advisers explained that when the President "first announced it, he said, 'Muslim ban.' He called me up. He said, 'Put a commission together. Show me the right way to do it legally.'" *Id.*, at 125. Plaintiffs also note that after issuing EO-2 to replace EO-1, the President expressed regret that his prior order had been "watered down" and called for a "much tougher version" of his "Travel Ban." More recently, on November 29, 2017, the President retweeted links to three anti-Muslim propaganda videos. In response to questions about those videos, the President's deputy press secretary denied that the President thinks Muslims are a threat to the United States, explaining that "the President has been talking about these security issues for years now, from the campaign trail to the White House" and "has addressed these issues with the travel order that he issued earlier this year and the companion proclamation." IRAP v. Trump, 883 F. 3d 233, 267 (CA4 2018)." (Opinion Brief of Donald J. Trump, President of the United States, Et At., Petitioners v. Hawaii by Chief Justice John Roberts, 2018).

This Opinion Brief by the Chief Justice of the Supreme Court in defending the actions of the other federal government branch should be a wake-up call for the sovereign states and their citizens. To defend the chief executive's actions in how he communicated to the American people is unsettling. To be honest, I never saw Associate Justice Jackson defend FDR's "Fireside Chats." Justice Jackson just attacked the rules of federalism and installed his own personal agenda rather than the agenda of the Constitutional framers. But to see Chief Justice Roberts offer in his opinion, the rants and raves of a commander in chief to prove his point that the travel ban is constitutionally acceptable. So now posts on Twitter, Facebook, Instagram are socially acceptable statements by public servants? These statements are now entered into evidence as pure facts while it brings disharmony and chaos to our American republic.

The proclamation does indicate that it restricts the entry of certain immigrants that are citizens or aliens of nations of Muslim heritage, despite statements by President Trump stating that it is just a travel security ban with no racist or demeaning tones against a group of people.

"The President of the United States possesses an extraordinary power to speak to his fellow citizens and on their behalf. Our Presidents have frequently used that power to espouse the principles of religious freedom and tolerance on which this Nation was founded. In 1790 George Washington reassured the Hebrew Congregation of Newport, Rhode Island that "happily the Government of the United States…gives to bigotry no sanction, to persecution no assistance [and] requires only that they who live under its protection should demean themselves as good citizens." 6 papers of George Washington 285 (D. Twohig ed. 1996)." (Opinion Brief of Donald J. Trump, President of the United States, Et At., Petitioners v. Hawaii by Chief Justice John Roberts, 2018).

Indeed, the president of the United States is a beacon of light figure to the nation and should have good standards of ethics and morality to share his beliefs onto the American people. Honestly, you truly cannot compare the distinguished manners and diplomacy of our first commander-in-chief to the meager and boorish ones of our current commander-in-chief.

George Washington was a unifier and he would do anything to unite a nation together away from violence and hatred. I'd rather listen to the speeches of the first commander in chief than the speeches of the second commander in chief. John Adams, the nation's second president, was not a unifier and created disharmony among the French, American citizens and anyone else who made contradictory opinions against his own policies. So, for Chief Justice Roberts to compare President Trump to President Washington is childish and demeaning to this jurist's emotional capacity. President George Washington would no way apply the same logic or share the emotionality and ethics of the 45th President of the United States.

"President Eisenhower, at the opening of the Islamic Center of Washington, similarly pledged to a Muslim audience that "America would fight with her whole strength for your right to have here your own church," declaring that "[t]his concept is indeed a part of America." Public Papers of the Presidents, Dwight D. Eisenhower, June 28, 1957, p. 509 (1957). And just days after the attacks of September 11, 2001, President George W. Bush returned to the same Islamic Center to implore his fellow Americans—Muslims and non-Muslims alike—to remember during their time of grief that "[t]he face of terror is not the true faith of Islam," and that America is "a great country because we share the same values of respect and dignity and human worth." Public Papers of the Presidents, George W. Bush, Vol. 2,

Sept. 17, 2001, p. 1121 (2001). Yet it cannot be denied that the Federal Government and the Presidents who have carried its laws into effect have—from the Nation's earliest days—performed unevenly in living up to those inspiring words." (Opinion Brief of Donald J. Trump, President of the United States, Et At., Petitioners v. Hawaii by Chief Justice John Roberts, 2018).

Again, Presidents Eisenhower and George W. Bush did not contradict their statements. I think they meant what they meant without creating disharmony and divisions. I believe both two presidents have good hearts and I do not see any similarities that Chief Justice is trying to compare with the current president.

I have an issue with the statement that Eisenhower made. He stated that "America will fight with her whole strength for the Muslim community to have their religious institutions." "I (do not) like Ike." He was a famous war hero that a major political party poached him to run for president without any knowledge of the Constitution. Otherwise he would have known that the First Amendment states quite clearly that governments -- both federal and sovereign states -- are not supposed to offer privilege to one religion. If he would have said that "America welcomes Muslims to practice their religion without any sense of bigotry or intolerance," then I would be more inclined to be supportive of Eisenhower's actions.

Now President George W. Bush's words are more sincere and more constitutional than Eisenhower's or Trump's words. After the terrible attacks of September 11, 2001, America was in a state of panic. And instead of President Bush initiating racist social media rants and outrageous statements, he unified a nation. I admit he may have unified it too much with the creation of the new bureaucratic train-wreck that is now the Department of Homeland Security. But still, President Bush unified America instead of separating it. I cannot therefore agree with the Chief Justice's defense and justifications of the current federal executive administration.

"If this Court must decide the question without this further litigation, I would, on balance, find the evidence of antireligious bias, including statements on a website taken down only after the President issued two executive orders preceding the Proclamation, along with the other statements also set forth in JUSTICE SOTOMAYOR's opinion, a sufficient basis to set the Proclamation aside. And for these reasons, I respectfully dissent." (Dissenting Brief of Donald J. Trump, President of the United States, Et At., Petitioners v. Hawaii by Associate Justice Stephen Breyer, 2018).

I not only dissent to the Opinion of this Court but to the dissent of Associate Justice Stephen Breyer. However, I am quite disappointed that Chief Justice Roberts knows very little to quote the rules of federalism in the matter of immigration. I am also disappointed, but not surprised, that Justice Breyer continues to support the idea of the federal government to enforce the Naturalization Clause. Whether it was to extend the detention timeframe on aliens and citizens, to now having the president use a "discretionary" power to arrest, imprison, detain, deport and now block anybody wishing to enter the sovereign states of this republic. I fully dissent with Justice Breyer's unconstitutional dissenting opinion.

But honestly, can we really think the federal government will ever give back the power to the sovereign states when since 1875, the federal government has forcibly removed it from the states. And in 1944, during war time, the federal executive branch established an (unconstitutional) executive order to arrest, imprison, detain and in some cases deport members of the the Japanese American community during World War II. For the Opinion of this Court to state that *Korematsu v. United States*, 1944 has no bearing on this court ruling and has no striking resemblance is insulting to every American that has studied the Constitution and the teachings of James Madison and Thomas Jefferson.

"Finally, the dissent invokes *Korematsu v. United States*, 323 U.S. 214 (1944). Whatever rhetorical advantage the dissent may see in doing so, *Korematsu* has nothing to do with this case. The forcible relocation of U.S citizens to concentration camps, solely and explicitly on the basis of race, is objectively unlawful and outside the scope of Presidential authority. But is wholly inapt to liken that morally repugnant order to a facially neutral policy denying certain foreign nationals the privilege of admission. See post, at 26-28. The entry suspension is an act that is well within executive authority and could have been taken by any other President—the only question is evaluating the actions of this particular President in promulgating an otherwise valid Proclamation. The dissent's reference to Korematsu, however, affords this Court the opportunity to make express what is already obvious: Korematsu was gravely wrong the day it was decided, has been overruled in the court of history, and—to be clear— "has no place in law under the Constitution." 323 U.S., at 248 (Jackson J., dissenting.)" (Opinion Brief of Donald J. Trump, President of the United States, Et At., Petitioners v. Hawaii by Chief Justice John Roberts, 2018).

I quite disagree with the Opinion of the Court that this ruling has no similarities with *Korematsu*. The rulings of 1944 and the 2018 have one thing in common. They were both initiated by a presidential executive decree, there is your first similarity. But the most important similarity is that it is an action of an arrogant and rogue federal government. An arrogant and rogue federal government placing an unconstitutional policy onto the sovereign states.

With the dissenting opinion regarding the comparison of *Korematsu*, I am troubled to be on their side simply because, this is their first time voicing their opinion against the federal government enforcing the Naturalization Clause. But why didn't they voice their contradictory opinion in 2003 or 2012? I, therefore, cannot stand with the majority or dissenting opinions.

"On December 8, 2015, Trump justified his proposal during a television interview by noting that President Franklin D. Roosevelt "did the same thing" with respect to the internment of Japanese Americans during World War II." (Dissenting Brief of Donald J. Trump, President of the United States, Et At., Petitioners v. Hawaii by Associate Justice Sonia Sotomayor, 2018).

"What I am doing is no different than FDR."

– Donald J. Trump on Good Morning America,
December 8, 2015.

When somebody decides to justify his/her actions by defending the actions of others, especially when those actions are unconstitutional and immoral, it is despicable. The basis of Proclamation No. 9645 is truly no different than Executive Order No. 9066. They both contain a sheer level of arrogance toward the rules of federalism. But we can expect nothing from populist demagogues.

The federal government administration of the Trump administration has showed from the beginning the continuation of a rogue and arrogant federal government that we have seen prior to Trump and prior to Barack Obama and so on. Not only a sense of arrogance, but a contempt for the residents and citizens of this land just because they are not of white descendant heritage.

As we have seen on many cases through America, *Buchanan v. Wharley*; *Brown v. Board of Education*; and

Loving v. Virginia. Is that the government, whether federal and state cannot show privilege to one race and contempt for another. That is exactly what President Trump proposed and has acted upon.

"Specifically, on December 7, 2015, he issued a formal statement "calling for a total and complete shutdown of Muslims entering the United States." App. 119. That statement, which remained on his campaign website until May 2017 (several months into his presidency), read in full:

"Donald J. Trump is calling for a total and complete shutdown of Muslims entering the United States until our country's representatives can figure out what is going on. According to a Pew Research, among others, there is great hatred towards Americans by large segments of the Muslim population. Most recently, a poll from the Center for Security Policy released data showing 25% of those polled agreed that violence against Americans here in the United States is justified as a part of the global jihad' and 51% of those polled 'agreed that Muslims in America should have the choice of being governed according to Shariah.'" (Dissenting Brief of Donald J. Trump, President of the United States, Et At., Petitioners v. Hawaii by Associate Justice Sonia Sotomayor, 2018).

"Mr. Trum[p] stated, 'Without looking at the various polling data, it is obvious to anybody that hatred is beyond comprehension. Where this hatred comes from and why we will have to determine. Until we are able to determine and understand this problem and the dangerous threat it poses, our country cannot be the victims of the horrendous attacks by people that believe only in Jihad, and I have no sense of reason or respect of human life. If I win the election for President, we are going to Make America Great Again.'— Donald J. Trump." *Id.*, at 158; see also *id.*, at 130-131." (Dissenting Brief of Donald J. Trump, President of the United States, Et At., Petitioners v. Hawaii by Associate Justice Sonia Sotomayor, 2018).

There are some major issues I had with then-presidential candidate Donald J. Trump and his ideas to let the federal government continue to enforce the Naturalization Clause. But I also see major issues with the dissenting opinion of Justice Sotomayor. Do not be fooled by Justice Sotomayor's stance. She is being anti-Trump rather than pro-federalism. She may very well be anti-Trump, but she remains a loyal supporter of an arrogant and over-growing federal government.

I also do not trust Justice Breyer in this dissenting opinion in which he advocated for the federal government to detain any alien, whether legal or illegal, for more than the 90 days required by law. Just because he dissented against this latest attack by the federal chief executive, he does not inspire any confidence that he stands for the rules of federalism.

Chief Justice Roberts may state that this Executive Proclamation does not resemble FDR's Executive Proclamation that lead to innocent aliens of Americans of Japanese descent to be imprisoned. And then later, the high court of the land decided to give legitimacy to a rogue and arrogant federal government administration of that time. I truly see a big similarity between Executive Order #90666 and Executive Proclamation (Order) #9645.

Justice Thomas' concurring opinion is still giving way to an arrogant and rogue federal government. He discusses extensively the threat of unruly injunctions by lower state and federal courts. It is not the job nor the responsibility of the judiciary system to correct the legislation. It is also not the job of the federal executive branch to pass legislation bypassing the national Congress.

One thing that Justice Thomas fails to point out, and that Chief Justice Roberts, and Justices Breyer and Sotomayor also forges is that it is the sole duty of each and all sovereign state to enforce the immigration clause.

A court may issue an injunction, but it must be handled with extreme thoughtfulness and care before passing judgment. It cannot pass any sort of judgment that bypasses the authority of the autonomous state. For Justice Thomas to issue a notice of care for more courts to act as a legislature, is a warning that the judiciary system cannot proceed anymore with that attitude. But also, the federal government cannot proceed with that attitude of arrogance.

"Our Constitution demands, and our country deserves, a Judiciary willing to hold to coordinate branches to account when they defy our most sacred legal commitments. Because the Court's decision today has failed in that respect, with profound regret, I dissent." (Dissenting Brief of Donald J. Trump, President of the United States, Et At., Petitioners v. Hawaii by Associate Justice Sonia Sotomayor, 2018).

Our Constitution demands, and our country rightly deserves, a return to federalism, that all our sovereign States hold the branches of the federal government accountable when they defy our most sacred legal commitments. Those commitments are the states enforcing the Naturalization Clause which is their sacred and legal duty to do.

Because of this court's decision has failed to restore the sovereignty of each State in the union, it is with heartfelt regret that I dissent not only with the Opinion brief but with the Dissenting brief.

I will only shout glory when the federal government has decided to fully understand the rules of federalism and when the federal government relinquishes that power and fully returns it to the states. I will also continue to criticize any overreach the federal government continues to make upon the sovereignty of the states, regardless of who is in power. For State Sovereignty … always!

* * *

Until recently, the federal government has not relinquished the enforcement power of the Naturalization Clause back over to the states. And today, sadly the sovereign states continue to be dependent on the national government. When will the federal government finally comprehend that they do not have the power to enforce the Naturalization Clause?

The Supreme Court heard a case on October 16, 2019. This case pertains to the sovereignty criminal enforcement issue of the State of Kansas in how to handle legal and illegal aliens in their state.

Since 1875, the federal government has grabbed with its slimy tentacles every aspect of the Naturalization Clause to enforce it on their own. It continues to this day and it will not end until the day one sovereign state says "enough" and nullifies all federal immigration acts of Congress. Nullification is the rightful remedy in restoring the sovereignty in all fifty states. By nullifying all unconstitutional federal immigration laws, we are telling the federal government, "Enough is Enough," and we will enforce the clause which is our duty to do.

* * *

I have analyzed the Supreme Court transcript of this case, *Kansas v. Garcia* and find it very disturbing. To this day, there is a belief from people that the federal government still has the ultimate authority in enforcing the Naturalization Clause. The federal government since 1875, has taken the reins of enforcing the immigration issue away from the sovereign states themselves.

We may see that some jurists do find their inner side of federalism, maybe not Justices Breyer, Sotomayor or Kagan … but anything is possible.

The people arguing for the sovereign state of Kansas were the Kansas Attorney General Derek Schmidt and Christopher G. Michel, Assistant to the Solicitor General. And arguing for the respondents' is Paul Hughes, Esq.

"That is why Kansas, like every other state, makes identity theft a crime. Our laws apply in all settings to all people, citizen and alien alike." (Oral Argument of Gen. Derek Schmidt, Kansas Attorney General in Kansas v. Ramiro Garcia, 2019).

"Respondents were convicted because they stole other people's personal information with intent to defraud. But, in Respondents' view, these state criminal laws that govern everybody else does not apply to them. They argue that Congress has, in effect, granted them special immunity because their intent was to obtain employment that Congress has forbidden." (Oral Argument of Gen. Derek Schmidt, Kansas Attorney General in Kansas v. Ramiro Garcia, 2019).

The chief enforcer of the laws of the state of Kansas knows two things about his role to protect the borders of the Sunflower State. Whoever resides in the state of Kansas, legally or illegally, must face the laws of that state if one commits a crime within their borders. General Schmidt is stating that the respondents are claiming that his case be heard at a federal level since Congress has enacted a federal law governing the employment status of all fifty states.

"Our view of what Congress did in 1986, against the backdrop of this Court's decision in *DeCanas*, that prior to IRCA the employment process generally was available to - - was within the scope of state criminal law. In 1986, Congress created something new and different. It created this I-9 system which was a novelty at the time. With the force of federal law, Congress was ordering millions of private employers around the country to gather up personal information of their employees or potential employees and to hold that information." (Oral Argument of Gen. Derek Schmidt, Kansas Attorney General in Kansas v. Ramiro Garcia, 2019).

"We concede that the state may not use the I-9 form." (Oral Argument of Gen. Derek Schmidt, Kansas Attorney General in Kansas v. Ramiro Garcia, 2019).

In 1986, the federal government passed and signed an unconstitutional legislation into law. States cannot be forced to use a federal form. There is nothing in the Constitution that says a state must comply with federal official forms.

"I don't believe you have a power as a state to prosecute crimes where the U.S. is a victim." (Associate Justice Sonia Sotomayor on the Arguments of Kansas v. Ramiro Garcia, 2019).

Well, we all can see where Justice Sotomayor holds her allegiance. To the federal government and against the rules of federalism. In response to her statement, "I don't believe, you or the federal government, have a power to prosecute crimes within the sovereignty of each state.

The federal government establishes the rules of immigration, hence the Naturalization Clause. Then it is the sovereign states that enforces these rules of immigration.

"Could you do this? Could a state have a law which says it is a crime for an alien to take information from the "S form" or other information that they give that's referred to in the federal statute, and it is a crime to do that and fraudulently give it to an employer for the purpose of obtaining a job." (Associate Justice Stephen Breyer on the Arguments of Kansas v. Ramiro Garcia, 2019).

I truly believe that someone needs to explain to Justice Breyer, the rules of federalism and how it applies in our federalism republic. From his majority opinion of *Zadvydas v. Davis*, to his dissent of *Trump v. Hawaii*. The States have every right to pass any legislative or referendum measure, if that measure does not contradict federal immigration constitutional law. Regardless of how this ruling will turn out, Justice Breyer will always come to the side of the federal government.

There are still individuals, whether on the judicial bench, legislative aisles, executive branch or individual citizens, who believe that the federal government is the answer to all the problems of each sovereign state and that includes immigration. As far as I can see from the respondent's legal counsel's arguments, he is incorrect in his interpretation of federal constitutional law and the rules of federalism.

"States may not prosecute individuals for using false information to demonstrate work authorization under federal immigration law." (Oral Argument of Paul Hughes, Esq., in Kansas v. Ramiro Garcia, 2019).

IRCA is nothing more than an unconstitutional piece of legislation. Quite frankly, lawyers today learn more about law jurisprudence than constitutional jurisprudence.

"Kansas is not trying to act as an immigration enforcer but to enforce our generally applicable identity theft laws." (Oral Argument of Gen. Derek Schmidt, Kansas Attorney General in Kansas v. Ramiro Garcia, 2019).

In conclusion, in trying to understand the transcripts of this Supreme Court case. I have come to an understanding that neither parties clearly understand the Naturalization Clause with being the enforcer of the law. If the respondent is legal or illegal alien, in this case, illegal. It is the responsibility of the state to prosecute the individual regardless of their legality status.

As we wait on the final judgment of this case, *Kansas v. Ramiro Garcia*, I truly hope that the Supreme Court gives the rightful power back to the states and away from the federal government, as this court did not return it in 2001, 2003, 2012, 2018. Let's truly hope that they regain their inner federalism wisdom and do the right thing.

A reminder to the Supreme Court of our land, the rights to enforce the Naturalization Clause belongs to the states. The power lies with us!

* * *

The judgment for the latest court ruling regarding which entity rightfully enforces the Naturalization Clause. It came on March 3, 2020, and I have to say that I was thrilled with the decision. This decision was a surprise to us all when the federal government gave sovereign and autonomous rights back to the States.

States can again prosecute and control their borders regarding the employment situation in the sovereign state of Kansas and among other states. It was a big surprise that five justices would affirm the power the sovereign states have over the federal government.

I can honestly say that the sovereign states have been returned their sovereign rights, but we still have a long way to go. This is the right step in the right direction to regain back our rights within the rules of federalism.

I am going to give a breakdown of how Justice Alito explains in his opinion how the states took the prosecutorial enforcement power away from the federal government.

This is an exciting time for our American republic. It is an exciting time because, finally the states were not silenced. They were given back their voice of sovereignty.

"Kansas law makes it a crime to commit "identity theft" or engage in fraud to obtain a benefit. Respondents—three aliens who are not authorized to work in this country—were convicted under these provisions for fraudulently using another person's Social Security number on state and federal tax-withholding forms that they submitted when they obtained employment. The Supreme Court of Kansas held that a provision of the Immigration Reform and Control Act of 1986 (IRCA), 100 Stat. 3359, expressly preempts the Kansas statutes at issue insofar as they provide a basis for these prosecutions. We reject this reading of the provision in question, as well as respondent's alternative arguments based on implied preemption. We therefore reverse." (Opinion Brief of Associate Justice Samuel Alito on Kansas v. Garcia, 2020).

The first sentence of Justice Alito's opinion should be eye opening to individuals who support the rules of federalism. "Kansas Law" is the first words out of Justice Alito's first statement. Each sovereign state has its own authority to create laws in accordance with the Constitution. It is a shame that the Kansas high court did not see the wisdom of the rules of federalism but fortunately the Supreme Court of the land did. But can we really blame a state court for being bamboozled by a rogue and arrogant federal government for all these years? A national law established to warn the state governments across this land to obey a central government autonomy.

Ever since 1942, the federal government whether the executive branch, national Congress or the high court, has taken it upon itself to establish a central government autonomy onto the sovereign states.

> The foundation of our laws on immigration does not reside with INA, IRCA or Patriot Act. It resides with the constitution.

Whether it be for education, healthcare, or immigration. I am just glad that today's court shut down the unconstitutional act of Congress passed in 1986 and returned the power to the states.

"The foundation of our laws on immigration and naturalization is the Immigration and Nationality Act (INA), 66 Stat. 163, as amended, 8 U.S.C Section 1101 et seq., which sets out the terms "terms and conditions of admission to the country and the subsequent treatment of aliens lawfully in the country." *Chamber of Commerce of United States of America v. Whiting*, 563 U.S. 582, 587 (2011). As initially enacted, the INA did not prohibit the employment of illegal aliens, and this Court held that federal law left room for the States to regulate in this field. See DeCanas v. Bica, 424 U.S. 351, 353 (1976)." (Opinion Brief of Associate Justice Samuel Alito on Kansas v. Garcia, 2020).

The foundation of our laws on immigration does not reside with INA, IRCA or Patriot Act. It resides with the constitution. And I am glad that Justice Alito quoted from the first court ruling that gave sovereignty rights back to the states. "States possess broad authority under their police powers to regulate the employment relationship to protect workers, *DeCanas v. Bica*, Associate Justice William J. Brennan, 1976. This court ruling gave precedence to this court to declare sovereignty back to the states in *Kansas v. Ramirez.*

It is a shame that we saw a tyrant-in-chief in the Eighties that signed and executed to increase the role of the federal government on immigration onto the States.

"With the enactment of IRCA, Congress took a different approach. IRCA made it unlawful to hire an alien knowing that he or she is unauthorized to work in the United States. 8 U.S.C Sub-Section1324a(a)(1)(A), (h)(3). To enforce this prohibition, IRCA requires employers to comply with a federal employment verification system. Section1324a(b). Using a federal work-authorization form (I-9), employers "must attest" that they "verified" that an employee "is not an unauthorized alien" by examining approved documents such as a United States passport or alien registration card. This requirement applies to the hiring of any individual regardless of citizenship or nationality. 8 U.S.C. Section1324a(b)(1). Employers who fail to comply may face civil or criminal sanctions. See sub-section1324a(e)(4), (f); 8 CFR Section274a.10. IRCA instructs employers to retain copies of the documents submitted by employees to show their authorization to work. 8 U.S.C. Sub-Section1324a(b) (3)—(4). IRCA concomitantly imposes duties on all employees, regardless of citizenship." (Opinion Brief of Associate Justice Samuel Alito on Kansas v. Garcia, 2020).

The first rule of federalism in this republic is that states do not have to comply with any law from the national government, unless it is in accordance with the Constitution. And quite frankly, IRCA is not in accordance with the Constitution. The sovereign states in this united republic have a solemn duty to refuse to cooperate with federal immigration authorities. IRCA imposes certain requirements onto the sovereign states which these requirements are unconstitutional.

"Although IRCA expressly regulates the use of I-9's and documents appended to that form, no provision of IRCA directly addresses the use of other documents, such as federal and state tax-withholding forms, that an employee may complete upon beginning a new job. Instead, the regulation provides that if an employee fails to provide a signed W-4, the employer must treat the employee "as a single person claiming no exemption." Section 31.3402(f)(2)-1(a). The submission of a fraudulent W-4, however, is a federal crime. 26 U.S.C Section 7205." (Opinion Brief of Associate Justice Samuel Alito on Kansas v. Garcia, 2020).

IRCA has supported the continuation of a rogue and arrogant federal government. It gives way too much power to a central autonomous government and makes the individual, sovereign states powerless. I know I sound like a federalism ideologue but this (IRCA) is not what the constitutional framers envisioned for our republic.

"Kansas uses a tax-withholding form (K-4) that is similar to the federal form. Kan. Stat. Ann. Section79-3298 (2018 Cum. Supp.); Kansas Dept. of Revenue. Employees must attest to the veracity of the information under the penalty of perjury. Finally, IRCA contains a provision that expressly "preempt[s] any State or Local law imposing civil or criminal sanctions (other than through licensing and similar laws) *upon those who employ, or recruit or refer for a fee for employment*, unauthorized aliens." 8 U.S.C. Section 1324a(h)(2)(emphasis added). This provision makes no mention of state or local laws that impose criminal or civil sanctions on employees or applicants for employment. See *Ibid.*" (Opinion Brief of Associate Justice Samuel Alito on Kansas v. Garcia, 2020).

As I stated before, IRCA has brought nothing but a rogue conduct and arrogance to the federal government in imposing unconstitutional enforcement.

"Like other States, Kansas has laws against fraud, forgeries and identity theft. These statutes apply to citizens and aliens alike and are not limited to conduct that occurs in connection with employment. The Kansas identity-theft statute criminalizes the "using" of any "personal identifying information" belonging to another person with the intent to "[d]efraud that person, or anyone else, in order to receive any benefit." Kan. Stat. Ann. Section 21-6107(a)(1). "[P]ersonal identifying information" includes, among other things, a person's name, birth date, driver's license number, and Social Security number. Section21-6107(e)(2). Kansas courts have interpreted the statute to cover the use of another person's Social Security number to receive the benefits of employment. See State v. Meza, 38 Kan. App. 2d 245, 247-250, 165P. 3d 298, 301-302

(2007)." (Opinion Brief of Associate Justice Samuel Alito on Kansas v. Garcia, 2020).

"The respondents in the three cases now before us are aliens who are not authorized to work in this country but nevertheless secured employment by using the identity of other persons on the I-9 forms that they completed when they applied for work. They also used these same false identities when they completed their W-4's and K-4's. All three respondents were convicted under one or both of the Kansas laws. We summarize the pertinent facts related to these three prosecutions." (Opinion Brief of Associate Justice Samuel Alito on Kansas v. Garcia, 2020).

If this nation was created to be a republic of sovereign states where each state is responsible for its border control and laws, then there is truly no need for IRCA (Immigration Reform and Control Act), INA, (Immigration and Nationality Act) or the Patriot Act. None is needed or wanted by the original standards of our constitutional framers.

The Founding Fathers knew that this republic was going to be bigger than its original and first thirteen states. That is the reason they created this system of federalism. Plus, they wanted to get away from the very idea of a central government authority which they endured during British colonial rule. You cannot have one law supersede the other because it creates disharmony and chaos. This is the reason the Kansas Supreme Court ignored the rules of federalism in where Kansas undoubtedly has the power to enforce the uniform code of naturalization. They decided to supersede it with a national law, a national law that involves budgetary funds from other states to enter the sovereign state of Kansas with no advisory discretion from the other states. That is strictly unconstitutional and would be repudiated by the Father of the Constitution, James Madison.

If the State of Kansas or any other state has a similar law alike as the national law of IRCA, then that law supersedes and preempts it. It is the responsibility of each state to handle their own budgetary and legislative needs as they see fit with no interference or intervention, militarily or fiscally, from the federal government.

It is the solemn duty of the sovereign and autonomous states to enforce the constitutional clause of Naturalization. And that is quite frankly what Kansas was doing and will continue to do it with or without the federal government guidance.

Let's give our brief interpretation of the crimes of the three respondents and see if their crimes were truly constitutionally upheld by the laws of the sovereign state of Kansas and not by the laws of the federal government.

"*Ramiro Garcia.* In August 2012, a local patrol officer stopped Garcia for speeding and learned that Garcia had been previously contacted by a financial crimes detective about possible identity theft, App. 39-44, 89-91; 306 Kan.113, 114, 401 P. 3d 588, 590 (2017). Local authorities obtained the documents that Garcia had completed when he began to work at a restaurant, and a joint state-federal investigation discovered that Garcia had used another person's Social Security number on his I-9, W-4, and K-4 forms. The State then charged Garcia with identity theft. The complaint alleged that, when he began to work at the restaurant, he used another person's Social Security number with the intent to defraud and in order to receive a benefit. App. 9-10. *Donaldo Morales.* A joint state-federal investigation of Morales began after the Kansas Department of Labor notified a Social Security agent that an employee at a local restaurant was using a Social Security number that did not match the identifying information in the department's files. A federal agent contacted the restaurant and learned that Morales had used another person's Social Security number on his I-9, W-4, and K-4 forms. The federal agent arrested Morales, who then admitted that he had bought the Social Security number from someone that he had met in a park. This information was turned over to state prosecutors, who charged Morales with identity theft and making false information. *Guadalupe Ochoa-Lara.* Ochoa-Lara came to the attention of a joint state-federal task force after officers learned that he had used a Social Security number issued to someone else when he leased an apartment. After contacting the restaurant where Ochoa-Lara worked, investigators determined that he had also used the same Social Security number to complete his I-9 and W-4 forms. Ibid. The State charged Ochoa-Lara with identity theft and making false information for using another's Social Security number on those documents." (Opinion Brief of Associate Justice Samuel Alito on Kansas v. Garcia, 2020).

These three cases have one similarity. They belong to be prosecuted at the bequest of the sovereign state of Kansas. They all had state-federal joint task forces working together in catching these three perpetrators. In my opinion, I find it very hard for the individual state governments to work together

> **The Sovereign State are in the need to cooperate, not in the need to work together with the federal government.**

with the federal government. That is one rule in the nullification process. It is an illusion that people have today of state and federal governments in the need to get along and corporate together. States need to work together with one another to be able to maintain "a more than perfect union." The federal government is not a sovereign entity, it is an administrative entity.

But since the national Congress and federal executive branch have overstepped their boundaries and forced their way into the sovereign states, and since the federal government has found ways to extort and blackmail several states. Then the states are bounded by threat to join in the federal task forces.

"In all three cases, respondents argued before the trial that IRCA preempted their prosecutions. They relied on 8 U.S.C. Section 1324a(b)(5), which, as noted, provides that

I-9 forms and "any information contained in or appended to enforcement of" the INA or other listed federal statutes. In response, the State dismissed the charges that were based on I-9's and agreed not to rely on the I-9's at trial. The State maintained, however, that Section 1324a(b)(5) did not apply to the respondents' use of false Social Security numbers on the tax-withholding forms. The trial courts allowed the State to proceed with the charges based on those forms. The State entered the K-4's and W-4's into evidence against Garcia and Morales, and Ochoa-Lara stipulated to using a stolen Social Security number on a W-4. Respondents were convicted, and three separate panels of the Kansas Court of Appeals affirmed their convictions." (Opinion Brief of Associate Justice Samuel Alito on Kansas v. Garcia, 2020).

This is the mess that the federal government has created upon the sovereignty of each state. The respondents tried to disavow the sovereign and autonomous laws of the state of Kansas and focus on the usurper laws of a rogue and arrogant federal government.

"A divided Kansas Supreme Court reversed, concluding that "the plain and unambiguous language of 8 U.S.C. Section 1324a(b)(5)" expressly prohibits a State from using "any information contained within [an] I-9 as the basi[s] for a state law identity theft prosecution of an alien who uses another's Social Security information in an I-9." The Court added "[t]he fact this information was included in the W-4 and K-4 did not alter the fact that it was also part of the I-9." Nevertheless, the court suggested that its holding did not sweep this broadly but was instead limited to the prosecution of aliens for using a false identity to establish "employment eligibility." *Id.*, at 1126, 1131, 401, P. 3d, at 596, 600." (Opinion Brief of Associate Justice Samuel Alito on Kansas v. Garcia, 2020).

It's a shame that the Kansas Supreme Court did not stand for the sovereignty of their state, but they instead stood for being puppets of a rogue and arrogant federal government. If the perpetrators falsified not only an I-9 document but also the state document of K-4, equivalent to the W-4., then by the rules of federalism, the state of Kansas, as well as any other state of this republic, has the right to prosecute citizens and aliens alike residing in their state. If the federal statute of IRCA notes that the prosecution of aliens falsifying on I-9 forms is a federal prosecutorial action, then it is the duty of the state to not proceed in prosecuting on that charge. But a state law does supersede a federal law, especially an unconstitutional one.

But the state of Kansas did the opposite and did not file charges for misusing this form. They only charged the respondents with misusing official sovereign state forms of Kansas and including the W-4 form which is like their own tax form.

What boggles the mind is that the Kansas high court has the audacity to claim that the state did not have enough evidence to hold these aliens for prosecution on behalf of "employment eligibility." These three respondents obtained and achieved employment eligibility via-the usage of fraudulent means of using other people's Social Security numbers. And therefore, violated the identity theft laws of the sovereign state of Kansas.

"Justice Luckert concurred based on implied, not express, preemption. In her view, IRCA occupies "the field" within which the prosecutions at issue fell, namely, "the use of false documents, including those using identity of others, when an unauthorized alien seeks employment." *Id.* At 1136, 401 P. 3d, at 602. Justice Luckert also opined that the Kansas statutes, as applied in these cases, conflict with IRCA because they "usur[p] federal enforcement discretion" regarding the treatment of aliens who obtain employment even though they are barred from doing so under federal law. *Ibid.*, 401 P. 3d, at 603." Two members of the court, Justices Biles and Stegall dissented, and we granted review. 586 U.S.___ (2019)." (Opinion Brief of Associate Justice Samuel Alito on Kansas v. Garcia, 2020).

For a state official to advise that her own sovereign state law is the usurper and that federal immigration law stomps over a state directive is a direct violation of the rules of federalism. This is the reason that our rules of federalism are crumbling because of ignorant state officials, and a rogue and arrogant federal government.

Therefore, we need to educate the public to advise their own state officials that the power of constitutional criminal and immigration enforcement lies within the states, not the federal government.

The Kansas Supreme Court became divided in this decision because sadly some jurists still believed in federal government authority towards immigration enforcement. I am glad that for once the federal high court decided to give it back to the states, not just to Kansas but to all fifty sovereign states.

"The Supremacy Clause provides that the Constitution, federal statutes, and treaties constitute "the supreme Law of the Land." Art V1, cl. 2. The Clause provides "a rule of decision" for determining whether federal or state law applies in a particular decision. Armstrong v. Exceptional Child Care, Inc., 575 U.S. 320, 324 (2015). If federal law "imposes restrictions or confers rights on private actors" and "a state law confers rights or imposes restrictions that conflict with the federal law," "the federal law takes precedence and the state law is preempted." *Murphy v. National Collegiate Athletic Assn.*, 584 U.S. ____, ____ (2018) (slip op., at 22)." (Opinion Brief of Associate Justice Samuel Alito on Kansas v. Garcia, 2020).

"In all cases, the federal restrictions or rights that are said to conflict with state law must stem from either the Constitution itself or a valid statute enacted by Congress. "There is no federal preemption in *vacuo*," without a constitutional text, federal statute, or treaty made under the authority of the United States. (Opinion Brief of Associate Justice Samuel Alito on Kansas v. Garcia, 2020).

"I agree that Kansas' prosecutions and convictions of respondents for identity theft and making false information are not preempted by Section101(a)(1) of the Immigration Reform and Control Act of 1986, 8 U.S.C. Section1324a. I write separately to reiterate my view that we should explicitly abandon our "purposes and objectives" preemption jurisprudence. (Concurring Opinion Brief of Associate Justice Clarence Thomas on Kansas v. Garcia, 2020).

"The Founders included a non- obstante provision in the Supremacy Clause. It directs that "Judges in every State shall be bound" by the "Constitution and the Laws of the United States which shall be made in Pursuance thereof; and all Treaties made, or which shall be made, or which shall be made, under the Authority of the United States,… any Thing in the standing." Art. V1, cl. 2. If we interpret the Supremacy Clause as the founding generation did, our task is straightforward. We must use the accepted methods of interpretation to ascertain whether the ordinary meaning of federal and state law "directly conflict"." *Wyeth v. Levine*, 555 U.S. 555, 590 (2009) (Thomas, J., concurring in judgment). "[F]ederal pre-empts state law only if the two are in logical contradiction." *Merck Sharp v. Dohme Corp. v. Albrecht*, 587 U.S. ____, ____ (2019) (Thomas, J., concurring) (slip-on., at 2); see also Nelson, *supra*, at 236-237." (Concurring Opinion Brief of Associate Justice Clarence Thomas on Kansas v. Garcia, 2020).

As I will always tend to agree with Justices Alito and Thomas, I have a feeling that they are not quite sure how to define the Supremacy Clause of the federal Constitution. These sovereign states must abide to the Constitution and laws of the United States but there is a slight error in Justice Thomas' statement. States should only abide by the laws passed by the national Congress if those laws are deemed constitutional and thus making them supreme. If such laws are deemed to be unconstitutional, then the sovereign states are required not to cooperate and nullify these laws.

"The doctrine of "purposes and objectives" pre-emption impermissibly rests on judicial guesswork about "broad federal policy objectives, legislative history, or generalized notions of congressional purposes that are not contained within the text of federal law." *Wyeth, supra*, at 587 (opinion of Thomas, J.); see also *Arizona v. United States*, 567 U.S. 387, 440 (2012) (Thomas, J., concurring in part and dissenting in part). I therefore cannot apply "purposes and objectives" pre-emption doctrine, as it is contrary to the Supremacy Clause." (Concurring Opinion Brief of Associate Justice Clarence Thomas on Kansas v. Garcia, 2020).

> **"[T]**he Supremacy Clause gives priority to 'the laws of the United States,' not the criminal law enforcement priorities or preferences of federal officers." - Associate Justice Clarence Thomas

"In these cases, the Court correctly distinguishes our "purposes and objectives" precedents and does not engage in a "freewheeling judicial inquiry into whether a state statute is in tension with federal objectives.'" *Wyeth, supra*, at 588 (opinion of Thomas, J.) (quoting *Bates v. Dow Agrosciences LLC*, 544 U.S. 431, 459 (2005) (Thomas J., concurring in judgment in part and dissenting in part). It also acknowledges that "[t]he Supremacy Clause gives priority to 'the laws of the United States,' not the criminal law enforcement priorities or preferences of federal officers." *Ante*, at 19. Because the Court rejects respondents' "purposes and objectives" argument without a textual speculation about legislative intentions, I join its opinion in full." (Concurring Opinion Brief of Associate Justice Clarence Thomas on Kansas v. Garcia, 2020).

What is a federal objective in my opinion? A federal objective is quite clear to me, a law passed in the halls of the national Congress that abides by the federal Constitution. A state statute cannot bring tension with a federal objective, if that objective is not contradictory to the state statute.

This statement by Justice Thomas speaks high volumes on the rules of federalism. "[t]he Supremacy Clause gives priority to 'the laws of the United States,' not the criminal law enforcement priorities or preferences of federal officers."

The Supremacy Clause does give priority to the "laws of the United States." I'd say it gives priority to the "constitutional laws of the United States." The federal government is not the policeman of each sovereign state. To me, this statement means that the police authority enforcement capabilities of the Immigration Code and Naturalization Clause rests in the hands of the sovereign State. In this case, in the hands of the sovereign State of Kansas.

The Supremacy Clause of the federal Constitution has been misconstrued and misinformed by many members of the federal court, federal executive branch and national Congress. The American citizenry has received erroneous information on what is the rightful definition of the Supremacy Clause.

In my opinion, the Supremacy Clause of the federal Constitution is quite simple to comprehend. Let me sum it up in just a few words. The federal government has such authority to enact laws onto the protection for the sovereign states, but these such laws must be in strict accordance with the Constitution. Hence making it the Supreme Law of the Land. Any laws not in strict accordance with the federal Constitution, are considered null and void. While the sovereign states have the right to nullify such unconstitutional laws and refuse to cooperate with federal government officials.

"In some cases, a federal statute may expressly preempt state law. See Pacific Gas & Electric. Co. v. State Energy Resources Conservation and Development Comm'n, 461 U.S. 190, 203 (1983) ("It is well established that within constitutional limits Congress may preempt state authority by so stating in express terms."). But it has long been established that preemption may also occur by virtue of restrictions or rights that are inferred from statutory law.

See, e.g., Osborn v. Bank of United States, 9 Wheat. 738, 865 (1824) (rejecting argument that a federal exemption from state regulation "not being expressed, ought not to be implied by the Court")." (Opinion Brief of Associate Justice Samuel Alito on Kansas v. Garcia, 2020).

It is not a well-established fact but a known fact that there are strict constitutional limits of not only congressional power but federal governmental power onto the states. Just if that power is strictly affirmed by the Constitution.

> **I** truly do not believe that such power of naturalization has been granted to the United States.

"And recent cases have often held state laws to be impliedly preempted. See, e.g., *Arizona* 567 U.S., at 400-408; *Kurns v. Railroad Friction Products Corp.*, 565 U.S. 625, 630-631 (2012); *PLIVA, Inc v. Mensing*, 564 U.S. 604, 617-618 (2011)." (Opinion Brief of Associate Justice Samuel Alito on Kansas v. Garcia, 2020).

Justice Alito mentions these three rulings allow federal law to preempt state law. We have reason to believe that in this glorious American republic, federal law does not preempt state law. State law is the preemptive measure to enforce. You will read about the court ruling of *Arizona v. United States*, 2012, on page 100 , and how the federal government greedily took away the states' power from enforcing the Naturalization Clause. I truly do not believe that such power of naturalization has been granted to the United States.

Let's just briefly the other two court rulings. The first ruling of *Kurns v. Railroad Friction Products Corp.*, 565 U.S. 625, 630-631 (2012) stated that state law must yield to a congressional act. I find it unnerving that the highest court of the land stated that each sovereign State cannot refuse to cooperate with the federal government. It's mind-boggling and unconstitutional. The second ruling of *PLIVA, Inc v. Mensing*, 564 U.S. 604, 617-618 (2011) stated the Supreme Court deferred to the direction of a federal government entity known as the Food and Drug Administration (FDA) regarding generic labeling regulations. Also, to affirm to give credit and openness to a federal government bureaucracy is frightening but also mind-boggling. These are one of those times that the federal government's High Court has granted unconstitutional power to the United States. But heading back to how the ruling Kansas v. Garcia, in where state law preempts over federal law and its riveting and music to my sovereign ears.

"As noted, IRCA contains a provision that expressly preempts state law, but it is plainly inapplicable here. That provision applies to the imposition of criminal or civil liability on employers and those who receive a fee for recruiting prospective employees. 8 U.S.C. Section1324a(h) (2). It does not mention state or local laws that impose criminal or civil sanctions on employees or applicants for employment. (Opinion Brief of Associate Justice Samuel Alito on Kansas v. Garcia, 2020).

"The Kansas Supreme Court did not base its holding on this provision but instead turned to Section1324a(b)(5), which is far more than a preemption provision. This provision broadly restricts any use of an I-9, information contained in an I-9, and any documents appended to an I-9. Thus, unlike a typical preemption provision, it applies not just to the States but also to the Federal Government and all private factors. The Kansas Supreme Court though that the prosecutions in these cases ran afoul of this provision because the charges were based on respondents' use in their W-4's and K-4's of the same false Social Security numbers that they also inserted on their I-9's. Taken at face value, this theory would mean that no information placed on an I-9—including an employee's name, residence address, date of birth, telephone number, and e-mail address—could ever be used by any entity or person for any reason." (Opinion Brief of Associate Justice Samuel Alito on Kansas v. Garcia, 2020).

"If this were not so, strange consequences would ensue. Recall that 8 U.S.C. Section1324a(b)(5) applies to the Federal Government. Under 26 U.S.C. Section7205, it is a crime to willfully supply false information on a W-4, and this provision is not among those listed in 8 U.S.C. Section7205 even if the Government made no use whatsoever of the I-9. And that is just the beginning." (Opinion Brief of Associate Justice Samuel Alito on Kansas v. Garcia, 2020).

The Kansas Supreme Court is playing politics with the rules of federalism. If the prosecution did not present the I-9 form in which the three respondents falsified the information, then this is an issue of state enforcement and not federal enforcement.

"The Kansas Supreme Court tried to fend off these consequences by suggesting that its interpretation applied only to the prosecution of aliens for using a false identity to establish "employment eligibility." 306 Kan., at 1126, 406 P. 3d, at 596. But there is no trace of these limitation in the text of Section1324a(b)(5). The point need not be belabored any further: The argument that Section1324a(b)(5) expressly bars respondents' prosecutions cannot be defended." (Opinion Brief of Associate Justice Samuel Alito on Kansas v. Garcia, 2020).

"Apparently, recognizing this, respondents turn to Section1324a(d)(2)(F), which prohibits use of the federal employment verification system "for law enforcement purposes other than" enforcement of IRCA and the same handful of federal statutes mentioned in Section1324a(b)(5); 18 U.S.C. Section1001 (false statements, Section1028 (identity theft), Section1546 (immigration-document fraud), and Section1621 (perjury). This argument fails because it rests on a misunderstanding of the meaning of the federal "employment verification system." The sole function of that system is to establish that an employee is not barred from working in this country due to alienage. As described in Section1324a(b), the system includes the steps that an employee must take to establish that he or she is not prohibited from working, the steps that an employer must take to verify the employee's status, and certain related matters—such as the preservation and copying of records that are used to show authorization to work. The federal employment verification system does not include things that an employee must or may do to satisfy requirements unrelated to work authorization. And completing tax-withholding documents plays no part in the process of determining whether a person is authorized to work. Instead, those documents are part of the apparatus used to enforce federal and state income tax laws. For all these reasons, there is no express preemption in these cases." (Opinion Brief of Associate Justice Samuel Alito on Kansas v. Garcia, 2020).

Aliens, whether legally or illegally in the United States and seeking employment in a sovereign state, are in the responsibility sphere of that state government. They are not in the responsibility sphere of the federal government. The issue is not the employment eligibility of the three respondents. The real issue is the magnitude of fraud that they caused for the state of Kansas.

The prosecution of these three individuals, legal or illegal, rests on the fact that they tried to defraud, not only the state of Kansas, but the employer. They supplied false documentation to prove their employment status.

The sovereign state of Kansas has every right to enforce its laws. The three criminals supplied false information on three documents. State law is above federal law in an American federalism republic.

There is a slight difference between this case and *Arizona*. And yet, both have a significant similarity with the two. *Arizona v. United States*, 2012, was an immigration enforcement legislation which may or not have had a provision of identity fraud for legal and illegal aliens. While this case is enforcing a state law of identity fraud of three individuals who just happened to be undocumented aliens.

"In order to determine whether Congress has implicitly ousted the States from regulating in a particular field, we must first identify the field in which this is said to have occurred. In their merits brief in this Court, respondents' primary submission is that IRCA preempts "the field of fraud on the federal employment verification system," Brief for the Respondents 41 (quotation altered), but this argument fails because, as already explained, the submission of tax-withholding forms is not part of that system." (Opinion Brief of Associate Justice Samuel Alito on Kansas v. Garcia, 2020).

"The submission of tax-withholding forms is fundamentally unrelated to the federal employment verification system because, as explained, those forms serve entirely different functions. The employment verification system is designed to prevent the employment of unauthorized aliens, whereas tax-withholding forms help to enforce income tax laws. And using another person's Social Security number on tax forms threatens harm that has no connection with immigration law." (Opinion Brief of Associate Justice Samuel Alito on Kansas v. Garcia, 2020).

In this case, the field and crime are identity theft and fraud. And just because the criminal perpetrators are undocumented, does not constitute that they be held under unconstitutional federal immigration law. The states are all within their legal right and obligation to protect their economy, society and borders.

"IRCA surely does not preclude the States from requiring and regulating the submission of all such information. Respondents suggest that federal law precludes their prosecutions because both the Kansas identity-theft statute and the Kansas false-information statute require proof that the accused engaged in the prohibited conduct for the purpose of getting a "benefit". Their argument is as follows. Since the benefit alleged by the prosecution in these cases was getting a job, and since the employment verification system concerns authorization to work, the theory of respondents' prosecutions is related to that system." (Opinion Brief of Associate Justice Samuel Alito on Kansas v. Garcia, 2020).

I truly despise *Hines v. Davidowitz*, 1941: Travel Registration Documents were never a part of the federal government's enumerated powers.

"Respondents argue that field preemption in these cases "follows directly" from our decision in Arizona, 567 U.S. 387, Brief doe Respondents 45-46, but that is not so. In Arizona, relying on our prior decision Hines v. Davidowitz, 312 U.S. 52 (1941), we held that federal immigration law occupied the field of alien registration. 567 U.S., at 400-

402. "Federal law," we observed, "makes a single sovereign responsible for maintaining a comprehensive and unified system to keep track of aliens within the Nation's borders." Id., at 401-402. But federal law does not create a comprehensive and unified system regarding the information that a State may require employees to provide. In sum, there is no basis for finding field preemption in these cases." (Opinion Brief of Associate Justice Samuel Alito on Kansas v. Garcia, 2020).

"We ultimately held in Arizona that the States thus may not make criminal what Congress did not, for any such state law "would interfere with the careful balance struck by Congress with respect to unauthorized employment of aliens." Id., at 406. Given that "obstacle to the regulatory system Congress chose," we concluded that the state law at issue conflicted with the federal Act and was therefore preempted. Id., 406-407." (Dissenting Brief of Associate Justice Stephen Breyer on Kansas v. Garcia, 2020).

> **"F**or local interests, the several States of this Union only exist, not for national purposes, not embracing the relations with foreign nations. Yes, we are one people, one REPUBLIC, BUT with 50 constitutional sovereign powers."
>
> — *Federico Lines, 2020*

I truly despise this 1941 federal court ruling. The Supreme Court at that time unconstitutionally held that federal law illegally occupied the field of alien registration.

Federal law has no bearing in the matter to control the borders of each of the fifty autonomous and sovereign states. The 1941 Supreme Court membership did not grant state sovereignty back then. But I am glad the 2020 Supreme Court membership did grant it.

"For local interests the several states of the Union exist, but for national purposes, embracing our relations with foreign nations, we are but one people, one nation, one power." (Opinion Brief of Associate Justice Hugo Black on Hines v. Davidowitz, 1941).

In response to Justice Black's statement, I speak for sovereignty. "For local interests, the several states of this Union only exist, not for national purposes, not embracing the relations with foreign nations. Yes, we are one people, one REPUBLIC, BUT with 50 constitutional sovereign powers."

Federal law should not have been demanding that the sovereign states comply with its statutes and rules. As in the beginning of the century, the state, city and port of New York had established immigration and naturalization standards for all individuals entering that port of entry. So do all other sovereign states have that right of established rule of immigration and naturalization.

In response to Justice Breyer's dissenting brief. Federal criminal immigration enforcement has no room of enforcement in the states.

"Nothing similar is involved here. In enacting IRCA, Congress did not decide that an unauthorized alien who uses a false identity on tax-withholding forms should not face criminal prosecution. On the contrary, federal law make it a crime to use fraudulent information on a W-4. 26 U.S.C. Section7205." (Opinion Brief of Associate Justice Samuel Alito on Kansas v. Garcia, 2020).

"The mere fact that state laws like Kansas provisions at issue overlap to some degree with federal criminal provisions does not even begin to make a case for conflict preemption. From the beginning of our country, criminal law enforcement has been primarily a responsibility of the states, and that remains true today. In recent times, the reach of federal criminal law has expanded, and there are now many instances in which a prosecution for a particular course of conduct could be brought by either federal or state prosecutors. Our federal system would be turned upside down if we were to hold that federal criminal law preempts state law wherever they overlap, and there is no basis for inferring that federal criminal statutes preempt state laws whenever they overlap. Indeed, in the vast majority of cases where federal and state laws overlap, allowing the states to prosecute is entirely consistent with federal interests." (Opinion Brief of Associate Justice Samuel Alito on Kansas v. Garcia, 2020).

The reason state provisions overlap with federal provisions is because federal provisions are overreaching. All enforcement since the inception of this republic has been handed down for the sovereign state to handle. No power of enforcement was ever given to the federal government regarding the issue of Immigration and Naturalization. The only duties, powers inscribed and enumerated and handed down to the federal government are to administer the functions of the sovereign states' activities, foreign affairs, defense and equality. The rest are given to the hands of each sovereign state at the consistency and administration of federal law.

"When we confront a question of implied preemption, the words of the statute are especially unlikely to determine the answer by themselves. Nonetheless, in my view, IRCA's text, together with its structure, context, and purpose, make it clear "'clear and manifest'" that Congress has occupied at least the narrow field of policing fraud committed to demonstrate federal work authorization. *Arizona v. United States*, 567 U.S. 387, 400 (2012) (quoting *Rice v. Santa Fe Elevator Corp.*, 331 U.S. 218, 230 (1947)); see Brief for United States as *Amicus Curiae* in *Puente Arizona v. Arpaio*, No. 15-15211 etc. (CA9), p. 15 (contending that the Act preempts state criminal laws "to the extent they regulate fraud committed to demonstrate authorization to work in the United States under federal immigration law")." (Dissenting Brief of Associate Justice Stephen Breyer on Kansas v. Garcia, 2020).

I am not one bit surprised that Justice Breyer is hypocritical and ignorant to the rules of federalism that establish our republic. States have all the legal right and obligation to prosecute anybody for work or legal status while residing within the borders of that sovereign state. State law always preempts federal law.

"Our precedent demonstrates that IRCA impliedly preempts state laws that trench on Congress' detailed and delicate design. In *Arizona*, we invalidated a state law that made it a crime for an unauthorized alien to work." (Dissenting Brief of Associate Justice Stephen Breyer on Kansas v. Garcia, 2020).

In your unconstitutional precedent, it demonstrates that the unconstitutional act of Congress known as IRCA, expressly does not preempt state law. In 2012, that Supreme Court also unconstitutionally had no right to invalidate the state enforcement law of the sovereign state of Arizona. If Justice Breyer is saying what I believe he is saying -- that states have no right to enforce the Immigration and Naturalization Clause of the Constitution, then according to his unconstitutional logic, they also do not have the right to enforce their laws of identity theft and fraud. Justice Breyer still wants to find a way to create a central planning committee under a federal government. Not under a President Trump planning committee, but under his own special interest plan.

Here is a jurist who tried to constrain the federal government executive power in *Trump v. Hawaii* but tried to take the power back with the other hand. The federal government surely has plenty of contradictory voices that the states are tired of following. The sovereign states cannot follow one central power entity with numerous voices. We need one voice coming from our sovereign state capital with the affirmation and blessing of its federal Constitution.

"Given that "obstacle to the regulatory system Congress chose," we concluded that the state law at issue conflicted with the federal Act and was therefore preempted. *Id.*, at 406-407." (Dissenting Brief of Associate Justice Stephen Breyer on Kansas v. Garcia, 2020).

Justice Breyer is plainly wanting to grant that unconstitutional power to the federal government and away from the states. "It is the federal law that at issue is at conflict with state law."

"For these reasons, I would hold that federal law impliedly preempted Kansas' criminal laws as they were applied in these cases. Because the majority takes a different view, with respect, I dissent." (Dissenting Brief of Associate Justice Stephen Breyer on Kansas v. Garcia, 2020).

"For these reasons, the judgments of the Supreme Court of Kansas are reversed, and these cases are remanded for further proceedings not inconsistent with this opinion, it is so ordered." (Opinion Brief of Associate Justice Samuel Alito on Kansas v. Garcia, 2020).

What I have learned from reading through all these court rulings and gaining a perspective on federalism, is that the power of naturalization lies with the sovereign states and not with the federal government. No matter what laws Congress passes, the federal executive branch signs into law or creates executive decrees, and the high court affirms... Power belongs to the states.

The power of naturalization as defined by the constitutional framers truly aligns with the protection and safety of all the sovereign states. States are in the certifiable position to enforce their safety and borders to protect their citizens and aliens alike.

The rulings indicate that the federal government granted the executive branch the right to detain and expel aliens and citizens alike; that the federal government told one sovereign state that they could not enforce their own borders; that the federal government has given absolute authority to the federal executive branch to enforce the naturalization power as they please. All these rulings to a true state sovereign advocate remain fictitious. We all know that such power of naturalization is reserved to the sovereign states and respectively the people.

Despite the sovereign victory of Kansas in 2020, we have a long way to go and it is an uphill battle. But people from across the nation in their respective sovereign states need to stand up and say "no more" to this rogue and arrogant federal government. We must educate our citizens about the true form of American government. An American federalism republic form of government.

Kansas was just the beginning in this new age and hopefully it would not be the end. We must "Return to Federalism." We must "Return to Sovereignty." For "State Sovereignty," always and always in order to keep this republic alive and well. Never again must we be beholden to a rogue and arrogant federal government on the issue of immigration and naturalization. Never again! For State Sovereignty, because the power lies with us.

FIVE

ACROSS STATE LINES AND GUN RIGHTS

"A well regulated Militia, being necessary to the security of a free State, the right of the people to keep and bear arms, shall not be infringed."

OF ALL THE GUARANTEED rights that our federal Constitution grants us, the Second Amendment has been the most controversial and provocative in the history of our republic. Since its inception in 1787, to the present, this amendment has been critical to our safety, security and ability to maintain a peaceful and more perfect union.

> "States can pass any legislation that they see fit, just as long as it doesn't contradict federal constitutional law."

But there are certain politicians and jurists in the federal government and state governments who have undermined this Amendment and with their efforts to prohibit the citizenry to exercise this right. It is to protect not only their private property from intruders, but to also protect them from the biggest intruder of them all: the federal government.

We have seen throughout the history of our republic, instances in which the government, whether federal or state, contradicts federal constitutional law with its attacks on the Second Amendment. I have said numerous times that "states can pass any legislation that they see fit, just as long as it doesn't contradict federal constitutional law."

States can find ways to regulate the said amendment to protect their residents, but they cannot prohibit or contradict. The federal Constitution is a guideline for states and the federal government to obey the rules of federalism and those rules are strictly self-explanatory, to not contradict the law.

After the shooting at Marjory Stoneman Douglas High School in Parkland, Fla., the Florida state legislature passed a measure to raise the age for gun ownership from 18 to 21 years of age. Many gun-rights advocates protested that this new regulatory law was an attack on the Second Amendment. That is false since states can regulate the amendment. However, what states can't do is prohibit the usage of this amendment. Also, there should never be any federal government interference and influence in prohibiting the use of the Second Amendment onto the states. It is a matter left up to the states. What the federal government is supposed to do is maintain the language of this Amendment true to its meaning and making sure that no state government contradicts the amendment as it pertains to all natural-born and naturalized citizens of our republic.

I am now going to reference different eras of our American republic where state legislators and jurists tended to contradict federal constitutional law on our Second Amendment. From the Black Codes in post-Civil War times to the progressives in the 20th century, there have been constant Second Amendment contradictions. I am going to discuss the court ruling that finally made it clear to the anti-constitutionalists that nobody, state or individuals, have a right to prohibit this right to any citizen and have no right to contradict the constitution. I am going to reference the late Associate Justice Antonin Scalia's definition on the Second Amendment and then I am going to define mine during our discussion of the ruling of *District of Columbia v. Heller*, 2008.

Where we see the abuse of a state government contradicting federal constitutional law on the Second Amendment toward its citizens, especially the newly made citizens of our republic, was in the State of Mississippi. The State of Mississippi's state constitution has a second amendment very similar to the federal Constitution's own second amendment.

"Article 1—Declaration of Rights: Sect 23. Every Citizen has a right to bear arms in defence of himself and of the state. (Race and Liberty in America: the essential reader, edited by Jonathan Bean, page 64, Mississippi Constitution, 1832).

To be honest, this right is very clear. "Every Citizen has a right to bear arms," it says. "Every Citizen." Regardless of social stature, race or background -- every citizen. And when the Fourteenth Amendment was added to the Constitution, all people born within the realm of this American republic, regardless of skin color, are citizens of this nation and of their respective state. There were some members of the white community that were former fighters of the Confederate Army or were descendants of those fighters that had animosity toward these new federal constitutional amendments. These former Confederate individuals still believed that they could return to the Antebellum days of the Old South. The law now prohibited the ownership of slaves, but they still wanted to keep the control over the newly made citizens. And how did they gain control, by prohibiting them the free exercise of their Second Amendment rights.

The Magnolia State's legislature then passed in 1866 a Black Code to prohibit the new citizens from engaging their gun-right privileges.

"Section 1: . . . That no freedman, free negro or mulatto, not in the military service of the United States government, and not licensed so to do by the board of police of his or her county, shall keep or carry fire-arms of any kind, or any ammunition, dirk or bowie knife, and on conviction thereof in the county court shall be punished by fine. . ." (Laws of the State of Mississippi, Passed at a Regular Session of the Mississippi Legislature, December 1865, Race and Liberty in America: the essential reader, edited by Jonathan Bean, page 64, Mississippi Constitution, 1832).

What is the first thing a state cannot do when passing state legislation for their own state? Even though, the Fourteenth Amendment had not been added to the constitution. States were denying basic rights to the newly freed slaves. After the Amendment passed, States cannot contradict federal constitutional law. These former slaves became citizens of this American republic, and in doing so were guaranteed the same rights and privileges as any other citizen. Just because the legislators of the Magnolia State fought, or had family members who fought, to preserve a human-rights violation, didn't give them the authority to contradict federal constitutional law after the fact.

When the federal government realized what these former rebellious states were doing, they enforced federal constitutional law through appropriate legislation allowed in the post-Civil War amendments. This era became known as "Reconstruction." Reconstruction never would have happened if those southern legislators would have accepted defeat and realized they cannot show any form of conflict with the federal Constitution because of race or color.

Almost a decade after Reconstruction ended, those states had to learn by force not to contradict federal constitutional law. I for one don't like the idea of the federal government using force to impose its will onto a sovereign state, but in the end if states like Mississippi and Louisiana were in violation of federal constitutional law, then so be it.

Now, in the modern days of our American republic, it is the federal government that is denying citizens their Second Amendment privileges. In the past, it was the sovereign states themselves who were denying their residents the rights protected under the federal Constitution. The federal government coming to their aid. Nowadays, it is the federal government denying this right while the States are trying to protect it and regulate it. The bottom line is that neither the central or state governments are allowed to contradict the constitution.

* * *

The Supreme Court during those Reconstruction years showed its ignorance in trying to interpret the words of our Founding Fathers. That is one thing that former Vice President of the Confederacy, Alexander Stephens, got wrong. After the passage of the Thirteenth, Fourteenth and Fifteenth Amendments to the federal Constitution, states would be subject to federal government control by a Republican-controlled central government during those times during and after the Civil War.

After the Civil War, there were Supreme Court cases that deny recognizing the rules of federalism and contradicted federal constitutional law.

In 1875, the Supreme Court of the land interpreted that the First Amendment and Second Amendment to the federal Constitution only applied to the federal government and not the states. Again, we come to the people that wanted the federal government off the backs of the states. These were former Confederate veterans or descendants of these veterans that still wanted to maintain the way of life they had before the Civil War. And since they were already attacking the 13th, 14th, and 15th Amendments, they decided to attack the two most important amendments to our republic.

"We have in our political system a government of the United States and a government of each of the several States. Each of one of these governments is distinct from the others, and each has citizens of its own who owe it allegiance, and whose rights, within its jurisdiction, it must protect. The same person may be at the same time a citizen of the United States and a citizen of a State, but his rights of citizenship under one of these governments will be different from those he has under the other. *Slaughter-House Cases*, 16 Wall. 74." (Opinion Brief of U.S v. Cruikshank, 92 U.S. 542, (1875), Chief Justice Morrison Waite).

You cannot be a sword with two blades. We are all citizens of these United States of America with rights granted by its governing document, the Constitution, as well as residents of those states uniting this union of sovereign states. The Founding Fathers, in their wisdom, saw how this nation was going to increase in size. That is the reason how our republic was established. Yes, every colony … state is different from one another. Every state will have the ability to have its own sovereignty and autonomy to make its own set of laws that govern its residents, but the federal Constitution must remain the guiding principle in creating their own state laws.

"The government of the United States is one of delegated powers alone. Its authority is defined and limited by the Constitution. All powers not granted to it by that instrument are reserved to the States or the people. No rights can be acquired under the constitution or laws of the United States, except such as the government of the United States has the authority to grant and secure. All that cannot be granted or secured are left under the protection of the States." (Opinion Brief of U.S v. Cruikshank, 92 U.S. 542, (1875), Chief Justice Morrison Waite).

"We now proceed to an examination of the indictment, to ascertain whether the several rights, which it is alleged the defendants intended to interfere with, are such as had been law in fact granted or secured by the constitution or laws of the United States" (Opinion Brief of U.S v. Cruikshank, 92 U.S. 542, (1875), Chief Justice Morrison Waite).

This whole case happened because of an electoral dispute after the 1872 elections in Louisiana. A federal judge ruled that the Republican-majority legislature can be seated. There was widespread resentment of this ruling by many members of the Democratic Party. And so, many of those members took to the streets and attacked newly freed black citizens and other citizens. Under the federal legislation of the Enforcement Act of 1870, those Democrat agitators were charged, and the victims of this attack protested that the attackers violated their First, Second, and Fourteenth Amendment rights. This is truly the first case where we see that many states and even the highest court of the land contradicting a wide variety of federal constitutional law.

"The first and ninth counts state the intent of the defendants to have been to hinder and prevent the citizens named in the free exercise and enjoyment of their 'lawful right and privilege to peaceably to assemble together with each other and with other citizens of the United States for a peaceful and lawful purpose.' The right of the people peaceably to assemble for lawful purposes existed long before the adoption of the Constitution of the United States. In fact, it is, and always has been, one of the attributes of citizenship under a free government. It 'derives its source,' to use the language of Chief Justice Marshall, in *Gibbons v. Ogden*, 9 Wheat. 211, 'from those laws whose authority is acknowledged by civilized man throughout the world.' It is found wherever civilization exists. It was not, therefore, a right granted to the people by the constitution. The government of the United States when established found it in existence, with the obligation on the part of the States to afford it protection. As no direct power over it was granted to Congress it remains according to the ruling in *Gibbons v. Ogden*, id. 203, subject to state jurisdiction. *552 Only such existing rights were committed by the people to the protection of Congress as came within the general scope

of the authority granted to the national government."
(Opinion Brief of U.S v. Cruikshank, 92 U.S. 542, (1875), Chief Justice Morrison Waite).

I can see now why ordinary American citizens had no interest then or now in following Supreme Court cases and the rulings. There have been justices who have invented their own opinions and dissents to satisfy their own personal agenda or a special-interest agenda. In this ruling, they were promoting the agenda of white supremacy over the newly freed black citizens. I cannot believe that these justices of the central court would add other rulings that have no constitutional basis to the one that they were discussing at that precise moment. In *Gibbon v. Ogden*, Marshall and the court were discussing the very idea of the Commerce Clause and navigational trade among across the states and if there would be any interference from the central government. What does the Commerce Clause have to do with the Colfax Massacre? Absolutely, nothing, it was just political theater to give credibility to the agitators and a reason to protest and protect their application of their "supposed" innocence.

The First Amendment is a 'Catch-22' theory from our founders. It is called tolerance and being non-violent. The words in this Amendment say it all: "Or the right of the people peaceably to assemble…." It does not advocate inciting violence from either side. There will be individuals or groups of individuals you may not agree with, but it is your right to listen or ignore, just as it is their right to say their grievances without a show of force. This was pure constitutional wisdom from our Founding Fathers.

"'The scope and application of these amendments are no longer subjects of discussion here.' They left the authority of the States just where they found it and added nothing to the already existing powers of the United States." (Opinion Brief of U.S v. Cruikshank, 92 U.S. 542, (1875), Chief Justice Morrison Waite).

The federal constitution gives each individual state the right to enforce not only the amendments to our Constitution, but to make sure that no laws are made that are contradictory to the national constitution. If states decide to not enforce a valid federal constitutional amendment and began to show privilege to one race and not the other, then it is the duty of the federal government to administer and advise the states in rebellion the appropriate steps to follow and constitutionally comply. But never by force, whether by regulation or military action.

"The second and tenth counts are equally defective. The right there specified is that of 'bearing arms for a lawful purpose.' This is not a right granted by the Constitution. Neither is it any manner dependent upon that instrument for its existence. The second amendment declares that it shall not be infringed; but this, as has been seen, means no more than that it shall not be infringed by Congress. This is one of the amendments that has no other effect than to restrict the powers of the national government, leaving the people to look for their protection against any violation by their fellow-citizens of the rights it recognizes, to what is called, in The City of New York v. Miln, 11 Pet. 139, the 'powers which relate to merely municipal legislation, or what was, perhaps, more properly called internal police', 'not surrendered or restrained' by the Constitution of the United States." (Opinion Brief of U.S v. Cruikshank, 92 U.S. 542, (1875), Chief Justice Morrison Waite).

If a citizen, or group of citizens, regardless of race, attacks another, the citizens being attacked have every right to defend themselves and use their right of the Second Amendment for that protection. To blatantly suggest that only a group of people have that right but not others, is giving privilege to the law to one group of citizens but not the other. That is not in the constitution. It clearly states, "All persons born within the realm of the United States and territories are citizens."

The following is the chief justice's explanation for giving privileges to one race of citizens but not the other:

"The fourteenth amendment prohibits a State from depriving any person of life, liberty or property, without due process of law; but this adds nothing to the rights of one citizen as against another. It simply furnishes an additional guaranty against any encroachment by the States upon the fundamental rights which belong to every citizen as a member of society. As was paid by Mr. Justice Johnson, in Bank of Columbia v. Okely, 4 Wheat. 244, it secures 'the individual from the arbitrary exercise of the powers of government, unrestrained by the established principles of private and distributive justice.' These principles in the indictment do not call for the exercise of any of the powers conferred by this provision in the amendment." (Opinion Brief of U.S v. Cruikshank, 92 U.S. 542, (1875), Chief Justice Morrison Waite).

"The fourth and twelve counts charge the intent to have been to prevent and hinder the citizens named, who were of African descent and persons of color, in 'the free exercise and enjoyment of their several right and privilege to the full and equal benefit of all laws and proceedings, then and there, before that time, enacted or ordained by the said State of Louisiana and by the United States; and then and there, at that time, being in force in the State and District of Louisiana aforesaid, for the security of their respective persons and property, then and there, at that time enjoyed at and within said the State and District of Louisiana by white persons, being citizens of said State of Louisiana and the United States, for the protection of the persons and property of said white citizens.' There is no allegation that this was done because of the race or color of the persons conspired against. When stripped of its verbiage, the case as presented amounts to nothing more than that the defendants conspired to prevent certain citizens of the United States, being within the State of Louisiana, from enjoying the equal protection of the laws of the State and of the United States." (Opinion Brief of U.S v. Cruikshank, 92 U.S. 542, (1875), Chief Justice Morrison Waite).

There you have it, folks, the first jurist trying to override the law and rewrite the law himself. The post-Civil War amendments were written after the bloody conflict that was fought to end the human-rights violations of slavery and discrimination. These amendments, including the Fourteenth Amendment, consist of equal protection and due process of the law for all citizens regardless of race.

This event took place before residents of the city of Colfax, the majority of whom were white and were unhappy with the outcome of the election and decided to pursue a form of illegal action against a group of people celebrating their electoral victory – the majority of whom were black American citizens. The people pursuing an illegal action against these black citizens were indeed violating their rights as American citizens. To say that, to remove the language that these citizens were just citizens with taking no account of their race, is contradictory to the Constitution.

"No question arises under the Civil Rights Act of April 9, 1866 (14 Stat. 27), which is intended for the protection of citizens of the United States in the enjoyment of certain rights, without discrimination on account of race, color, or previous condition of servitude, because as has already been stated, it is nowhere alleged in these counts that the wrong contemplated against the rights of these citizens was on account of their race or color." (Opinion Brief of U.S v. Cruikshank, 92 U.S. 542, (1875), Chief Justice Morrison Waite).

Many of these agitators who attacked this peaceful assembly of black citizens were white. This ruling was and only to contemplate satisfaction of white privilege which at the time was the majority race in America. The constitution with the Fourteenth Amendment sees no color, only sees equality.

"I concur that the judgment in this case should be arrested, but for the reasons quite different from those given by the court." (Dissenting Brief of U.S v. Cruikshank, 92 U.S. 542, (1875), Associate Justice Nathan Clifford).

"Persons born on naturalized in the United States, and subject to the jurisdiction thereof, are citizens thereof; and the fourteenth amendment also provides, that no State shall make or enforce any law which shall abridge the privileges or immunities of citizens of the United States. Congress may, doubtless, prohibit any violation of that provision, and may provide that any person convicted of violating the same shall be guilty of an offence, and be subject to such reasonable punishment as Congress may prescribe." (Dissenting Brief of U.S v. Cruikshank, 92 U.S. 542, (1875), Associate Justice Nathan Clifford).

"What is charged in the fourteenth count is, that the defendants did combine, conspire, and confederate the said citizens of African descent and persons of color to injure, oppress, threaten, and intimidate, with the intent the said citizens thereby to prevent and hinder in the free exercise and enjoyment of the right and privilege to vote *at any election to be thereafter had and held* according to law by the people of the State, or by the people of the parish; they, the defendants, well knowing that the said citizens were lawfully qualified to vote at any such election thereafter to be had and held." (Dissenting Brief of U.S v. Cruikshank, 92 U.S. 542, (1875), Associate Justice Nathan Clifford).

Justice Clifford is quite clear in how our rules of federalism must be applied in our American federalism republic. The federal constitution is the principled governing document that governs our individual and sovereign states and we must abide to it. States cannot

> States cannot contradict the constitution by creating a new set of legislation to please a group of citizens and deny others the same rights and privileges.

contradict the Constitution by creating a new set of legislation to please a group of citizens and deny others the same rights and privileges.

And another valid and constitutional point, Justice Clifford points out is that the said victims of the altercation were within their legal and rightful bounds to participate in the American electoral process without the hint of oppression, threat, or cause of injury.

The First Amendment was put in place to be accepting of all forms of speech and opinion without the use of agitation or force. There will be views of other citizens that we may not like or agree with, but it's our duty as citizens to simply ignore it. And if our rights are threatened by a voice of opposition then it is our right as citizens of this country to invoke the Second Amendment. These two amendments are equally important to preserve, protect and maintain our republic.

"Certain other causes for arresting the judgment are assigned in the record, which deny the constitutionality of the Enforcement Act; but, having come to the conclusion that the indictment is insufficient, it is not necessary to consider that question." (Dissenting Brief of U.S v. Cruikshank, 92 U.S. 542, (1875), Associate Justice Nathan Clifford).

Remember Section V of the Fourteenth Amendment, it states that Congress will have the authority to enforce this amendment with the appropriate legislation. Whether States ratified or not the Post-Civil War Amendments had to abide to them. They were indeed the Supreme law of the land because it was in the constitution. And so, I agree with Justice Nathan Clifford in his dissenting opinion. States cannot let dogs lie and ignore federal constitutional law. It truly goes against our rules of federalism. Once the state breaks these rules, you will have anarchy and further infiltration of the federal government, which is one thing our Founding Fathers never dreamed would happen. And so, I dissent.

* * *

Once a state starts to break the rules of federalism and contradicts federal constitutional law, the federal government will begin to move in, infiltrate, oppress and impose new rules. New rules that are not one of the enumerated powers of the federal government.

There was a period when the highest court of the land was filled with progressive jurists who truly had no idea how our rules of federalism work. And the national Congress also did not know any better, and so from 1933 to 1947 this republic had enacted by congress, progressive and anti-federalism legislation that went against the rules of federalism and the very idea of state sovereignty.

In 1934, the distinguished members of our 73rd United States Congress passed The National Firearms Act. An act that was intended to regulate the transfer of firearms and impose a tax upon transferred firearms. (National Firearms Act S 1 et., 26 U.S.C.A S 1132 et seq.)

This ruling was passed with a unanimous vote and with one jurist recusing himself. Not a single jurist decided to defend the rules of federalism, nor federal constitutional law. This quite frankly is an attack on our rights. I will show you excerpts of this sole unanimous attack on our federalism liberty.

Justice James McReynolds, appointed by President Woodrow Wilson, delivered the opinion of the court in *United States v. Miller*, 1939.

"An indictment in the District Court Western District Arkansas, charged Jack Miller and Frank Layton 'did unlawfully, knowingly, willfully, and feloniously transport in interstate commerce from the town of Claremore in the State of Oklahoma to the town of Siloam Springs in the State of Arkansas a certain firearm, to wit, a double barrel less than 18 inches in length, bearing identification number 76230, said defendants, at the time of so transporting said firearm in interstate commerce as aforesaid, not having registered said firearm as required by Section 1132d of Title 26, United States Code, 26 U.S.C.A. s 1132d (Act of June 26, 1934, c. 757, Sec. 5, 48 Stat), and not having in their possession a stamp-affixed written in order for said firearm as provided by Section 1132C, Title 26, United States 26 U.S.C.A. s. 1132c, (June 26, 1934, c. 757, sec 4, 48 Stat. 1237) and the regulations issued under authority of the said Act of Congress known as the 'National Firearms Act' approved June 26, 1934, contrary to the form of the statute in such case made and provided, and against the peace and dignity of the United States." (Opinion Brief of U.S. Miller, 307 U.S. 174, 1939 by Associate Justice James McReynolds).

I am disgusted by the unanimous decision of the highest court of our republic, but I'm mainly disgusted by the states that bowed down to an act of Congress. Since when do the individual and autonomous states must abide by the legislative acts of Congress, especially if the said act of Congress is so blatantly unconstitutional. Legislatures in the sovereign States should have stated that they will not enforce this unconstitutional act of Congress and refused to cooperate with union officials. It truly appears that many states have not applied the teachings of Madison and Jefferson to pass nullification legislation and refuse solely to cooperate with central government officials.

There was a lack of refusal to cooperate against union officials when it came to the issue of the Second Amendment. That is until recently, when the Montana state legislature proposed, passed and signed, by then governor Brian Schweitzer, the 'Montana Firearms Freedom Act, MT HB 246. This legislative act reinforces that the individual and sovereign states are not beholden to the central government and will not cooperate with federal government agencies that are deemed unconstitutional.

The federal government agency of Alcohol, Tobacco and Firearms (ATF) has made it clear that this legislation cannot cross state lines into neighboring states of Montana or other states that wish to do business with Montana regarding this firearms legislation. States are not infringing on the rules of federalism, it is the federal government who is infringing upon them. And I do believe, these states are not contradicting federal constitutional law. Since there is nothing in the Constitution that allows the central government to prohibit the usage of weapons to its states and citizenry. After 2009, other states (Kansas, Tennessee, Wyoming, South Dakota, Utah, Arizona Idaho and Alaska), finally continued the model of Madison and Jefferson to nullify federal acts of Congress that are deemed unconstitutional.

"A duly interposed demurrer alleged: The National Firearms Act is not a revenue measure but an attempt to usurp police power reserved to the States, and is therefore unconstitutional. Also, it offends the inhibition of the Second Amendment to the Constitution, U.S.C.A.-'A well regulated Militia, being necessary to the security of a free State, the right of the people to keep and bear arms, shall not be infringed.' The District Court held that Section 11 of the Act violated the Second Amendment. **818 It accordingly sustained the demurrer and quashed the indictment." (Opinion Brief of U.S. Miller, 307 U.S. 174, 1939 by Associate Justice James McReynolds).

The American people must truly comprehend the views and opinions of most of the membership of this court. From 1933 to 1945, there was a sentiment of central government control. Many bureaucrats in the city of Washington were supporters of a new progressive mentality movement known as the Bolshevik-Leninist movement where the central (federal) government has the ultimate right to install authoritarian views onto its states and people.

"The Constitution, as originally adopted, granted to the Congress the power "to provide for calling forth the Militia to execute the Laws of the Union, suppress Insurrections and repel invasions; To provide for organizing, arming, and disciplining, the Militia, and for governing such Part of them as may be employed in the Service of the United States, reserving to the States respectively, the Appointment of the

Officers, and the Authority of training the Militia according to the discipline prescribed by Congress. U.S.C.A Const. art. 1, s 8. With obvious purpose to assure the continuation and render possible the effectiveness of such forces the declaration and guarantee of the Second Amendment were made. It must be interpreted and applied with that end in view." (Opinion Brief of U.S. Miller, 307 U.S. 174, 1939 by Associate Justice James McReynolds).

In another court ruling discussion, I will let Associate Justice Antonin Scalia give his definition of the right known as the Second Amendment. I will now give my definition of the Second Amendment and shoot down this centrist opinion of Justice McReynolds in how he is trying to gain control of the central government authority onto the states and its residents by limiting this right.

> "*A well regulated Militia, being necessary to the security of a free State, the right of the people to keep and bear arms, shall not be infringed.*"

Justice McReynolds has it all wrong with his interpretation and definition of the Second Amendment. A nation must have a government militia to preserve and protect the republic. But in the meantime, that the nation has a standing government militia to quell any domestic rebellion or foreign invasion, the government has no right to infringe on the citizens' arms and confiscate them. Justice

McReynolds failed to point that out in his interpreted definition. Instead he states that the people are the militia hired by their respective state to help to quell and assist when a rebellion or foreign invasion is taking place.

"The militia which the States were expected to maintain, and train is set in contrast with Troops which they *179 were forbidden to keep without the consent of Congress. The sentiment of the time strongly disfavored standing armies; the common view was that adequate defense of country and laws could be secured through the Militia-civilians primarily, soldiers on occasion." "The signification attributed to the term Militia appears from the debates in the Convention, the history and legislation of the colonies and States, and the writings of approved commentators. These show plainly enough that the Militia comprised all males physically capable of acting in concert for the common defense. 'A body of citizens enrolled for military discipline.' And further, that ordinarily when called for service these men were expected to appear bearing arms supplied by themselves and of the kind in common use at the time." (Opinion Brief of U.S. Miller, 307 U.S. 174, 1939 by Associate Justice James McReynolds).

This is not the exact interpretation of the Second Amendment. This justice says everything to have the people have the right to keep and bear arms but for all the wrong reasons. The phrase that dictates this amendment is so simple, founders made it quite clear. And below Justice McReynolds points out during colonial times in America where they installed gun control measures. I will explain in detail the reason behind the Framers persistence that its new citizens must have the need to maintain its new citizenry the right to keep and not have their weapons confiscated.

"'The American Colonies In the 17th Century,' Osgood, Vol. 1, ch. XIII, affirms in reference to the early system of defense in New England." 'In all the Colonies, as in England, the militia system was based on the principle of the assize of arms. This implied the general obligation of all adult male inhabitants to possess arms, and, with certain exceptions to *180 cooperate in the work of defense.' 'The possession of arms also implied the possession of ammunition, and the authorities paid quite as much attention **819 to the latter as to the former.' 'A year later (1632) it was ordered that any single man who had not furnished himself with arms might be put out of service, and this became a permanent part of the legislation of the colony (Massachusetts)." (Opinion Brief of U.S. Miller, 307 U.S. 174, 1939 by Associate Justice James McReynolds).

It's absurd to bring up the American colonial times under British rule and give a new meaning to the Second Amendment. If this justice and other progressive jurists, past and present, never understood the main reason this new nation broke away from a central-style of government. During the Revolutionary War, the British army began to confiscate the arms of the colonists. Even with this confiscation rule, colonists were forced to join the British army but not with their weapons but with an army registered weaponry. So, I am afraid to say that Justice McReynolds may have been curtailing the truth.

"The General Assembly of Virginia, October, 1785 (12 Hening's Statutes c. 1, p. 9 et seq.), declared: 'The defense and safety of the Commonwealth depend upon having its citizens properly armed and taught the knowledge of military duty.'" (Opinion Brief of U.S. Miller, 307 U.S. 174, 1939 by Associate Justice James McReynolds).

To even suggest that the Commonwealth of Virginia would be a totalitarian system of government is ludicrous and untrue. The General Assembly of that state knew perfectly how to interpret the Second Amendment to our federal Constitution and applied it well to their constitution. They knew that to maintain a secure and free state within the borders of the Commonwealth of Virginia, they needed to reassure their citizens' right to maintain their weapons would not be infringed by the government of the Commonwealth of the federal government.

Some people suggest that when the Union Army invaded the City of Alexandria, Virginia and other parts of Northern Virginia, the Army of the Potomac confiscated the weapons of those residents and prohibited their Second Amendment usage. Some will argue that the Union Army and the government of Washington City acted very tyrannical, and others may argue that if they were to quell a domestic rebellion that certain constitutional rights were to be suspended. That issue is not the topic of this discussion, but again, there is nothing in the Constitution that grants the central government or state governments the right for gun confiscation unless the individual has committed a crime and is found guilty of that crime.

"Most if not all of the States have adopted provisions touching the right to keep and bear arms. Differences in the language employed in these have naturally led to somewhat variant conclusions concerning the scope of the right guaranteed. But none of them seem to afford any material support for the challenged ruling of the court below. In the margin some of the more important opinions and comments by writers are cited. We are unable to accept the conclusion of the court below and the challenged judgment must be reversed. The cause will be remanded for further proceedings. Reversed and remanded." (Opinion Brief of U.S. Miller, 307 U.S. 174, 1939 by Associate Justice James McReynolds).

All states have added a provision confirming from the federal Constitution to their own constitution for their residents the guarantee to keep and bear arms. If the Supreme Court made the opinion well known that same-sex marriage and the right to abort a baby is guaranteed in the federal Constitution, and all states have to abide it, then why couldn't the Supreme Court then and now comprehend that the right to keep and bear arms is in the Constitution and it is allowed that all states abide by it. As I have said before, states can pass whatever legislative measure or plebiscite referendum as a law, just if it does not contradict federal constitutional law.

Associate Justice Williams O. Douglas recused himself in this case and took no part in any opinion of this ruling. People that fail to take a stand to protect the rules of federalism and contradict the American republic's rules are unfit to serve any kind of public office. The Second Amendment is the second most important guaranteed right to our republic and its citizenry. When the federal government and state governments start to prohibit, confiscate, and contradict the constitution. We have truly lost our sense of liberty. I, as a citizen of this republic, stand in dissent against this unconstitutional ruling.

* * *

It will take years that the American Republic finally comprehended that states and federal government cannot conflict and contradict federal constitutional law. Regarding the Second Amendment, there is no contradiction or conflict.

The Supreme Court ruling that I am going to discuss is to establish that citizens have a right to keep and bear, or in English terms, "a right to carry", firearms without being persecuted or prohibited by an authority figure without proper and reasonable cause. Now I am going to discuss the ruling that clearly defined what this amendment means and how it applies to our rules of federalism.

"We consider whether a District of Columbia prohibition on the possession of **2788 usable handguns in the home violates the Second Amendment to the Constitution. The District of Columbia generally prohibits the possession of handguns. It is a crime to carry an unregistered *575 firearm, and the registration of handguns is prohibited. See D.C. Code Section 7—2501. 01 (12), 7—2502.01 (a), 7—2502(a)(4) (2001). Wholly apart from that prohibition, no person may carry a handgun without a license, but the chief of police may issue licenses for 1—year periods. See Section 22—4504(a), 22—4506. District of Columbia law also requires residents to keep their lawfully owned firearms, such as registered long guns, "unloaded and dissembled or bound by a trigger lock or similar device" unless they are located in a place of business or are being used for lawful recreational activities. See Section 7—2507.02." (Opinion Brief of the District of Columbia v. Heller, 554, U.S. 570 (2008), Associate Justice Antonin Scalia).

It is the opinion of this author that the Federal District of Columbia's anti-gun prohibition upon its residents is indeed a violation and contradiction towards federal constitutional law and affects our rules of federalism. When is it a crime for an American citizen to be denied all his or her constitutional rights and that includes the Second Amendment. The Second Amendment is in our Bill of Rights and is equally as important as our First Amendment right or our Thirteenth or Fourteenth Amendment rights. As for the District of Columbia, a federal territory not following federal constitutional law is a disgrace. All states, federal territories -- and that includes the District of Columbia and territories and Native American land -- are still American soil and therefore governed by the federal Constitution. All our citizens, born or naturalized, are entitled to the same rights as other citizens.

Another issue I have with this D.C. regulation is that the Washington, DC chief of police is the only authority figure to issue gun licenses and permissions. Are we to treat the chief of police as a monarchial figure, anointed by God? No. That was one reason we broke away from Great Britain. The federal, state and local governments have made it a habit to give privilege to certain citizens. And one thing that our federal Constitution makes clear is that it gives privilege to no one. We are all equal under the law and no one should be denied or granted privileges at the bequest of a police or military authority figure. In this republic, we the people are the rulers and the government is the servant. But, sadly, in recent times, we have seen these roles reversed.

Associate Justice Antonin Scalia in this brilliant opinion brief gives an excellent definition of the meaning of the Second Amendment. This opinion brief will finally settle the question as to how people are to treat the Second Amendment. We have seen time and time again where federal legislators and state legislators pass their own form of Second Amendment legislation to satisfy their emotional egos and disregard the rules of federalism and federal constitutional law. But now Justice Scalia will finally put everybody – past, present and future legal scholars and legislators -- in their place by closing the matter in a clear and plain English definition of the "right to bear arms."

"We turn first to the meaning of the Second Amendment. The Second Amendment provides: "A well regulated Militia, being necessary to the security of a free State, the right of the people to keep and bear Arms, shall not be infringed." In interpreting this text, we are guided by the principle that the [t]he Constitution was written to be understood by the voters; its words and phrases were used in their normal and ordinary as distinguished from technical meaning." *United States v. Sprague,* 282 U.S. 716, 731, 51 S. Ct. 220, 75 L.Ed. 640 (1931); see also *Gibbons v. Ogden*, 9 Wheat. 1, 188, 6 L. Ed. 23 (1824). Normal meaning may of *577 course include an idiomatic meaning, but it excludes secret or technical meanings that would not have been known to ordinary citizens in the founding generation." (Opinion Brief of the District of Columbia v. Heller, 554, U.S. 570 (2008), Associate Justice Antonin Scalia).

Every single item in the federal Constitution was and is guided and written by the will of the people. The Founding Fathers did not mention anywhere that the government whether, federal or state would control the weapons owned by the citizenry. The words in all the amendments are easily to comprehend, and they truly do not have any hidden meaning on the verbiage.

"The two sides in this case have set out very different interpretations of the Amendment. Petitioners and today's dissenting Justices believe that it protects only the right to possess and carry a firearm in connection with military service. See Brief for Petitioners 11-12; post at 2822 (STEVENS, J, dissenting). Respondents argues that it protects an individual right to possess a firearm unconnected with service in a militia, and to use that arm for traditionally lawful purposes, such as self-defense within the home. See Brief for Respondent 2-4." (Opinion Brief of the District of Columbia v. Heller, 554, U.S. 570 (2008), Associate Justice Antonin Scalia).

The United States of America until recently has had two sides in the discussion of the Second Amendment. Since 1934 to the present, the American liberal-progressive mentality has had this belief that the "Right to Bear Arms" refers to a branch of military service, but nothing could be further from the truth.

"The Second Amendment is naturally divided into two parts: its prefatory clause and its operative clause. The former does not limit the latter grammatically, but rather announces a purpose. The Amendment could be rephrased, "Because a well-regulated Militia is necessary to the security of a free State, the right of the people to keep and bear arms shall not be infringed." See J. Tiffany, A Treatise on

Government and Constitutional Law S 585, p. 394 (1867).
Although this structure of the Second Amendment is unique
in our Constitution, other legal documents of the founding
era, particularly individual-rights provisions of state
constitutions, commonly included a prefatory statement of
purpose. See generally Volokh, The Commonplace Second
Amendment, 73 N.Y. U.LRev. 793,814-81 (1998)."
(Opinion Brief of the District of Columbia v. Heller, 554, U.S. 570
(2008), Associate Justice Antonin Scalia).

"Logic demands that there be a link between the stated
purpose and the command. The Second Amendment would
be nonsensical if it read, "A well regulated Militia, being
necessary to a free State, the right of the people to petition for
redress of grievances shall not be infringed." That requirement
of logical connection may cause a prefatory clause to resolve an
ambiguity in the operative clause." "The preface makes clear
that the operative clause refers not to canons of interpretation
but to clergymen. But apart from that clarifying function, a
prefatory clause does not limit or expand the scope of the
operative clause. Therefore, while we will begin our **2790
textual analysis with the operative clause to ensure that
our reading of the operative clause is consistent with the
announced purpose." (Opinion Brief of the District of Columbia v.
Heller, 554, U.S. 570 (2008), Associate Justice Antonin Scalia).

I truly believe that you do not need that much logic or
common sense in defining all our amendments in the Bill of
Rights, including the Second Amendment. It is quite clear

what the "Operative Clause" means and how Americans -- from ordinary citizens to the high-level bureaucrats -- need to follow this important liberty amendment to our Constitution.

*579 1. Operative Clause.

a. "Right of the People." "The first salient feature of the operative clause is that it codifies a "right of the people." The unamended Constitution and the Bill of Rights use the phrase "right of the people" two other times, in the First Amendment's Assembly—and—Petition Clause and in the Fourth Amendment's Search—and—Seizure Clause. The Ninth Amendment uses a very similar terminology ("The enumeration in the Constitution, of certain rights, shall not be construed to deny or disparage others retained by the people"). All three of these instances unambiguously refer to individual rights, not "collective" rights, or rights that may be exercised only through participation in some corporate body. Nowhere in the Constitution does a "right" attributed to "the people" refer to anything other than an individual right. (Opinion Brief of the District of Columbia v. Heller, 554, U.S. 570 (2008), Associate Justice Antonin Scalia).

"This contrasts markedly with the phrase "the militia" in the prefatory clause. As we will describe below, the "militia" in colonial America consisted of a subset of the "the people"—those who were male, able bodied, and within a certain age range. Reading the Second Amendment as protecting only the right *581 to "to keep and bear Arms" in an organized militia therefore fits poorly with the operative clause's description of the holder of that right as "the people." We start therefore with a strong presumption that the Second Amendment right is exercised individually and belongs to all Americans." (Opinion Brief of the District of Columbia v. Heller, 554, U.S. 570 (2008), Associate Justice Antonin Scalia).

The inception of this republic was built into one premise and one premise only. "The laws of these United States will be dictated and brought forth for them to obey and not be able to lose rights of these laws that are from "we the people" of this republic."' Once the government decides that we are not a republic formed by "we the people," we will lose all our rights. We the people's rights begin at the state level with our rights protected and the federal government serving as an administrative tool to remind us that the Constitution must never be misinterpreted and contradicted.

> **W**e the people's rights begin at the state level with our rights protected and the federal government serving as an administrative tool to remind us that the constitution must never be misinterpreted and contradicted.

b. "Keep and Bear Arms." "We move now from the Second Amendment—the people"—to the substance of the right:

"to keep and bear arms." (Opinion Brief of the District of Columbia v. Heller, 554, U.S. 570 (2008), Associate Justice Antonin Scalia).

Before Justice Scalia addressed the verbs of "keep" and "bear" in the amendment's language, he addressed the word "Arms." In the version of the dictionary of Samuel Johnson, the term "Arms" means "weapons of offense, or armor of defense." Another definition of this word that he used was from Timothy Cunningham's 1771 legal dictionary and its definition of "Arms" is "any thing that a man wears for his defense, or takes into his hands, or uses in wrath to cast at or strike another." We can see from these definitions that arms does mean weapons of action, but it does not specifically specify anything to be for military use.

"The term was applied, then as now, to weapons that were not specifically designed for military use and were not employed in a military capacity. For instance, Cunningham's legal dictionary gave as an example of usage: "Servants and labourers shall use bows and arrows on *Sundays*, & c. and not bear other arms." (Opinion Brief of the District of Columbia v. Heller, 554, U.S. 570 (2008), Associate Justice Antonin Scalia).

If bows and arrows are not described to be arms for defense, then why are rifle or handgun? They are just as dangerous as a rifle or a handgun. This is one of the contradictions always shown to the anti-gun establishment. They are all arms and by that meaning, are defined as a right to keep and bear arms for defense of each citizenry.

"Some have made the argument, bordering on the frivolous, that only those arms in existence in the 18th century are protected by the Second Amendment. We do not interpret constitutional rights that way. Just as the First Amendment protects modern forms of communications, *e.g. Reno v. American Civil Liberties Union*, (1997), and the Fourth Amendment applies to modern forms of search, *e.g. Kyllo v. United States* (2001), the Second Amendment extends, **2792 prima facie, to all instruments that constitute bearable arms, even those that were not in existence at the time of the founding." (Opinion Brief of the District of Columbia v. Heller, 554, U.S. 570 (2008), Associate Justice Antonin Scalia).

Every single amendment to our Bill of Rights in the federal Constitution stands firm as it did in 1787 to the present. Individual Americans, whether right-wing, conservative, liberal,

> Congress cannot prohibit and deny the usage of these amendments to each and every American.

progressive cannot pick and choose how to interpret each amendment to satisfy their own personal agenda. Each amendment is there to represent the right of all Americans and the beauty of it all is that Congress cannot prohibit the usage of these amendments to the American citizenry.

"We turn to the phrases "keep arms" and "bear arms." No party has apprised us of an idiomatic meaning of "keep arms" and "bear arms". Johnson defined "keep" as, most relevantly, "[t]o retain; not to lose," and "[t]o have in custody." Johnson 1095. Webster defined it as "[t]o hold; to retain in one's power or possession." No party has apprised us of an idiomatic meaning of "keep Arms". Thus, the most natural reading of "keep Arms" in the Second Amendment is to "have weapons". The phrase "keep arms" was not prevalent in the written documents of the founding period that we have found, but there are a few examples, all of which favor viewing the right to "keep Arms" as an individual right unconnected with militia service. (Opinion Brief of the District of Columbia v. Heller, 554, U.S. 570 (2008), Associate Justice Antonin Scalia).

"Although the phrase implies that the carrying of the weapon is for the purpose of "offensive or defensive action," it in no way connotes participation in a structured military organization." (Opinion Brief of the District of Columbia v. Heller, 554, U.S. 570 (2008), Associate Justice Antonin Scalia).

> **I**t is a shame that the dissenters and petitioners, rather than uphold the federal Constitution and abide by the rules of federalism, would instead contradict them and ignore these important rules.

I understand Justice Scalia is stating that the Second Amendment does not apply to people in military service or retired military service. The said amendment applies to everyone regardless of present or retired military service.

"In any event, the meaning of "bear arms" that petitioners and Justice STEVENS propose is not even the (sometimes) idiomatic meaning. Rather, they manufacture a hybrid definition, whereby "bear arms" connotes the actual carrying of arms (and therefore is not really an idiom) but only in the service of an organized militia. No been apprised of no source that indicates that it carried that meaning at the time of the founding. But it is easy to see why petitioners and the dissent are driven to the hybrid definition. Giving "bear arms" its idiomatic meaning would cause the protected right to consist of the right to be a soldier or to wage war—an absurdity that no commentator has ever endorsed. See L. Levy, Origins of the Bill of Rights 135 (1999). Worse still, *587 the phrase "keep and bear arms" would be incoherent. The word "Arms" would have two different meanings at once: "weapons" (as the object of "keep") and (as the object of "bear") one-half of an idiom. It would be rather like saying "He filled and kicked the bucket" to mean "He filled the bucket and died." Grotesque." (Opinion Brief of the District of Columbia v. Heller, 554, U.S. 570 (2008), Associate Justice Antonin Scalia).

Scalia always made his point quite clear in defending our federal constitution and the rules of federalism. It is a shame that the dissenters and petitioners, rather than uphold the federal Constitution and abide by the rules of federalism, would instead contradict them. The language in the Second Amendment is crystal clear that does not need Supreme Court clarification. A citizen's right to "keep and bear Arms" is a matter of liberty for our established republic to prevent a government from becoming tyrannical.

One thing that I have become expert in is reading and learning the writings and words of our third chief executive of our republic and father of the Constitution, James Madison. It upsets me when an activist judge, whether conservative or liberal, take the liberty to falsely interpret the words of a founding father, especially James Madison.

> **A** citizen's right to "keep and bear arms" is a matter of liberty for our established republic to prevent a government in becoming tyrannical.

"Justice STEVENS places great weight on James Madison's inclusion of a conscientious-objector clause in his original draft of the Second Amendment: "but no person religiously scrupulous of bearing arms, shall be compelled to render military service in person." Creating the Bill of Rights 12 (H. Veit, K. Bowling, & C. Bickford eds. 1991) (hereinafter Veit). He argues that this clause establishes that the drafters of the Second Amendment intended "bear arms" to refer only *590 to military service. See post, at 2836. It is always perilous to derive the service meaning of an adopted provision from another provision deleted in the drafting process. In any case, what Justice STEVENS would conclude from the deleted provision does not follow. It was not meant to exempt from military service those who objected to going to war but had no scruples about personal gunfights. Quakers opposed the use of arms not just for militia service, but for any violent purpose whatsoever—

so much so that Quaker frontiersmen were forbidden to use arms to defend their families, even though "[i]n such circumstances the temptation to seize a hunting rifle or knife in self-defense…must sometimes have been almost overwhelming. Thus, the most natural interpretation of Madison's deleted text is that those to carrying weapons for potential violent confrontation would not be "compelled to render military service," in which such carrying would be required." (Opinion Brief of the District of Columbia v. Heller, 554, U.S. 570 (2008), Associate Justice Antonin Scalia).

For someone to be a conscientious objector, does not mean that he or she should be stripped of their Second Amendment rights. This person does not believe in entering a war conflict because of his or her religion. Progressives and jurists like Justice STEVENS have always linked the Second Amendment to military service and that is not the case at all. And to quote mistakenly the father of the Constitution, James Madison, on this is simply ludicrous and an outright false interpretation of Madison's writings. Madison has never once showed anything but allegiance to the federal Constitution and rules of federalism. But what does it matter to a progressive jurist like Justice Stevens, his whole life has been to mislead the truth from the American people.

I will give a better interpretation of the Second Amendment against of Justice STEVENS and BREYER's dissenting opinions. I will also give a better reason in why they are wrong in contradicting federal constitutional law.

Just as many southern and Rocky Mountain states were contradicting federal constitutional law while passing segregation laws, advocates in the District of Columbia, New York City, Chicago, Los Angeles, San Francisco are all contradicting the Second Amendment.

"**c. Meaning of the Operative Clause.** Putting all these textual elements together, we find that they guarantee the individual right to possess and carry weapons in case of confrontation. This meaning is strongly confirmed by the historical background of the Second Amendment. We look to this because it has always been widely understood that the Second Amendment, like the First and Fourth Amendments codified a *pre-existing* right. The very text of the Second Amendment implicitly recognizes the pre-existence of the right and declares only that it "shall not be infringed." As we said in *United States v. Cruikshank*, 92 U.S. 542, 553, 23 L.Ed. 588 (1876), "[t]his is not a right granted by the constitution. Neither is it any manner dependent upon that instrument for its existence. The second **2798 amendment declares it shall not be infringed," (Opinion Brief of the District of Columbia v. Heller, 554, U.S. 570 (2008), Associate Justice Antonin Scalia).

At the beginning of this chapter, I point out the 1875 ruling of *United States v. Cruikshank*, (see page 227). This ruling was beyond unconstitutional and contradictory to our principled document. For Chief Justice Waite to state that the Second Amendment is not a right granted by the Constitution, just because now the newly freed blacks became citizens and obtained these rights under the Constitution, is ludicrous and obscene.

If everybody recognizes that the First and Fourth amendments have a pre-existing right, then the Second Amendment has that same right and it shall not be infringed or confiscated. The Third Amendment may sound outdated, but it is not. The principle still stands. "No soldier shall, in time of peace be quartered in any house, without the consent of the Owner, nor in time of war, but in a manner to be prescribed by law." As I stated, the principle stands for all time just as the Second Amendment does. No soldier may take refuge or lodging at a private house or domicile without the consent of the owner. The Second Amendment clearly states, "The right of the people to keep and bear arms, shall not be infringed." Both amendments speak volumes on the rights of the American citizen, one says the "owner," the other says "the people." So, in conclusion, both amendments should be respected across this republic by the rightful owner, the citizenry.

Member of the progressive movement, whether left or right, who want to disrupt our rules of federalism, want to rewrite it to please their own personal agenda or some agenda by some special interest organization. Let's now discuss the "Prefatory Clause in the Second Amendment:

"A well regulated militia, being necessary to the security of a free state," by Justice Antonin Scalia.

"a. "Well-Regulated Militia." In *United States v. Miller* 1939, explain[s] that "the militia comprised all males physically capable of acting in concert for the common defense." That definition comports with the founding-era sources. See e.g. Webster ("The militia of a country are the able bodied men organized into companies, regiments and brigades...and required by law to attend military exercises on certain days only, but at other times left to pursue their usual occupations"); The Federalist No. 46, pp 329, 334 (B. Wright ed. 1961) (J. Madison) ("near half a million of citizens with arms in their hands"); Letter to Destutt de Tracy (Jan 26, 1811), in The Portable Thomas *596 Jefferson 520, 524 (M. Peterson ed. 1975) ("the militia of the State, that is to say, of every man in it able to bear arms"). (Opinion Brief of the District of Columbia v. Heller, 554, U.S. 570 (2008), Associate Justice Antonin Scalia).

"Finally, the adjective "well-regulated" implies nothing more than the imposition of proper discipline and training. See Johnson 1619 ("Regulate": "To adjust by rule or method"); Rawle 121-122; cf. Va. Declaration of Rights S13 (1776), in 7 Thorpe 3812, 3814 (referring to "a well -regulated militia, composed of the people, trained for arms"). (Opinion Brief of the District of Columbia v. Heller, 554, U.S. 570 (2008), Associate Justice Antonin Scalia).

"b. "Security of a Free State." The phrase "security of a Free State meant "security of a free polity," not security of each of the several States as the dissent below argued, see 478 F 3d, at 405, and n. 10 Joseph Story wrote in his treatise on the Constitution that "the word 'state' is used in various senses [and in] its most enlarged sense it means the people composing a particular nation or community. 1 Story S208; see also 3id., S 1890 (in reference to the Second Amendment's prefatory clause: "The militia is the "State" elsewhere in the Constitution refers to individual States, but the phrase "Security of a free State" and close variations seem to have been terms of art in 18th-century political discourse, meaning a 'free country' or free polity. See Volokh, "Necessary to the security of a Free State," 83 Notre Dame L. Rev. 1, 5 (2007); see e.g., 4 Blackstone 151 (1769); Brutus Essay III (Nov. 15, 1787), in The Essential Antifederalist 251, 253 (W. Allen & G. Lloyd eds., 2d ed. 2002). (Opinion Brief of the District of Columbia v. Heller, 554, U.S. 570 (2008), Associate Justice Antonin Scalia).

I also touch on in this chapter this unconstitutional and contradictory Supreme Court ruling known as, *United States v. Miller*, 1939. To understand this ruling, you must understand that the Supreme Court at that time had jurists of deep anti-federalism thinking who were subjected to personal and special-interest agendas. Justice McReynolds and Justice Kennedy truly missed the point in the "Prefatory Clause." When I read this clause and put it together with the "Operative Clause," I know what the Founding Fathers were trying to say for the republic of these United States to prevail. Within the free state, a well established and regulated militia, in other words, present words today, the armed forces, the right of the people of the right to keep and bear arms shall not be infringed. What was happening before and during the American Revolutionary War? The British Colonial government in almost all the colonies received a decree from the King of England, George the III, to confiscate the arms of all residents in the American colonies. Now, that is not a "free state."

The founders saw the wisdom in avoiding these tyrannical acts of central government power, the framers gave power to the citizens of the new nation to fight off tyranny. That to me, is what the Second Amendment stands for. "In order to maintain a non-tyrannical nation, the government must have a national militia but cannot be tyrannical in their powers by restricting and prohibiting Arms to their citizenry."

"3. Relationship Between Prefatory Clause and Operative Clause. We reach this question now: Does the preface fit with an operative clause that creates an individual right to keep and bear arms? It first perfectly, once one knows the history that the founding generation knew and that we have described above. That history showed that the way tyrants had eliminated a militia consisting of all able-bodied men was not by banning the militia but simply by taking away the people's arms, enabling a select militia or standing army to suppress political opponents. This is what had occurred in England that prompted codification of the right to have arms in the English Bill of Rights." (Opinion Brief of the District of Columbia v. Heller, 554, U.S. 570 (2008), Associate Justice Antonin Scalia).

This amendment's language fits perfectly with the formation of our union. Not only does Justice Scalia mention the history of why a tyrannical government came to their senses after they established an anti-gun legislation or executive decree and gave the English people back their right to keep and bear arms.

"Federalists responded that because Congress was given no power to abridge the ancient right of individuals to keep and bear arms, such a force could never oppress the people. Remarks on the Amendments to the Federal Constitution, Nov, 7, 1788, in *id.*, at 556. It was understood across the political spectrum that the right helped to secure the ideal of a citizen militia, which might be necessary to oppose an oppressive military force if the constitutional order broke down." (Opinion Brief of the District of Columbia v. Heller, 554, U.S. 570 (2008), Associate Justice Antonin Scalia).

I only wish that Justice Scalia showed this paragraph to Chief Justice Waite and could have explained to Justice McReynolds the true definition of the Second Amendment. Justice McReynolds, as a good progressive model, never took a moment to read the amendment more clearly. While not just the amendment but the writings of our founders in trying to explain to the American citizenry the real and clear definition of this right.

This amendment gives the right for all citizens, regardless of race, sex, or creed the right to keep and bear arms against possible oppressive federal and state governments. While the citizens still have this right, the federal and state governments cannot contradict the meaning of this right, and this goes for all amendments.

This amendment gives the right for all citizens, regardless of race, sex, or creed the right to keep and bear arms against possible oppressive federal and state governments.

Also, the government, whether federal and/or state cannot prohibit the usage of this amendment towards its citizenry. They, of course, can regulate it and only prohibit it when that citizen has committed an infraction against our union. State legislatures can raise the gun ownership age from 18 to 21 years of age. This legislative act by a state can be done quite constitutionally. They did not deny anybody the right to keep and bear arms, they decided to regulate it until the appropriate age of twenty-one. The Bill of Rights has no age limit. Just like the Twenty-First Amendment, the Constitution gives states the right to regulate alcohol-related products and not prohibit them. It gives that discretion to the states to regulate it.

Jurists like Waite, McReynolds and certain members of today's court would completely be against our founding principle of our republic and liberty.

"Justice BREYER's "subsidiary assertion that individual self-defense is merely a "subsidiary interest" of the right to keep and bear arms, *see post*, at 2841 (dissenting opinion), is profoundly mistaken. He bases that assertion solely upon the prologue—but that can only show that self-defense had little to do with the right's *codification*; it was the *central component* of the rights itself." (Opinion Brief of the District of Columbia v. Heller, 554, U.S. 570 (2008), Associate Justice Antonin Scalia).

We shall discuss further Justice BREYER's dissenting opinion and find out why he decided to contradict federal constitutional law. Justice BREYER and his colleagues on the bench, past and present that have a continuing passion to enact conflict with constitutional law, truly does not understand it.

"Our interpretation is confirmed by analogous arms-bearing rights in state constitutions that preceded and immediately *601 followed adoption of the Second Amendment. Four states adopted analogues to the Federal Second Amendment in the period between independence and the ratification of the Bill of Rights. Two of them—Pennsylvania and Vermont—clearly adopted individual rights unconnected to militia service. Pennsylvania's Declaration of Rights of 1776 said: "That the people have a right to bear arms *for the defence of themselves and the state…*" S XIII, in 5 Thorpe 3082, 3083 (emphasis added). In 1777, Vermont adopted the identical provision, except for punctuation and capitalization. See Vt. Const., ch. 1, S XV, in 6 *id.*, at 3741." "North Carolina also codified a right to bear arms in 1776: "That the people have a right to bear arms for the defence of the state…" Declaration of Rights S XVII, in 5 id., at 2787, 2788. This could plausibly be read to support only a right to bear arms in a militia—but that is a peculiar way to make the point in a constitution that elsewhere repeatedly mentions the militia explicitly. Many colonial statutes required individual arms bearing for public-safety reasons—such as the 1770 Georgia Law that "for the security and *defence of this province* from internal dangers and insurrections" required those men who qualified for militia duty individually "to **2803 carry firearms" "to places of public worship." "The 1780 Massachusetts Constitution presented another variation on the theme: "The people have a right to keep and bear arms for the common defence…" Once again, if one gives narrow meaning to the phrase "common defence" this can be thought to limit the right to the bearing of arms in a *602 state-organized military force. But once again the State's highest court thought otherwise. Writing for the court in an 1825 libel case, Chief Justice Parker wrote: "The liberty of the press was to be unrestrained, but he who used it was to be responsible in cases of its abuse; like the right to keep and bear arms, which does not protect him who uses them for annoyance or destruction." Commonwealth v. Blanding, 20 Mass. 304, 313-314. The analogy makes no sense if firearms could not be used for individual purpose at all... (19th century courts never read "common defence" to limit the use of weapons to militia service." (Opinion Brief of the District of Columbia v. Heller, 554, U.S. 570 (2008), Associate Justice Antonin Scalia).

"We therefore believe that the most likely reading of all four of these pre-Second Amendment state constitutional provisions is that they secured an individual right to bear arms for defensive purposes. Other states did not include rights to bear arms in their pre-1789 constitutions—although in Virginia a Second Amendment analogue was proposed (unsuccessfully) by Thomas Jefferson. (It read: No freeman shall ever be debarred the use of arms [within his own lands or tenements]." The Papers of Thomas Jefferson 344 (J. Boyd ed. 1950)." Between 1789 and 1820, nine States adopted Second Amendment analogues. Four of them—Kentucky, Ohio, Indiana, and Missouri—referred to the right of the people to "bear arms in defence of themselves and the State." Another three States—Mississippi, Connecticut and Alabama—used the even more individualistic phrasing that each citizen has the "right to bear arms in defence of himself and the State." Finally, two States—Tennessee and Maine—used the "common defence" language of *603 of Massachusetts... That of the nine state constitutional protections for the right to bear arms enacted immediately after 1789 at least seven unequivocally protected an individual citizen's right to self-defense is strong evidence that is how the founding generations conceived of the right." (Opinion Brief of the District of Columbia v. Heller, 554, U.S. 570 (2008), Associate Justice Antonin Scalia).

These examples that Justice Scalia has shown that individual states added to their own state constitutions to create a Second Amendment are very clear. States can create their own laws and rights if they do not contradict the federal Constitution. No where in these separate state constitutions do, they state that the Second Amendment is to be used as a right to create a state militia by able-bodied men to protect their own sovereignty and the sovereignty of the United States. It is quite clear that most of these states created their own version of Second Amendment to protect the common sense of "self-defense" to the individual right of the American citizenry to bear arms for their defense of their life, property and individualism against a tyrannical federal government or state government.

Even Thomas Jefferson introduced, but sadly not admitted, that freemen shall not be debarred (prohibited) the right to bear arms in protection of their property. Sadly, slavery was continuing in the United States at that time and so a legality of emancipation was still no where near. But it was a step in the right direction made by our future third president to propose to allow all citizens regardless of race, color the right to bear arms.

Pre-Civil War (prior to 1875 and 1939), Supreme Court cases did interpret the Second Amendment correctly as far as that citizens have a right to bear and keep arms for defense of their property and life. Nowhere in those cases, do they mention that owning arms was connected to military duty. One flaw in these post-civil war rulings is that the Supreme Court gave privilege to one race but not the other.

"**2. Pre-Civil War Case Law.** The 19th Century cases that interpreted the Second Amendment universally support an individual right unconnected to militia service. In *Houston v. Moore*, 5 What. 1, 24, 5 L.Ed. 19 (1820), this Court held that States have concurrent power over the militia, at least where not pre-empted by Congress. Agreeing in dissent that States could "organize, arm, and discipline" the militia in the absence of conflicting federal regulation, Justice Story said that the Second Amendment "may not, perhaps, be thought to have any important bearing on this point." Of course, if the Amendment simply "protect[ed] the right of the people of each of the several States to maintain a well-regulated militia," post, at 2822 (STEVENS, J., dissenting), it would have enormous **2808 and obvious bearing over the militia from the nonexclusive nature of federal power, not from the Second Amendment, whose preamble merely "confirms and illustrates" the importance of the militia. Even clearer was Justice Baldwin, sitting as a Circuit Judge, cited both for his conclusion that a citizen has "a right to carry arms in defense of his property or person, and to use them, if either were assailed with such force for the protection or safety of either." (Opinion Brief of the District of Columbia v. Heller, 554, U.S. 570 (2008), Associate Justice Antonin Scalia).

When I read excerpts of these pre-civil war cases, I can also understand the true meaning of the Second Amendment. I also understand that the States must abide and create legislation to reflect on the Amendments in question without contradicting them.

"Many early-19ᵗʰ century state cases indicated that the Second Amendment right to bear arms was an individual right unconnected to militia service, though subject to certain restrictions. A Virginia case in 1824 holding that the Constitution did not extend to free blacks explained: "[N]umerous restrictions imposed on [blacks] in our Statute Book, many of which are inconsistent with the letter and spirit of the Constitution, both of this State and of the United States as respects the free whites, demonstrate, that, here, those instruments have not been considered to extend equally to both classes of our population. We will only instance the restriction upon the migration of free blacks into the State, and upon their right to bear arms." *Aldridge v. Commonwealth*, 4 Va. 447, 2 Va. Cas. 447, 449 (Gen. Ct.). The claim was obviously not that blacks were prevented from carrying guns in the militia. See also *Waters v. State*, Md. 1843, (because free blacks were treated as a "dangerous population," "laws have been passed to prevent the migration into the State; to make it unlawful for them to bear arms; to guard even their religious assemblages with peculiar watchfulness").") (Opinion Brief of the District of Columbia v. Heller, 554, U.S. 570 (2008), Associate Justice Antonin Scalia).

This is where I disagree with many state Supreme Court cases and with some cases that came before the highest court of the land. As the Fourteenth Amendment reaffirmed our Constitution that any citizen that is born or naturalized within the boundaries of the United States of America and its official territories are citizens of this great republic. The amendment also reaffirmed and reassured that all citizens regardless of their skin color are citizens and have the same rights and privileges as any other citizen. That means that everybody, all citizens are entitled to that right.

Now still some states prior to the Civil War and later post-Civil War, were reaffirming that the Second Amendment stands for defense of the American citizenry's life and property but giving privilege to one race and not the other in some cases.

"**2809 In *Nunn v. State*, 1 Ga. 243, 251 (1846), the Georgia Supreme Court construed the Second Amendment as protecting the "*natural right of self-defence*" and therefore struck down a ban on carrying pistols openly. Its opinion perfectly captured the way in which the operative clause of the Second Amendment furthers the purpose announced in the prefatory clause, in continuity with the English right: "The right of the whole people, old and young, men, women and not militia only, to keep and bear arms of every description, and not such merely as are used by the militia, shall not be infringed, curtailed, or broken in upon, in the smallest degree; and all this for the important end to be attained: the rearing up and qualifying a well-regulated militia, so vitally necessary of a free state." (Opinion Brief of the District of Columbia v. Heller, 554, U.S. 570 (2008), Associate Justice Antonin Scalia).

> **T**oday's jurists should take a lesson from these Georgia jurists and learn how to apply the rules of federalism in our everyday American republic life.

Contradiction of the Constitution by legislators is not a new thing. Apparently, legislators back then found ways to create conflict with the national principle document. But at least there were wise members of state supreme courts that truly knew the rules of federalism and how to interpret the Constitution. To read this opinion of the Georgia high court, makes me proud that there were people that knew how to apply the rules of federalism. Today's jurists should take a lesson from these Georgia jurists and learn how to apply the rules of federalism.

Other cases after *Nunn*, took effect in favor of the Constitution and Second Amendment. If only this correct interpretation of this amendment would have continued, we would not have had multiple contradictory opinions on this amendment and further congressional legislation that prohibited the usage of this amendment.

After the Civil War, when newly freed slaves became citizens of this republic of ours, they were routinely being denied their citizen's rights and especially their Second Amendment rights.

"Blacks were routinely disarmed by Southern states after the Civil War. Those who opposed these injustices frequently stated that they infringed blacks' constitutional right to keep and bear arms. A report of the Commission of the Freedmen's Bureau in 1866 stated plainly: "[T]he civil law [of Kentucky] prohibits the colored man from bearing arms...Their arms are taken from them by the civil *615 authorities...Thus the right of the people to keep and bear arms as provided in the constitution is *infringed*." "The understanding of that the Second Amendment gave freed blacks the right to keep and bear arms was reflected in congressional *616 discussion of the bill, with even an opponent of it saying that the founding generation "were for every man bearing his arms about him and keeping them in his house, his castle, for his own defense." Cong. Globe, 39th Cong., 1st Sess., 362, 371 (1866) (Sen. Davis)." (Opinion Brief of the District of Columbia v. Heller, 554, U.S. 570 (2008), Associate Justice Antonin Scalia).

Slavery was wrong not by a violation of state sovereignty but by a violation of human rights. When slavery was abolished, and former slaves became citizens, by law, they had the same rights and privileges as a white citizen.

During post-Civil War days, most state legislatures across the country, mainly in the South, were giving privilege to one race and denying it to the other race. So that is why the national Congress decided to act and add a Fourteenth Amendment to clarify that all citizens regardless of race, skin or color were citizens of this country, entitled equality and allowed due process of the law. But even with this amendment and several acts of congress, still many state legislatures and state courts granted a privilege division.

"It was plainly understanding in the post-Civil War Congress that the Second Amendment protected an individual right to use arms for self-defense." (Opinion Brief of the District of Columbia v. Heller, 554, U.S. 570 (2008), Associate Justice Antonin Scalia).

As it is to Justice Scalia's understanding and mine as well that the Second Amendment, and frankly all amendments, are guaranteed the same rights and privileges for all individual citizens -- all individual citizens regardless of race.

"United States v. Cruikshank, 92 U.S. 542, 23 L. Ed. 588, in the course of vacating the convictions of members of a white mob for depriving blacks of their right to keep and bear arms, held that the Second Amendment does not apply by its own force apply to anyone other than the Federal Government. The opinion explained that the right "is not a right granted by the Constitution [or] in any manner dependent upon that instrument for its existence. **2813. The Second Amendment...means no more *620 than that it shall not be infringed by Congress." Id., at 553. States, we said, were free to restrict or protect the right under their police powers. The limited discussion of the Second Amendment in Cruikshank supports, if anything, the individual-rights interpretation." (Opinion Brief of the District of Columbia v. Heller, 554, U.S. 570 (2008), Associate Justice Antonin Scalia).

The Second Amendment means no more than that it shall not be infringed by Congress and the state governments across this republic. Justice Scalia forgot to add "state governments" in this statement. Congress and the state governments in practice do not have the right to prohibit or infringe on the constitutional duty and right of all citizens to keep and bear arms. They may when necessary regulate the amendment to make their state and nation a better place to live.

"*636 We are aware of the problem of handgun violence in this country, and we take seriously the concerns raised by the many *amici* who believe that prohibition of handgun ownership is a solution. The Constitution leaves the District of Columbia a variety of tools for combating that problem, including some measures regulating handguns, see supra, at 2816-2817, and n. 26. But the enshrinement of constitutional rights necessarily takes certain policy choices off the table. These include the absolute prohibition of handguns [other arms], held and used for self-defense in the home. Undoubtedly some think that the Second

Amendment is outmoded in a society, and where gun violence is a serious problem. That is perhaps debatable, but what is not debatable is that it is not the role of this Court to pronounce the Second Amendment extinct. We affirm the judgment of the Court of Appeals. It is so ordered." (Opinion Brief of the District of Columbia v. Heller, 554, U.S. 570 (2008), Associate Justice Antonin Scalia).

The current gun violence in this republic is a problem. It is a problem that has occurred since the inception of this amendment to the present time. Many people on the contradictory side of this amendment believe and seek to not only prohibit the rights granted by this amendment but to erase it from our federal Constitution. Prohibiting a right that is granted by our federal Constitution is explicitly going against the basic principles of this republic.

This court's ruling and its dissenting opinion's main objective was to terminate this amendment from our Constitution. Quite frankly, Justice Scalia said the truth at the end of his opinion, that this court (or any other interpreting court) does not have the right to terminate and dissolve this right. It is not the duty of the court to interpret laws with accordance of the Constitution. Justice Scalia and the members that share the same opinion are quite right in interpreting this ruling correctly and with accordance to the federal Constitution and with the rules of federalism. This ruling in my humble opinion is so ordered and in no conflict with federal constitutional law.

"The question presented by this case is not whether the Second Amendment protects a "collective right" or an "individual right." Surely it protects a right that can be enforced by individuals. But a conclusion that the Second Amendment protects an individual right does not tell us anything about the scope of that right." (Dissenting Brief of the District of Columbia v. Heller, 554, U.S. 570 (2008), Associate Justice John Paul Stevens).

The first paragraph from Justice Stevens upsets me, and it upsets me in ways that would upset an individual that supports the federal Constitution and rules of federalism. It states that the Second Amendment protects the individual right but that the Court did not find ways the individual is protected by the magnitude of this right.

The first paragraph is full of contradictions. It is fair to say that Justice Stevens, along with his colleagues in that day's dissent, presented to the American people a perfect view of their contradiction of federal constitutional law.

"Guns are used to hunt, for self-defense, to commit crimes, for sporting activities, and to perform military duties. **The Second Amendment plainly does not protect the right to use a gun to rob a bank**; it is equally clear that it does encompass the right to use weapons for certain military purposes. Whether it also protects the right to posses and use guns for nonmilitary purposes like hunting and personal self-defense *637 is the question presented by this case. The text of the Amendment, its history, and our decision in United States v. Miller, 307 U.S. 174, 59 S. Ct. 816, 83 L. Ed. 1206 (1939), provide a clear answer to that question." (Dissenting Brief of the District of Columbia v. Heller, 554, U.S. 570 (2008), Associate Justice John Paul Stevens).

> "The Second Amendment plainly does not protect the right to use a gun to rob a bank."

In reading the first paragraph of Justice Stevens' dissent, I can plainly state that I cannot take him or the other dissenters seriously. "The Second Amendment plainly does not protect the right to use a gun to rob a bank," is an ignorant and uneducated statement from anybody and that includes an Associate Justice to the Supreme Court. Of course, all sensible and common-sense American citizens know that the Second Amendment does not give us the right to rob a bank. There are not only state laws but federal precedent that makes bank robberies a federal offense. How can an American citizen rob a bank because its his Second Amendment right while there is a federal law establishing the opposite of committing a felony? Justice Stevens is not only contradicting federal constitutional law but also contradicting federal laws against bank robberies.

A progressive, whether a legislator or jurist, will cling to an unconstitutional law and/or ruling. I understand that the court are supposed to interpret a law with accordance to the Constitution, and their final say is final as to how the law is constitutionally interpreted. But even the highest court of the land can make mistakes. And one ruling is nothing more than a federal constitutional law contradiction, and that is the ruling of *United States v. Miller*, 1939.

United States v. Miller was based to state that the act of Congress in 1934, to enact the National Firearms Act of 1934 was constitutional. Not only did Justice McReynolds and Justice Stevens totally disregarded the definition of this amendment but also the rules of how this republic was established, the rules of federalism. They also misinterpreted how these rules need to be played out in our republic.

"The Second Amendment was adopted to protect the right of the people of each of the several States to maintain a well-regulated militia. It was a response to concerns raised during the ratification of the constitution that the power of congress to disarm state militias and create a national standing army posed an intolerable threat to the sovereignty of the several States. Neither the text of the Amendment nor the arguments advanced by its proponents evidenced the slightest interest in limiting any legislature's authority to regulate private civilian uses of firearms. Specifically, there is no indication that the Framers of the Amendment intended to enshrine the common-law right of self-defense in the Constitution. In 1934, Congress enacted the National Firearms Act, the first major federal firearms law. Sustaining an indictment the **2823 Act, this Court held that, "[i]n the absence of any evidence tending to show that possession or use of a 'shotgun having a barrel of less than eighteen inches in length' at this time has some reasonable relationship to the preservation or efficiency of a well-regulated militia, we cannot say that the Second Amendment guarantees the right to keep and bear such an instrument. Since our decision in *Miller*, hundreds of judges have relied on the view of the Amendment we endorsed here; we ourselves affirmed it in 1980. See Lewis v. United States, 445 U.S. 55, 65-66, n. 8, 100 S. Ct. 915, 63 L.Ed.2nd 198 (1980). No new evidence has surfaced since 1980 supporting the view that the Amendment was intended to curtail the power of Congress to regulate *639 civilian use or misuse of weapons." (Dissenting Brief of the District of Columbia v. Heller, 554, U.S. 570 (2008), Associate Justice John Paul Stevens).

If I could not believe my eyes in Justice McReynolds' opinion of the court on *Miller*, I cannot believe my eyes on this dissent. The continuing contradiction of federal constitutional law and constant denial of recognizing the definition of this amendment. To the dissenters that read this brief and still believe every word that came out of Justice Stevens' handy work, let me expressly tell you, dissenter readers that you and Justice Stevens are wrong. And let me tell you why.

The Second Amendment was adopted to protect the right of the people of each state (and federal territory including the District of Columbia), not to maintain a well-regulated militia but to do the opposite. The amendment is quite clear, I do not understand the constant denial and contradiction. "A well regulated Militia, being necessary to the security of a free State, the right of the people to keep and bear Arms, shall not be infringed".

It does not say, "A well regulated militia organized by the citizens of this republic to being necessary to the security of a free State." Progressives like McReynolds and Stevens decided to rewrite the Second Amendment to their personal agenda and ignore the wishes of the framers.

After the *Miller* ruling came out, so did other rulings that ruled in favor to be against the Second Amendment. The definition of the Second Amendment and the infringement of state sovereignty from an intrusive federal government. But that is because the judges who presided over these rulings did not know any better. They were taught from previous precedents to praise

> "**T**he Framers were not denying the right for the nation to obtain a well-regulated national militia, they were only stating that the citizens' right to keep and bear arms shall not be confiscated to maintain a secure, free State."

a centralized form of federal government and undermine the principled document and rules that initially governs our republic. No new evidence is needed to show to the American citizenry to defend the Second Amendment. The evidence is quite clear. The Framers were not denying the right for the nation to obtain a well-regulated national militia, they were only stating that the citizens' right to keep and bear arms shall not be confiscated to maintain a secure, free state.

"In this dissent I shall first explain why our decision in Miller was faithful to the text of the Second Amendment and the purposes revealed in its drafting history. I shall then comment on the post-ratification history of the Amendment, which makes abundantly clear that the Amendment should not be interpreted as limiting the authority of Congress to regulate the use of possession of firearms for purely civilian purposes." (Dissenting Brief of the District of Columbia v. Heller, 554, U.S. 570 (2008), Associate Justice John Paul Stevens).

> "**F**ederal and state governments are not here to prohibit our rights; they are here to administer them."

Federal and state governments are not here to prohibit our rights; they are here to administer them. Furthermore, federal law cannot consist of prohibiting and/or regulating the use of possession of firearms, we leave that to the individuality and sovereignty of each state. Now a state has much power to create any laws to the definition and meaning of the Second Amendment, but what they cannot do is contradict that definition and meaning. It will be a violation of the rules of federalism.

Justice Stevens goes into his own semantics of Second Amendment defining moments in detailing his own definition and meaning of the Second Amendment. In his own personal defining moments of the Second Amendment, he still holds onto the ruling of *Miller*, 1939, as if it was holier than our Constitution. I am just going to examine a few excerpts from his dissent and prove to you that his dissent is strictly unconstitutional and contradictory.

"[T]o keep and bear Arms". Although the Court's discussion of these words treats them as two "phrases"—as if they read "to keep" and "to bear"—they describe a unitary right: to possess arms if needed for military purposes and to use them in conjunction with military activities. **2828 As a threshold matter, it is worth pausing to note an oddity in the Court's interpretation of "to keep and bear Arms." Unlike the Court of Appeals, the Court does not read that phrase to create a right to possess arms for "lawful, private purposes." *Parker v. District of Columbia*, 478 F3d 370, 382 (C.A.D.C2007). Instead, the Court limits the Amendment's protection to the right "to possess and carry weapons in case of confrontation." *Ante*, at 2797. No party or *amicus* urged this interpretation; the Court appears to have fashioned it out of whole cloth. But although this novel limitation lacks support in the text of the Amendment, the Amendment's text *does* justify a different limitation: The "right to keep and bear Arms" protects only a right to possess and use firearms in connection with service in a state-organized militia." (Dissenting Brief of the District of Columbia v. Heller, 554, U.S. 570 (2008), Associate Justice John Paul Stevens).

Post-Supreme Court cases and lower court cases that came after the *Miller* ruling are just as unconstitutional and contradictory as the grandfather of high-court rulings that set this precedent in 1939. Justice Stevens and his dissenting gang of contradictory justices against the Second Amendment will never tire of repeating this ruling. In their conflicting minds, they still agree to this day that the Second Amendment is a right for the citizen to be involved in a government-run state or national militia. The American citizenry does not need to belong to a government-sponsored militia to obtain this right.

"The proper allocation of military power in the new Nation was an issue of central concern for the Framers. The compromises they ultimately reached, reflected in Article I's Militia Clauses and the Second Amendment, represent quintessential examples of the Framers' "split[ting] the atom of sovereignty. *653 Two themes relevant to our current interpretative task ran through the debates on the original Constitution. "On the one hand, there was a widespread fear that a national standing Army posed an intolerable threat to individual liberty and to the sovereignty of the separate States." Perpich v. Department of Defense, 496 U.S. 334, 340, 110 S.Ct. 2418, 110 L.Ed.2d 312 (1990). Governor Edmund Randolph, reporting on the Constitutional Convention to the Virginia Ratification Convention, explained: "With respect to a standing army, I believe there was not a member in the federal convention, who did not feel indignation at such an institution." (Dissenting Brief of the District of Columbia v. Heller, 554, U.S. 570 (2008), Associate Justice John Paul Stevens).

"On the other hand, the Framers recognized the dangers inherent in relying on inadequately trained militia members "as the primary means of providing for the common defense," Perpich, 496 U.S., at 340, 110 S. Ct. 2418; during the Revolutionary War, "[t]his force, though armed, was largely untrained and its deficiencies were the subject of bitter complaint." Wiener, The Militia Clause of the Constitution, 54 Harv. L.Rev. 181, 182 (1940). *654 In order to respond to those twin concerns, a compromise was reached: Congress would be authorized to raise and support a national Army and Navy, and also to organize, arm, discipline, and provide for the calling forth of "The Militia." U.S. Const., Art. I, Section 8, cls. 12-16. The President, at the same time, was empowered as the "Commander in Chief of the Army and Navy of the United States, and of the Militia of the several States, when called into the actual Service of the United States." Art. II, Section 2. But, with respect to the militia, a significant reservation was made to the States: Although Congress would have the power to call forth, organize, arm, and discipline the militia, as well as to govern "such Part of them as may be empowered in the Service of the United States," the States respectively would retain the right to appoint officers and to train the militia in accordance with the discipline prescribed by Congress. Art

I, Section 8, cl. 16." (Dissenting Brief of the District of Columbia v. Heller, 554, U.S. 570 (2008), Associate Justice John Paul Stevens).

It's one thing to rewrite the Constitution for their own personal agenda, and another to rewrite American Revolutionary War history. The war that lead to the creation of this federalism republic, which makes these United States of America. The Continental Army was made up of various people in the fight for liberty against the British crown. Yes, most of the soldiers were farmers, ranchers, small business entrepreneurs that decided to take a stand and join the cause of liberty. And some were inexperienced in the art of war. But they were quickly trained to be part of the Continental Army. Just because these men were inexperienced in the common military tactics of war, does not mean that the framers of the Constitution wanted to restrict the future citizens of this land the right to keep and bear arms. When the war was over, and America became independent from Great Britain, the dissenting justices would have you believe that the Continental Army then confiscated the arms of the once inexperienced minutemen, but that of course is false.

The Continental Army was not even close in resemblance to

> **"B**ut you must also encounter that the Framers, also known as the Founding Fathers of the Constitution to maintain the peace between these inexperienced minutemen now newly-American citizens, they were not about to confiscate their arms."

the British Army. Before and during the war of American independence, the British Army confiscated the weapons of the colonists to avoid civil disobedience and disruptions. As the war for American independence began and concluded, with an American independent victory and later the ratification of the Second Amendment, not once were the guns confiscated from these inexperienced individuals. These contradictory jurists would still have you believe that the Continental Army and the idea of the framers were to prohibit and confiscate the arms from the citizens of this new nation. A lie which you see here in this dissent.

No one is denying that the Founding Fathers wanted to establish a national militia and navy to guard this new nation and let Congress prescribe the rules of war and national militia preparedness. But you must also understand that the framers, also known as the Founding Fathers of the Constitution, in order to maintain the peace between these inexperienced minutemen, now newly minted American citizens, that they were not about to confiscate their arms. Also no one is disputing that Congress has the power to delegate war approvals and make it an obligation law to command its citizens to prepare for war to defend this federalism republic.

> "The language of the Second Amendment is so simple to comprehend, why are these contradictory jurists being so stubborn to continue with their actions of conflicted opinions against the Constitution."

But as Congress calls up for a draft as constituted in the Constitution, it is also stated that Congress cannot confiscate/infringe the rights of the American citizenry's right to keep and bear arms. The language of the Second Amendment is so simple to comprehend. Why are these contradictory jurists being so stubborn to continue with their actions of conflicted opinions against the Constitution?

"Notably, each of these proposals used the phrase "keep and bear arms," which was eventually adopted by Madison. And each proposal embedded the phrase within a group of principles that are distinctly military in meaning. By contrast, New Hampshire's proposal, although it followed another proposed amendment that echoed the familiar concern about standing armies, described the protection involved in more clearly personal terms. Its proposal read: "Twelfth, Congress shall never disarm any Citizen unless such as are or have been in Actual Rebellion." Id., at 758, 761." (Dissenting Brief of the District of Columbia v. Heller, 554, U.S. 570 (2008), Associate Justice John Paul Stevens).

James Madison, who incidentally was the father of the Constitution and our fourth president, did in fact write the Constitution. He knew perfectly how to establish the true meanings of all our citizen's Bill of Rights, including the Second Amendment. There is no evidence to point out that Madison, when he wrote the Second Amendment, truly did not mean to state that the right to "keep and bear arms" was for military use only.

Justice Stevens' statement indicating the law passed by the twelfth Congress, that they have a right to deny that citizen's right to "keep and bear" arms if they have committed a rebellious infraction, is just as ludicrous as his statement in the beginning of this dissent. "The Second Amendment plainly does not protect the right to use a gun to rob a bank." It's mind-boggling that he would even put that on paper. There were laws established even before the Second Amendment, even before the ratification of the 1787 Constitution, that anybody who committed a crime against federal or state governments, that they would lose their rights.

"In addition, Madison had been a member, some years earlier, of the committee tasked with drafting, the Virginia Declaration of Rights. That committee considered a proposal

> **T**hen do we, as citizens, wait for the police or militia for them to assist us and not fend for ourselves?

by Thomas Jefferson that would have included within the Virginia Declaration the following language: "No freeman shall ever be debarred the use of arms [within his own lands or tenements]." 1. Papers of Thomas Jefferson 363 (J. Boyd ed. 1950). But the committee rejected that language…" (Dissenting Brief of the District of Columbia v. Heller, 554, U.S. 570 (2008), Associate Justice John Paul Stevens).

Justice Stevens and the dissenting members of the Supreme Court loved to twist and turn the words of our Founding Fathers to please their own anti-Constitution agenda. We all know it to be true that Thomas Jefferson and James Madison were men who abhorred slavery. But they were living in a state where slavery was still in high demand. They were a minority voice in the Commonwealth of Virginia, and they tried their best to adopt a measure that made the African-American citizen a part of this new nation.

"The Court suggests that by the post-Civil War period, the Second Amendment was understood to secure a right to firearm use and ownership for purely private purposes like personal self-defense. While it is true that some of the legislative history on which the Court relies support that contention, see ante, at 2809–2011, such sources are entitled to limited, if any weight. All of the statements the Court cites were made long after the framing of the Amendment and cannot possibly supply any insight into the intent of the Framers; and all were made during pitched political debates, so that they are better characterized as advocacy than good-faith attempts at constitutional interpretation. What is more, much of the evidence the Court offers is decidedly less clear than its discussion allows. The Court notes: 'Blacks were routinely disarmed by Southern States after the Civil War. Those who opposed these injustices frequently stated that they infringed blacks' constitutional right to keep and bear arms.' *Ante*, at 2810. The Court hastily concludes that "[n]eedless to say, the claim was not that blacks were being prohibited from carrying arms in an organized state militia," *ibid.* But some of the claims of the *671 sort, the Court cites may have been just that. In some Southern States, Reconstruction-era Republican governments created state militias in which both blacks and whites were permitted to serve." (Dissenting Brief of the District of Columbia v. Heller, 554, U.S. 570 (2008), Associate Justice John Paul Stevens).

As we discussed, the first Supreme Court ruling of *United States v. Cruikshank*, 1876, in the beginning of this chapter that denied the newly made citizens of this republic the right to "keep and bear arms" for their own protection and self defense. The justices back then, and the justices now, are being contradictory to the United States Constitution and violating the rules of federalism. These justices cannot give privilege to one race and not the other. The Constitution is quite clear that all citizens regardless of race and color are equal under law per the Fourteenth Amendment. The background that lead to this contradicting ruling was the denial of the basic rights of the newly made citizens who just happened to be black Americans.

After the 1872 Louisiana gubernatorial election, the Republicans won a majority in the state legislature and governor's seat. While most of these Republican voters were black Americans, the Democrat voter, predominantly white, got upset and took to the streets to disrupt the rally headed by many black Republican voters. The instigators behind this counter-protest were Democrat, white voters. The newly made citizens had every right to protect their life and property if they agreed they were in danger, but the Supreme Court, past and present, saw it differently.

If Justice Stevens makes these claims that white and black citizens belonging to a militia have the right to keep and bear arms, but not ordinary citizens, then must we, as citizens, wait for the police or militia to assist us and not fend for ourselves? I hate to disappoint Justice Stevens, but our Second Amendment DOES NOT apply to militia officers based on race or color. The Second Amendment is APPLIED for all citizens the right to "keep and bear Arms." If the black American citizens would have been allowed to carry Arms during their protest in Colfax, Louisiana, the outcome would have been differently, the justices would have respected the rules of federalism and federal constitutional law.

"In *United States v. Cruikshank*, 92 U.S. 542, 23 L.Ed. 588 (1876), the Court sustained a challenge to respondent's convictions under the Enforcement Act of 1870 for conspiring to deprive any individual of " 'any right or privilege granted or secured to him by the Constitution or the laws of the United States.' "*Id.*, at 548: "This is not a right granted by the Constitution. Neither is it any manner dependent on *673 that instrument for its existence. The second amendment declares that it shall not be infringed; but this, as has been seen, means no more than it shall not be infringed by Congress. This is one of the Amendments that has no other effect than to restrict the powers of the national government." (Dissenting Brief of the District of Columbia v. Heller, 554, U.S. 570 (2008), Associate Justice John Paul Stevens).

"The majority's assertion that the Court in *Cruikshank* "described the right protected by the Second Amendment as "bearing arms for a lawful purpose," ' " *ante*, at 2813 (quoting *Cruikshank*, 92 U.S., at 553), is not accurate. The Cruikshank Court explained that the defective indictment contained such language, but the Court did not itself describe the right, or endorse the indictment's description of the right." (Dissenting Brief of the District of Columbia v. Heller, 554, U.S. 570 (2008), Associate Justice John Paul Stevens).

"Moreover, it is entirely possible that the basis for the indictment's counts 2 and 10, which charged the respondents with depriving the victims of rights secured by the Second Amendment, was the prosecutor's belief that the victims—members of a group of citizens, mostly black but also white, who were rounded up by the Sheriff, sworn in as a posse to defend the local courthouse, and attacked by a white mob—bore sufficient resemblance to members of a state militia that they were brought within the reach of the Second Amendment. See generally C. Lane, The Day Freedom Died: The Colfax Massacre, The Supreme Court, and the Betrayal of Reconstruction (2008)." (Dissenting Brief of the District of Columbia v. Heller, 554, U.S. 570 (2008), Associate Justice John Paul Stevens).

The events before the ruling of *Cruikshank* were quite simple, black American citizens were celebrating a Republican statewide electoral victory. Because of this electoral victory in Louisiana, many members, mostly white, loyal to the party that supported the human-rights violation of labor known as slavery took to the streets to counter the protest.

> **"In** my eyes, you have the right 'to keep and bear arms' as long as you do not cause any disruptions to the day-to-day activities of your community."

All citizens, regardless of race, are protected by the Second Amendment even though many former Confederate veterans and sympathizers find ways to contradict federal constitutional law. Those black American citizens have every right to defend themselves with or without the help of an integrated or non-integrated federal or state militia. Justice Stevens wants to make you believe that all citizens have a right to "keep and bear arms" if you belong to the federal or state militia. But what he states is that plain citizens do not have that right. That is simply wrong.

Justice Stevens wants you to also believe that he is being fair to everybody by saying that only militia members have that right. In my eyes, you have the right "to keep and bear arms" if you do not cause any disruptions to the day-to-day activities of your community. Once you break that community trust, you lose all benefits and rights as an American citizen. That is the principle of all our Bill of Rights, they are all a "Catch-22." How much tolerance can the American citizen endure and how much can we take?

What is the role of the federal government in all of this? Are they to regulate and prohibit the sale, distribution, and usage of our Second Amendment Bill of Right? Or are they here to administer and to make sure the states ensure that all citizens have access to maintain that right? In my opinion, the role of the federal government is the latter of administrative services. Their duty is to instruct the states that their residents are entitled to this Second Amendment right. Especially when the country has accepted that all citizens of all races are equal under law. All of them deserve equal access. We come to the other question of whether the federal government has the right to regulate the Second Amendment.

"**2844 In 1901, the President revitalized the militia by creating " 'the National Guard of the several States.' " Perpich, 496 U.S., at 341, and nn. 9—10, 110 S. Ct. 2418; meanwhile, the dominant understanding of the Second Amendment's inapplicability to private gun ownership continued well into the 20th century. The first two federal laws directly restricting civilian use and possession of firearms—the 1927 Act of prohibiting mail delivery of "pistols, revolvers, and other firearms capable of being concealed on the person," ch. 57, 44 Stat. 1059, and the 1934 Act prohibiting the possession of sawed-off shotguns and machine guns—were enacted over minor Second Amendment objections dismissed by the vast majority of the legislators who participated in the debates. Members of Congress clashed over the wisdom and efficacy of such laws as crime-control measures. But since the statutes did not infringe *676 upon the military use or possession of weapons, for most legislators they did not even raise the specter of possible conflict with the Second Amendment." (Dissenting Brief of the District of Columbia v. Heller, 554, U.S. 570 (2008), Associate Justice John Paul Stevens).

Justice Stevens and the dissenting justices of this brief had to come to terms with the political and culture climate that was affecting these United States during the beginning and middle of the 20th century. There was a movement in America in those times, trying to change our American founding principles from the First Amendment, Second Amendment, Fourth Amendment and even the representation of each individual state sovereignty.

At first it was the Republican Party making these radical changes to our American founding principles and then it was the Democratic Party. Maybe John Adams was right that political parties would be the death of the republic. These progressives of both parties never understood the meaning of America's principle of the Second Amendment and neither did Justice Stevens. The Second Amendment is very clear in its role of arms. The Federal government and state governments can establish a national and state militia to maintain a free state BUT to maintain that free state, the prohibition/infringement of citizen's right to "keep and bear" arms will be considered illegal.

Years later, the court foisted the first gun-control policy onto the states and its citizenry. Congress established legislation that banned certain arms onto its people and made strong restrictions and prohibitions upon its people. And the Supreme Court of this land ruled in favor of this legislation while contradicting the rules of federalism and the Constitution. This was a time in America, where government took advantage on the American people and passed legislation without hesitation or consideration of the will of the people.

This must never happen again. Members of Congress, jurists, past and present, must never do anything that takes advantage of the very same people and Constitution they are here to represent, maintain and defend.

"The Court properly disclaims that any interest in evaluating the wisdom of the specific policy choice challenged in this case, but it fails to pay heed to a far more important policy choice—the choice made by the Framers themselves. The Court would have us believe that over 200 years ago, the Framers made a choice to limit the tools available to elected officials wishing to regulate civilian use of weapons, and to authorize this

> **F**or over 200 years, the Framers decided to have a well-regulated government army but to also have an army. They also made the decision to coexist with the army and not lose their right to have Arms.

Court to use common-law process of case-by-case judicial lawmaking to define the contours of acceptable gun-control policy. Absent compelling evidence that is nowhere to be found in the Court's opinion., I could not possibly conclude that the Framers made such a choice. For these reasons, I respectfully dissent." (Dissenting Brief of the District of Columbia v. Heller, 554, U.S. 570 (2008), Associate Justice John Paul Stevens).

For over 200 years, the framers decided to have a well-regulated government army but to also have an army. Our Founding Fathers agreed on the decision to let our citizens coexist with the right to keep and bear arms. It is also stated in the amendment's language. "The right of the people to keep and bear arms, shall not be infringed." Infringement means that the government has no right to regulate, prohibit or much less confiscate the arms of their citizenry. There is no such thing as "acceptable gun-control policy" by Congress. But that will never happen because we still live in a republic and the people still reign over their representatives.

For these very reasons, I cannot join in celebration with the dissenting opinion of Justice Stevens and I must respectfully dissent to his dissent.

This Supreme Court ruling had not one but two dissenting opinions and alas two opinions contradicting the Constitution and the rules of federalism. I have said it before in interpreting Justice Stevens' dissent -- members of today's court plainly do not understand the basic language of this amendment and the correct interpretation by the framers.

They still believe in their minds that the amendment speaks of militia service and not citizen service. I am just going to grab a few excerpts from Justice Breyer because reading his dissent is like reading Steven's dissent, repetitive and contradicting.

"We must decide whether a District of Columbia law that prohibits the possession of handguns in the home violates the Second Amendment. The Court, relying upon its view that the Second Amendment seeks to protect a right of personal self-defense, holds that this law violates that Amendment. In my view, it does not." (Dissenting Brief of the District of Columbia v. Heller, 554, U.S. 570 (2008), Associate Justice Stephen Breyer).

"The majority's conclusion is wrong for two independent reasons. The first reason is that set forth by Justice STEVENS—namely, that the Second Amendment protects militia-related, not self-defense-related, interests. These two interests are sometimes intertwined. To assure 18th century citizens that they could keep arms for militia purposes would necessarily have allowed them to keep arms that they could have used for self-defense as well. But self-defense alone, detached from any militia-related objective, is not the Amendment's concern." (Dissenting Brief of the District of Columbia v. Heller, 554, U.S. 570 (2008), Associate Justice Stephen Breyer).

"The second independent reason is that the protection the Amendment provides is not absolute. The Amendment permits government to regulate the interests that it serves. Thus, irrespective of what those interests are—whether they do or do not include an independent interest in self-defense—the majority's view cannot be correct unless it can show that the District's regulation is unreasonable or inappropriate in Second Amendment terms. This the majority cannot do." (Dissenting Brief of the District of Columbia v. Heller, 554, U.S. 570 (2008), Associate Justice Stephen Breyer).

> The federal government does not have the power to regulate, prohibit and confiscate the arms of its citizens. Again, it is plainly stated in the Amendment's language: "The right of the people to keep and bear arms, shall not be infringed."

These first three paragraphs of Justice Breyer's dissent tells me all I need to know about where he truly stands. He is just repeating Justice Steven's words, and even worse the words in Justice McReynolds' opinion of *U.S. v. Miller*. These two jurists love to quote from and set that precedent. The issue is that Justice McReynolds just gave an opinion but he, thanks be to God, was not a founding member of this republic. So, his opinion should stand as just an opinion, and nothing more.

The American citizenry does not realize that the Supreme Court is a branch of the federal government. Sadly, they are not the last word to tell the country which law passed by the national Congress is and is not constitutional. That power has been reserved to the states with the act of nullification. After the ruling of Miller, we have seen several states passed legislation nullifying, not overriding that ruling by stating, "Even though, the Supreme Court of the United States has ruled this law constitutional, it is our sovereign state duty to still refuse to cooperate with federal union officials in the enforcement of that law/ruling."

That is also one fact that Justices Stevens and Breyer fail to point out-- that the states are more powerful than the federal government. They can bring out the imaginary giant of the federal government but in the end, it is the states that are bigger giants and we have the rules of federalism on our side.

The federal government does not have the power to regulate, prohibit and confiscate the arms of its citizens. Again, it is plainly stated in the amendment's language:

"The right of the people to keep and bear arms, shall not be infringed."

"The argument About method, however, is by far the less important argument surrounding today's decision. Far more important are the unfortunate consequences that today's decision is likely to spawn. Not at least of these, as I have said, is the fact that the decision threatens to throw into the doubt the constitutionality of gun laws throughout the United States. I can find no sound legal basis for launching the courts on so formidable and potentially dangerous a mission. In my view, there simply is no untouchable constitutional right guaranteed by the Second Amendment to keep loaded handguns in the house in crime-ridden urban areas. For these reasons, I conclude that the District's measure is a proportionate, not disproportionate, response to the compelling concerns that led the District to adopt it. And, *723 for these reasons as well as the independently sufficient reasons set forth by Justice STEVENS, I would find the District measure consistent with the Second Amendment's demands. With respect, I dissent." (Dissenting Brief of the District of Columbia v. Heller, 554, U.S. 570 (2008), Associate Justice Stephen Breyer).

The Second Amendment does not go into specifics on what arms is allowed its citizens to own and operate. One argument that these progressives throw against the Second Amendment is that if "the citizens are allowed to own and operate a Nuclear Arm?" As of now, the federal government has not given the states their sovereign right to grant their citizens, the right to keep and bear nuclear arms. But that arm is more dangerous than a regular handgun. It is a silly argument and holds no common-sense knowledge with the Second Amendment's language.

The Second Amendment does not discriminate as to who should own and operate an Arm as it does not discriminate as to what arms should be allowed to be owned and operated. In due time, the federal government will grant these allowances or not. The only way that they would allow these allowances or disallow is if they create a revised amendment or repealing the said amendment. Until that day, the government cannot pick and choose which arm is lawful and deny the pride of ownership of their citizenry. And for that matter, I also dissent in Justice Breyer's dissent. That's the reason the Second Amendment is only second to the First Amendment. It is to protect the free speech of its citizen by peaceful measures and if necessary, by force if that protection is infringed.

So, to bring this conclusion to a close, I stand with the Second Amendment, our second Bill of Rights and with the former Associate Justice Antonin Scalia. A man who truly knows the rules of federalism and how it needs to be played in our American federalism republic.

BIBLIOGRAPHY

Chapter One

Scalia's Court on Abortion, Kevin A. Ring, 2004, 2016

Opinion Brief on Planned Parenthood SE PA v. Casey, 1992

Dissenting Brief on Planned Parenthood SE PA v. Casey, 1992

Opinion Brief on Buck v. Bell, 1927

Chapter Two

Scalia's Court on Homosexuality, Kevin A. Ring, 2004, 2016

Opinion Brief of *Bower v. Hardwick*, 1984, Associate Justice Byron White

Concurrence Brief of *Bower v. Hardwick*, 1984, Associate Justice Lewis F. Powell, Jr.

Concurrence Brief of *Bower v. Hardwick*, 1984, Chief Justice Warren E. Burger

Dissenting Brief of *Bower v. Hardwick*, 1984, Associate Justice Harry Blackmun

Opinion Brief of *Lawrence v. Texas*, 2003, Associate Justice Anthony Kennedy

Dissenting Brief of *Lawrence v. Texas*, 2003, Associate Justice Antonin Scalia

Dissenting Brief of *Lawrence v. Texas*, 2003, Associate Justice Clarence Thomas

Chapter Three

Scalia's Court on Obamacare, Kevin A. Ring, 2004, 2016

Unanimous Opinion Brief of Wickard, Secretary of Agriculture v. Filburn, 1942, Associate Justice Robert Jackson

Opinion Brief of Alberto R. Gonzales, Attorney General v. Angel McClary Raich, Associate Justice John Paul Stevens, 2005

Concurring Opinion Brief of Alberto R. Gonzales, Attorney General v. Angel McClary Raich, Associate Justice Antonin Scalia, 2005

Dissenting Brief of Alberto R. Gonzales, Attorney General v. Angel McClary Raich, Associate Justice Clarence Thomas, 2005

Chapter Four

Opinion Brief of Associate Justice Stephen Breyer on Zadvydas v. Davis, et., al, 2001

Dissenting Brief of Associate Justice Antonin Scalia on Zadvydas v. Davis, et., al, 2001

Syllabus of Arizona, ET AL., Petitioners v. United States, SB1070 legislation, 2012

Opinion Brief of Anthony Kennedy on Arizona, ET AL., Petitioners v. United States, 2012

Concurring and Dissenting Opinion Brief of Associate Justice Antonin Scalia on Arizona, ET AL., Petitioners v. United States, 2012

Concurring and Dissenting Opinion Brief of Associate Justice Clarence Thomas on Arizona, ET AL., Petitioners v. United States, 2012

Concurring and Dissenting Opinion Brief of Associate Justice Samuel Alito on Arizona, ET AL., Petitioners v. United States, 2012

Opinion Brief of Demore, District Director, San Francisco District of Immigration and Naturalization Service, v. Kim, Chief Justice William D. Rehnquist, 2003

Dissenting Brief of Demore, District Director, San Francisco District of Immigration and Naturalization Service, v. Kim, Associate Justice Sarah Day O'Connor, 2003

Opinion Brief of Donald J. Trump, President of the United States, Et At., Petitioners v. Hawaii by Chief Justice John Roberts, 2018

Concurring Brief of Donald J. Trump, President of the United States, Et At., Petitioners v. Hawaii by Associate Justice Clarence Thomas, 2018

Dissenting Brief of Donald J. Trump, President of the United States, Et At., Petitioners v. Hawaii by Associate Justice Stephen Breyer, 2018

Dissenting Brief of Donald J. Trump, President of the United States, Et At., Petitioners v. Hawaii by Associate Justice Sonia Sotomayor, 2018

Oral Argument of Gen. Derek Schmidt, Kansas Attorney General in Kansas v. Ramiro Garcia, 2019

Associate Justice Sonia Sotomayor on the Arguments of Kansas v. Ramiro Garcia, 2019

Associate Justice Stephen Breyer on the Arguments of Kansas v. Ramiro Garcia, 2019

Oral Argument of Paul Hughes, Esq., in Kansas v. Ramiro Garcia, 2019

Opinion Brief of Associate Justice Samuel Alito on Kansas v. Garcia, 2020

Concurring Opinion Brief of Associate Justice Clarence Thomas on Kansas v. Garcia, 2020

Dissenting Brief of Associate Justice Stephen Breyer on Kansas v. Garcia, 2020

Opinion Brief of Associate Justice Hugo Black on Hines v. Davidowitz, 1941

Chapter Five
Race and Liberty in America: the essential reader, edited by Jonathan Bean, page 64, Mississippi Constitution, 1832

Laws of the State of Mississippi, Passed at a Regular Session of the Mississippi Legislature, December 1865, Race and Liberty in America: the essential reader, edited by Jonathan Bean, page 64, Mississippi Constitution, 1832)

Opinion Brief of U.S v. Cruikshank, 92 U.S. 542, (1875), Chief Justice Morrison Waite

Dissenting Brief of U.S v. Cruikshank, 92 U.S. 542, (1875), Associate Justice Nathan Clifford

Opinion Brief of U.S. Miller, 307 U.S. 174, 1939 by Associate Justice James McReynolds

Opinion Brief of the District of Columbia v. Heller, 554, U.S. 570 (2008), Associate Justice Antonin Scalia

Dissenting Brief of the District of Columbia v. Heller, 554, U.S. 570 (2008), Associate Justice John Paul Stevens

Dissenting Brief of the District of Columbia v. Heller, 554, U.S. 570 (2008), Associate Justice Stephen Breyer

STATES RIGHTS RADIO

E-Mail: *statesrightsradio@mail.com*
TikTok: *@statesrightsradio*